Your Soaring Phoenix

Profound Tools for

Spiritual Ascension

With 26 Spiritual Teachers

Written and Edited by

Carol Francis, Psy.D., MFT, MCHt

and

Mary O'Maley, MSHN, CHtI

Dear Natalie,
You can Soar!
Mary O'Maley
11/11/22

Contributing Spiritually Attuned Authors

Michael Almaraz, Alberto Amura, Peter Blum, Andrew Cort, Brigit Esselmont, **Debra Fentress**, Belinda Ferrell, Carol Francis, Dennie Gooding, Michael Ortiz Hill, Steve G. Jones, Kathi Kenedi, Raven Keyes, **Cynthia Sue Larson**, Susan Mann, Marjorie Miles, Mary O'Maley, **Shelley Stockwell-Nicholas**, Heather Friedman Rivera, Michael Rogalski, Donald Saunders, Barbara Schiffman, Jane Sibbett, **Edie Summers**, Carolyn White, Sara Wiseman

-Topics-

Higher Self, Hypnosis, Reiki, Healing Energy, Shamanism, Vibrational Medicine, Healers, Light Healing, Tarot Cards, Meditation, Self-Discovery, Soul Retrieval, Shamanic Journeys, Remote Viewing, Astral Projection, Law of Attractions, Walk-Ins, Dream Work, Reiki and Medicine, Quantum Physics, Quantum Leap, Camino, Synchronicity, Cancer and Poetry, Power of Writing, Channeling, Mediumship, Mediums, Psychics, Psychic Readings, Time Travel, 3-D, Time Space, Akashic Records, Faith Healers, Spontaneous Healing, Spiritual Eating, Yoga, Mindfulness, Past Life Regression, Regression Therapy, Clair-cognizance, Spiritual Downloads, Chakra Systems, Huna Magic, Love, Buddhism, Hinduism, Christianity, Judaism, Muslim, Compassion, Angels, Guides, Death, Near Death Experiences, Money, Law of Manifestation, Full Living, Meaning of Life, Metaphysics, Mysticism, Occult, Nature and Spirituality, Metaphysics and Cellular Biology, Medicine and Spirituality, Math and Metaphysics, Cosmology and Metaphysics, Soul Journeys, Psychology

Make Life Happen Publishing * Rancho Palos Verdes * 2014

Your Soaring Phoenix

Into flaming death, our burdens surrender.

Beyond death's embers, our soul peeks out.

Out of the ashes of dying fires, we rise like the Magician's Phoenix.

Newly hatched, we suckle the magic of our neonatal Phoenix-Self.

Clumsily flitting and flapping with novice wings, we risk flight.

Flying the skies of Roaring Fire Spirit, we survive and sense the More.

Daring to join Cosmos, our Phoenix-filled Cosmic Selves,

We expand our wings fully,

Freely,

Hugely creating flames of our own...

... Then we do the dare...

We soar.

Dr. Carol Francis

DEDICATIONS

I would like to dedicate this book to all of my teachers, family, friends, clients, and mentors. I would especially like to thank Dr. Shelley Stockwell Nicholas for opening my mind and Dr. Carol Francis for encouraging my soaring spirit. And, I thank my son, Vincent for teaching me perfect love and simple faith. Vince, you are the oldest soul I know.

Mary O'Maley

Marjorie teaches me to travel beyond the veil of death and listen to the music of the Universe. Charles fuels my skeptic scientific investigations and keen curiosities about the forces of Source. Matthew challenges me to scrutinize everything and articulate the unusual and spiritual domains with simplicity and everyday language. Jonathan helps me laugh, discern, prioritize people, and boldly live without limits. Mary O'Maley metabolizes the spiritual world with ease and gracious heartedness and listens discerningly to the essence of my many peculiar spirit-world experiences. Thank you each. Much love and appreciation.

Dr. Carol Francis

CONTENTS

Section II

Healing Powers: Ancient to Post-Modern Phoenix Healing Energies

Section III

Beyond the Veil: Psychic Tools, Mediumship and Beyond

Section IV - Spiritual Journeys When Your Phoenix-Soul Take Flights

Annotated Table of Contents

Section I

Love as the Primary Power Source of

Phoenix Ascension

Depth of spiritual progression is embedded essentially in power, intent, and flow of Love. These six authors help us transcend into many dimensions of Love beginning our Soaring Phoenix Journey.

Chapter 1 - Sara Wiseman, best-selling inspirational author, reveals the stages of love's progressive spiritual development in **The Heart is Where the Soul Resides.**

Chapter 2 - Peter Blum, hypnotherapist, musician, and shamanic practitioner, discloses the singularity of all that is. From that unity-consciousness springs forth spiritual love for all brethren in **All My Relations - Ah Ho Mitakuye Oyasin.**

Chapter 3 - Dr. Carol Francis, Clinical Psychologist, author and spiritual counselor, encourages being expansive and powerfully fueled by Love in **Being Small Takes Too Much Space.**

Chapter 4 - Michael Ortiz-Hill, best-selling author, shamanic journeyman, and nurse, teaches the *Craft of Compassion* extending Buddhist principals to love of self, others, and the All in **The Craft of Compassion.**

Chapter 5 - New Testament Paraphrase of I Corinthians 13 explains Love is the supreme spiritual power in **Love-Greater than All Spiritual Gifts**.

Chapter 6 - **A Galactic Fairy Tale** reminds all spiritually awakened individuals to enjoy the gifts of love and light which we can share with each other. This tale is included here with permission from the author, **Michael Lightweaver** to playfully inspire.

Section II

Healing Powers and Energy Work,

Ancient to Post-Modern

When it comes to healing practices it looks as though we may be coming full circle. We know that healing in ancient times always included the spiritual aspects. A little more than one hundred years ago, practical science took hold in the Western nations as the best way, and perhaps the only way, to heal the body. Today, largely due to public intervention, spiritual healing has found its way back and is often walking hand in hand with Western medicine. Clearly, of course, if everything is energy, then healing must be energy, too. In Section II, spiritual healing arts and energy work are revealed as spiritual partners.

Chapter 7 - Reiki Energy and Western Medicine, by Raven Keyes, bestselling author of *The Healing Power of Reiki*, introduces us to the power of energy healing when combined with surgery. The addition of Reiki Energy not only lessens the trauma of surgery, but also facilitates faster healing. Raven Keyes journeys into the surgery rooms, Ground Zero of 911, and private lives of cancer and cardiac victims touching our hearts as Raven Keyes's Reiki energizes their bodies.

Chapter 8 - Kathi Wolfrum, DC, shares with us her personal journey of becoming a spiritual healer who performs the mechanical and soulful aspects of Chiropractic care in **A Healer's Journey to Mastery.**

Chapter 9 - Chiropractor **Dr. Andrew Cort** reminds us that we also learn valuable **Lessons from the Patient.** Dr. Cort reminds us to live more fully and with more kindness by remembering that we too will die.

Chapter 10 - Reiki Master, **Alberto Amura,** eloquently reminds us that it is our personal responsibility to both heal ourselves and heal Earth in **Healing the Individual and Humanity.** He explores how obvious environmental transgressions need our attention since the human effects of subtle energies impact our environment as well.

Chapter 11 - We have all heard the wisdom of only needing faith the size of a mustard seed. **Jane Sibbett's, All You Need is One Percent**, tells the story of a miraculous healing journey. Using Braco's gazing healing work, Sibbett explains how one percent faith that healing can occur may be all that is necessary to heal.

Chapter 12 - **Michael Almaraz, CHt.,** uses the art of Hypnosis to reach the thought, spirituality, and healing processes of body, mind and spirit through one's Higher Consciousness in his chapter, **Harnessing the Light.**

Chapter 13 - **Belinda Farrell, CHt.,** illustrates the absolute power of our thoughts in the healing of our bodies and the world in **Explaining the Unexplainable**, from her book, *Find Your Friggin' Joy*. She shares a unique process of thought forms taught by the Hawaiian Huna Shamanic practices.

Chapter 14 - **Dr. Marjorie Miles, DCH,** tells her personal story of healing by commanding her body to heal with heart-centered poetry. **Spirituality, Cancer, and Poetic Healing** will inspire you with the elegant simplicity of Haiku healing energies.

Chapter 15 - The blueprint that is uniquely you can be found in your chakras. **Dr. Carolyn White** explains the concept of energy in color, sound, and movement and gives us the steps to know and to heal ourselves through our chakra centers in **Chakra Energy Healing**.

Chapter 16 - Mary O'Maley, MSHN, CHtI, demonstrates how using the energy of colors and nature can empower us to change the way we feel and respond to life stressors while having a great deal of fun in **Playing with Energy.**

Section III

Beyond the Veil

Psychic Tools, Mediumship, and Guides

In this section we share many experiences and applications of psychic work from those who use these gifts in their daily practice. Psychics routinely are consulted by people from all walks of life and religious practices. Celebrities and government officials use the services of psychics as do many of who are simply seeking practical advice on love, finances, business, and health. Psychics are no longer relegated to the archetype of the turbaned-mystic reading palms at the carnival. Many dimensions of psychic-based tools are discussed in Section III.

Chapter 17 - Mike Rogalski's Remote Viewing chapter provides exercises for honing remote viewing skills. These skills are akin to those which help develop many aspects of ESP, PSI, or the Sixth Sense. He also reveals some fascinating history of the U.S. Government's Remote Viewing programs, including scientific confirmation of psychic spying using remote viewing.

Chapter 18 - Dennie Gooding's chapter, **Psychic from Birth,** flows through her childhood and adult experiences as a psychic and a medium. Her unique perceptions were sometimes judged and silenced. Yet, Dennie persevered providing a worthy template for others to develop their psychic proclivities. Dennie

Gooding's work with the government, law enforcement agencies, and private clientele is well known and proven to date.

Chapter 19 - Mary O'Maley's chapter, **I'm A Medium, Too?,** treats readers to the joy and work of a medium who facilitates the spiritual journeys of the living and the dead. Since 1997, Mary has heard and conveyed messages verified by the living and shared by those from beyond the thin veil.

Chapter 20 - Dr. Carol Francis's chapter **Channeling, How, Who, Why?** examines the steps, experiences and tasks of channeling spiritual guides. To illustrate the process of interfacing with channeled guides, Dr. Francis details four channeled sessions and the personal characteristics of four channeled guides to help others understand the process and results of spiritual channeling.

Chapter 21 - Changing of the Guides by Mary O'Maley, playfully illustrates the ebb and flow of human relationships with spiritual guides and the progressive, ever-changing flow of interactions with various assistants and angels.

Chapter 22 - Psychic Animal Interventions By Mary O'Maley, Demonstrates how animals too, can telepathically communicate with their human friends, if only someone will listen.

Chapter 23 - In **Tarot Meditations for Soulful Connections**, world-renowned **Brigit Esselmont** o f *biddytarot.com* urges readers to expand their meditative spiritual growth using the art and mystical messages of the Tarot Cards. Consider here how to use this oracular tool to access the mysteries of your own extraordinary awareness.

Section IV

Spiritual Journeys

When Your Phoenix Takes Flight

With your physical body or without your physical body, you can travel without regard to time, space, or third dimensional realms. You can visit souls who passed over, other astral realms, past lives, Akashic Records, or soulful retreats of the Camino.

Chapter 24 - Communicate Beyond the Veil of Death by **Dr. Carol Francis** encourages journeying into the locations where loved-ones who have passed-on now reside: a tricky journey?

Chapter 25 - Discover Through Past Life Explorations by **Dr. Heather Friedman Rivera** demonstrates the use of Past Life Regression work which is a spiritual journey into lives you have yet to remember and their impact on your present.

Chapter 26 - Dr. Shelley's Time Travel © by **Shelley Stockwell-Nicholas, Ph.D.**, demonstrates journeys of your consciousness used to heal and relieve current life situations. This a chapter from her bestselling book, *Time Travel.*

Chapter 27 - The Wild and Whacky World of Regression Therapy by **Mary O'Maley, MSHN, ChtI**, demonstrates other journeys associated to regression therapies which help you leap beyond your fear of time travel.

Chapter 28 - Shamanic Journeys by **Dr. Carol Francis,** explains soul retrieval, journeys to different realms of reality, and use of trance work shamanically. Also, a meditation is included to help you enter into the process of shamanic exploration.

Chapter 29 - Shamanic Soul Retrieval: The Glass Soul by **Debra Fentress,** shows how shamanic techniques become a beautiful gentle journey on behalf of another aching soul who needs a lost part of her returned home safe and sound.

Chapter 30 - Dr. Steve G. Jones, a bestselling author and creator of thousands of hypnosis audio tools, wished to share his **Four Tools for Spiritual Journeys** associated to his progression as a seeker.

Chapter 31 - Disengaging from your physical form and the limits of your five senses allows free-floating journeys throughout this planet, 3-D regions, and beyond time and space as explored by **Dr. Carol Francis** in **Astral Projection, How and Why**.

Chapter 32 - Data collecting, life-reviews, autobiographical writings, explanations, perspective, purpose and personal discoveries await the traveler who journeys to the Akashic Records as discussed by author and lecturer **Barabara Schiffman, Cht., ARCT,** in **New Frontier of Conscious Evolution: The Akashic Records.**

Chapter 33 - Susan Mann journeyed the **Camino de Santiago de Compostela,** a physically strenuous 500 kilometer pilgrimage that creates a soulful ascension, as well as communion with nature, the Divine and diverse humankind. Susan Mann describes lessons to be learned while on the Camino in **Spiritual Journeys on Physical Paths: Camino and Synchronicity**

Chapter 34 - Donald Saunders' Spiritual Messages Downloaded is about profound and enlightening information that was spiritually downloaded during one seemingly random morning. That instantaneous download or "knowing" resulted in clarifications about how life's manifestations and spiritual power tools are gained. Donald Saunders explains 10 basic tenants of such wisdom in his chapter. This chapter is a partial synopsis of insights gained in his powerful book *The Knowledge* and his associated series by the same name.

Chapter 35 - Kathi Kenedi describes the Walk-In experience in **The Dream and The Walk-In** wherein one spirit suddenly appears within the body and life of another. This unique experience is rarely shared openly.

Section V

Scientific Research and

Metaphysical Experiences

New discoveries and paradigms associated to scientific research and theory provide yet other explanations and avenues for clearer understanding of metaphysical and spiritual experiences and tools.

Chapter 36 - Cynthia Sue Larson, graduate of UC Berkeley in Physics explores the last hundred years in the field of Physics and Computer Science and the direct applications to spiritual manifestation. This chapter, **Welcome to the Quantum Age,** is an excerpt from Cynthia Sue Larson's many works, and is a small taste of her amazing best-selling book, *Quantum Jumps: An Extraordinary Science of Happiness and Prosperity.* Integrating life and all its fields of exploration is what many hope Quantum Mechanics and its discoveries will allow.

Chapter 37 - Examining the spiritual paths that are revealed in nature and revealed in hard sciences is the focus of the chapter **Interdisciplinary Consciousness: Nature, Science, Aesthetics and Spirituality** adapted from the book *Spiritual Paths, Spiritual Gurus: Your Choice,* by **Dr. Carol Francis**.

Chapter 38 - During the last 60 years, enumerable scientific research confirms spiritual concepts such as multiverses, parallel universes, life after death, law of manifestation through thought and emotion, power of prayer, ESP, PSI, Reiki, effectiveness of meditation, remote viewing, holographic data likened to Akashic records, bi-location, synchronicity, healing via belief, and much more. The final chapter in this section is **Science of Metaphysical and Spiritual Phenomenon: A Brief Annotated Bibliography** by **Dr. Carol Francis,** is a guide for those who are keenly intrigued by the scientific methodology of investigation about spiritual awareness.

Section VI

Humanly Grounded While

Spiritually Soaring

Your human need for money, exercise, food, breath, psychological health, and rest are set before you in Section VI as yet other ways to expand your spiritual consciousness in your vision quest as an Earth-bound physical form.

Chapter 39 - First, best-selling author **Belinda Ferrell** integrates emotional and psychological health with spiritual awakening, Huna style, from her inspiring book, *Find Your Friggin' Joy* in her chapter **Shifting from Anger, Fear, and Guilt**.

Chapter 40 - Nutrition Expert and Alternative Treatment Practitioner, **Mary O'Maley, MSHN, CHtL,** holistically examines nutrition as the multi-leveled process of simultaneously feeding our body, mind, and soul with more than merely good whole foods in **Holistic Health Primer.**

Chapter 41 - Health and fitness coach and author, **Edie Summers**, weaves physical exercise with nutrition and with spiritual mindfulness and soulful connections in **Eating, Exercising, and Sensing within the Body-Mind Spirit Triad**.

Chapter 42 - **Dr. Carol Francis** examines strategies for building businesses, wealth, and attaining goals with 16 exercises including spiritual consciousness, Laws of Manifestation, Attraction and Intentionality. This last chapter, **Spiritually Mindful Tools for Financial and Business Growth**, is adapted from her book *Spiritual Gurus, Spiritual Paths: Your Choice*.

ACKNOWLEDGMENTS

Vincent, Matthew, and Jonathan
100 Years of Spiritual Teachers
12 Decades of Real Living

Two Very Helpful Editors
Toni Martinovich and Sandy Pierce

EDITORS' NOTES

WHAT'S NEXT SPIRITUALLY?

INTRODUCTION BY MARY O'MALEY

How many times in your life have you burned to ash and been reborn? Life, just before the burn, can seem harsh and difficult, a sure sign that something needs to change. Yet, the joy, life, and passion that emerge from the ashes create a longing and a burning desire for more.

The *more* that you desire is what you will find in this book: more knowledge, more love, more hope, more healing, more joy, life, and passion. You will experience a deeper, more satisfying connection to self, spirit, the earth, and your companions on this journey.

As your old, unhelpful paradigms burn, so will your self-imposed boundaries. The burn releases light, and light begets new ideas. Like the Phoenix, you can rise from the ashes and soar.

No matter where you are on your journey, whether you are ready to burn or ready to rise from the ashes, you will find something in this book to fuel the fire of your creation.

You can read this book any way you choose. You may read it slowly, cover to cover, savoring, learning, and expanding your own possibilities with each chapter. Or, you may pick and choose what seems interesting at the time. You may use it as a reference when your spirit is asking you, "What's next?"

If you have questions or just crave more information you will find that the contributing authors are accessible and willing to mentor this leg of your adventure, with their own books and in person. Examine your life honestly and thoroughly. Find those places within that are ready to burn and be reborn. Close your eyes and open the book to see where spirit leads you.

Your Phoenix is ready to soar!

SOAR EVEN HIGHER SPIRITUALLY

INTRODUCTION BY DR. CAROL FRANCIS

One day, your spiritual self rose from
The ashes of your fear of death and life:
Your Phoenix was resurrected, but have you soared yet?

You rose above your limited five senses. You recognized the blindness of your myopic materialistic living. Then enumerable amazing "ah-has" and some transcendent experiences swirled into your life. Perhaps to feed your newly hatched Phoenix-self, you likely honed tools of meditation, prayer, attunements, studying with gurus, or communing with like-minded spiritual seekers.

Sometime during these spiritual journeys, you were urged out of the nest and encouraged to fly. You, as this adolescent Phoenix-Spirit, felt confined, frustrated with the limits of nesting. Mouth-to-mouth feeding by nurturing spiritual teachers no longer satisfied. Newer Phoenix hatchlings needed what no longer nourished your growing spirit.

It was time to fly.

Perhaps you flew out of the nest with attitudes of intrigue, adventure, reluctance, and even inhibition. Next, you experimented beyond your initial mentors and uncovered secrets and forged new paths. Sometimes you hid behind old teachings and embraced ancient dogmas out of fears of being too weird, too grandiose, too tired, or too alone.   Other moments you shouted and broke out of choking restraints which pinched and limited your flight. Even as an experienced flying Phoenix, you and others clipped your wings, inhibited your powers.

Yet, you were made to fly, free, huge, and high.
You were resurrected to soar.
You are a Phoenix ready to soar.
You are a Spiritual Phoenix
Who long-ago rose from your ashes
Left your nest and learned to fly.

It is time now to soar.

For those spiritually awake who are wishing to soar, this collection of writings are offered. So now, join each author as you further unclip your wings, daily. Read, practice, experience.

Fly beyond perceptions of time and space.   Embrace the omnipotence and omnipresence of Love.   Discern depressing creeds about death or ill-health and rise above death.   Learn to soar while healing your human self and others. Face clearly the constraints of materialistic economics; transcend above such needs. Journey with your soul into domains both known and unknown. Look into death, the past, the present, the future with multiverse eyes. See beyond the borders of finitude. Embrace the human tools of scientific investigations while simultaneously springing into the beyond where you can finally spread your magnificent firebird wings – and soar.

Soar, Phoenix, soar.
Let the journeys begin.

YOUR SOARING PHOENIX

FRANCIS & O'MALEY

SECTION I

LOVE

PRIMARY
POWER SOURCE
FOR
TRUE ASCENSION

FRANCIS & O'MALEY

INTRODUCTION

LOVE AS THE SOURCE OF MYSTICAL MAGIC

BY DR. CAROL FRANCIS

Source of Mystical Magic
Fuel of Spiritual Energies
Unifying Principal of the All
Namaste's Trajectory
Love
Broth for the Stew of Awakening

We contend that the beginning, end, and middle of all spiritual journeys and mystical magics spring out of the fluid, the fuel, the Source called LOVE.   Six authors ground us in Love's sophisticated levels, acts, and magic.   These six spiritual teachers will focus us on Love in order to expand our mystical skills while bathing in the Singularity of the Universe which is flowing in the juices of LOVE.

Sara Wiseman, best-selling inspirational author, reveals the stages of love's progressive spiritual development in **The Heart is Where the Soul Resides**.

Peter Blum, musician and shamanic practitioner, discloses the singularity of all that is. From that unity-consciousness springs forth spiritual love for all brethren in **All My Relations - Ah Ho Mitakuye Oyasin**.

Dr. Carol Francis, Clinical Psychologist, author, and spiritual counselor, encourages being expansive, powerful, and fueled by Love in **Being Small Takes Too Much Space**.

Michael Ortiz-Hill, best-selling author, shamanic journeyman, and nurse, teaches the Craft of Compassion extending Buddhist principals to love of self, others, and the All in **The Craft of Compassion.**

New Testament Paraphrase of I Corinthians 13 decrees Love as supreme above all else in **Love-Greater Than All Spiritual Gifts**.

A Galactic Fairy Tale reminds all spiritually awakened individuals to enjoy the gifts of love and light which we have to share with each other. This story is included here with permission from the author, **Michael Lightweaver**.

CHAPTER 1

THE HEART IS WHERE

THE SOUL RESIDES

BY SARA WISEMAN

The heart is contained in four ways: first by the physical body, next by the emotional armor we all carry, next by the physical heart itself, and finally, at the very center of everything, is the inner heart, the heart within the heart: Ananda Khanda.

This is what desires to be cracked open to the world.

Heart opening is a symptom of personal growth. We might call this emotional opening, or psychological breakthrough. But if we use the lens of spirituality, of soul growth, and we accept the idea that *the heart is where the soul resides,* what then?

What do we mean then, when we talk about heart's opening?

Obviously, we are not talking about a physical opening in the heart; it is energetic, just as all things are energetic. Heart's opening is not a one-time thing, either. Instead, it is a progressive opening, a series of passages from one state of consciousness to another. And it does not happen all at once—that would be too much, too fast, a shock to the system.

Instead, our heart opens slowly, when we are ready. We move through each passage as part of our soul growth, in Divine time.

Some folks bust their hearts open at a young age, determined from the get-go to live life at full throttle—to accept what life brings without hesitation, and to live their days in love and light regardless of situation.

This is a great way to live!

Others of us take longer, opening our hearts slowly as we move through our lessons of soul growth, as our experiences on earth teach us the lessons of wisdom.

Still others stay stuck for years, even decades, entombed in anger, sadness, and shame.

You will find yourself in one of these places, now.

Right now, you have either a heart - fully open, partly open, or mostly shut.

If your heart is fully open, congratulations. It is lovely to be here.

If your heart is partly open, you can learn to open it farther.

If your heart is mostly shut, you may feel quite vulnerable as you explore the idea of opening, and consider what might happen if you dared to open your heart to the light.

The four passages

The heart does not open at random. Instead, it opens in four sequential and progressive stages, each expansion building on the next. These four passages are:

- Heart of pain
- Heart of compassion

• Heart of connection

• Heart of love

Depending on where you find yourself on your own personal journey of soul growth, you will be in the midst of or embarking upon one of these passages right now.

Let's take a look at what each passage means, and how it might show up in your life:

If you are in *heart of pain*, the first passage, you are becoming aware; you are becoming a conscious person. This is a good thing! But at this first stage, you are examining your own unhappiness. For the first time, you are considering the idea of facing pain directly, rather than avoiding it, numbing out, or blaming others for your troubles.

For most people, heart of pain is the most difficult passage. Entering this passage signifies the clear desire to change your life from the inside out, and to become awake after years or decades of living life asleep.

If you are in *heart of compassion*, the second passage, you have moved completely through pain, and are ready to hold compassion for others and for yourself. It does not mean you never feel pain again. It means you have a new way to think about pain, as something that is universal to the human condition. This passage allows you to understand that we are all, at our core, the same— divine beings in human bodies, facing human challenges. At this stage, you are becoming more conscious.

If you are in *heart of connection*, the third passage, you have become conscious. You have expanded your awareness to a level in which you recognize yourself as one of One. You see yourself first as a spiritual being. Earthly concerns fade, as you connect yourself to the Oneness that surrounds us and is us. Spiritual and/or intuitive awakening are the hallmarks of this passage.

If you are in *heart of love*, the fourth passage, you will be in a state of nirvana, bliss, true healing, fulfillment, peace, and happiness—if not all of the time, then most of the time.

This is the state of *Ananda Khanda*, loosely translated as the high heart, the spiritual heart, the heart within the heart. It is the opening of the deepest heart within all your hearts, the innermost heart under all of your layers, armors, resistances and distractions, into the state of pure love.

It is a state of transcendence, and of transmutation into grace.

The heart opens over and over again, until the heart within the heart, the Ananda Khanda, finally is able to become illuminated and infused with light. These openings happen in the most ordinary moments of every lifetime. When the inner heart opens fully, this is known as bliss, transcendence, nirvana. There is no going back from this opening; the inner heart, once opened, always remains open. If this happens to you, your life will be forever changed. In this fourth passage, in this state of pure love, you are fully conscious; the most conscious a human can be. There is nothing withheld; you are conscious of everything, in all moments.

Many of us can access these higher states some of the time; we can go to this state of love momentarily, or even for longer. Yet in true heart of love, you live there all the time, in every moment of your existence. At this point in time, very few people on earth have the ability to remain in this passage all the time—only the saints, the holy ones, the ascended masters. Thus, most of us might expect to learn how to go into heart of love; but the journey to stay there, to reside in that place, will be a journey of all lifetimes.

Have patience with yourself, on your journey of soul growth.

Please know that your understanding will unfold in correct timing; there is no hurry or concern for the pace of your awakening. Simply begin, and trust in the journey and know that every person on the planet also walks the same path.

About Sara Wiseman

Sara Wiseman is a spiritual teacher, intuitive and author of six insightful books on spirituality and intuition including *Living The Life of Gratitude* and *Your Psychic Child*. She is the founder of Intuition University, hosts the popular radio show Ask Sara, and is a top contributor to DailyOM, VividLife, InspireMeToday Aspire Magazine and more. Visit her at www.sarawiseman.com.

FRANCIS & O'MALEY

CHAPTER 2

ALL MY RELATIONS
"AH HO MITAKUYE OYASIN"
BY PETER BLUM

"Ah Ho Mitakuye Oyasin."

I was taught this phrase, in the language of the Lakota, in the first sweat lodge ceremony that I attended, over 25 years ago. I was also told that it meant "All My Relations." As a novice, who did not know much about the tradition, I honored the request to say "All My Relations" even though I did not understand what it signified. We said it every time we entered the sweat lodge, when the rocks were brought in, as well as when it was time for the flap to be opened at the end of one of the four "rounds."

For those not familiar, this ancient purification ceremony was practiced by many of the plains Indians, and variations of it can be found all over the world. Also called a "stone people's lodge" by some, it involves heating stones in a fire until they are red hot, and then placing them in a pit in the earth in the center of a hemisphere made of saplings which have been trimmed and bent over to be tied, and then covered with layers of blankets until the interior is completely dark.

After this is done, participants enter and sit on the ground while water is poured over the stones, ceremonial songs are sung and prayers are offered. There are many variations of this ceremony. But my story is not so much about the sweat lodge ceremony as this idea of "all my relations." What did it mean, I wondered? Growing up, my idea of my "relations" was my blood family - grandparents, parents, aunts, uncles, cousins, siblings...

As I spent more time with indigenous elders, wisdom keepers from the earth-based spiritual traditions, I began to get a better idea. It became even clearer when another teacher explained that "Mitakuye Oyasin" could also be translated as "We are all related." The stones that are heated in the fire are considered alive (and, we are told, they give their lives, so we two-legged can sweat and purify ourselves) and are called "stone people." Thusly, we are taught to regard everything as alive. It is a vast connected web of what the Buddhists would call "interdependence."

To realize in my life what it means to be related to everything, is to live in balance, to walk in balance, to be in "right relationship" with my friends and associates, my community, my environment. And, to remember how easy it is for me to forget this, to fall back into old patterns of self-centeredness. So, in their wisdom, the ancient medicine people, mystics, shamans, and visionaries from all cultures encouraged the people to develop ceremonies. By participating regularly in ceremony, I am reminded of "all my relations."

Years ago, while exploring other spiritual traditions, I learned some of the Dances of Universal Peace, sometimes called "Sufi dances," because they were created and brought to the public by Sufi Sam, or Murshid Sam Lewis of the Chisti order of Sufism. These spiritual folk dances combine chanting, whirling, and singing from a number of sources. What I remember most about them was the intention of interacting on a deeply personal level with every person involved in the dances. In a brief time, during a dance, I had eye contact and was brought in intimate relationship with people I had never met. In this way, group dance and song can serve as a communal ritual to remind us of the fact that we are all related.

After being in sweat lodge ceremonies for a number of years, I was fortunate enough to be asked to help build several new lodges, as well as collect more "stone people." The way that my teachers showed me was to ask each sapling, before cutting it down, if it was willing to give its life, and then thanking it and honoring it by placing tobacco at its roots as an offering. This again illustrated the meaning of "everything is alive." They are the "tree people," just as the stones that we gathered were the "stone people." Before lifting them from the earth to be used, placed in the fire for the lodge, we thanked them for giving their life.

During the 60's, which was my coming of age, it was popular to call each other "brother" and "sister," but it made me uncomfortable. It seemed like more of an affectation - something that we did because it was cool. It took decades for me to "own" that - to genuinely feel that all men are my brothers and all women my sisters. Do I always act that way, or have that foremost in my consciousness? Not yet. But in moments when I do, it is a feeling of such connectedness, of such gentle spaciousness. I may not agree with you, but it is like having a disagreement with a family member. We are all related.

One definition of the Buddhist practice of "metta" (loving kindness) is that it is "the first of four kinds of contemplation designed to develop a sound pacific relationship to other living beings." Ahhh... there's that "relationship" word again; I would add "all" before "other living beings." So in an individual or group meditative practice, which is a form of ceremony, there is the opportunity to make this connection on the mental/emotional plane with all my relations.

I love the story of Hotei, the "laughing Buddha." Statues of him often show him sitting with a fat belly. In this story he is walking with a linen sack on his back. Anecdotes conjecture what was in it: rice plants, food, candy for children, or, some say, the woes of the world.

Hotei was an Enlightened One, but he never spoke, only laughed. A spiritual aspirant approached him and said, "Hotei, what is the meaning of Zen?" Hotei smiled and took his sack off his shoulder and placed it on the ground. The student had sudden insight, but, still seeking more asked, "Hotei, what is the actualization of Zen?" Hotei laughed, and picked up his sack and kept walking.

My understanding of my relationship to all - on an intellectual level, even on a heart level - is meaningless, unless it shows up in my behavior. So, as with all spiritual teachings, repeating something until it is integrated, I have learned to use the phrase "Ah Ho Mitakuye Oyasin" as a greeting. It is a constant reminder to me of our vast and continuous interconnectedness.

In closing, I thank my many teachers - any true wisdom that comes through in my words, I have learned from them; any foolishness or errors I claim as my own.

About Peter Blum

As a senior instructor for the National Guild of Hypnotists since 1993, Peter Blum has trained hundreds in the spiritual art of hypnosis. A student of trans-cultural shamanism, Peter considers himself fortunate to have had training from Native American mystic and visionary Beautiful Painted Arrow for over 25 years. He has also studied with Dr. Lewis Mehl-Madrona, a healer of Cherokee and Lakota heritage who integrates shamanic techniques in his psychiatric practice. When he is not practicing hypnosis, Peter loves to participate in sweat lodge ceremonies, and make healing sounds with his collection of sacred singing metals. Since 1999, he has produced 7 CD's in the "Sounds for Healing" series.

Peter Blum and his musical meditations can be reached at 845-247-8839, though Facebook, or through his website: www.soundsforhealing.com.

CHAPTER 3

BEING SMALL TAKES TOO MUCH SPACE

BY DR. CAROL FRANCIS

Relinquishing Smallness – Loving the Whole Self

Taught to be humble, meek, or reserved? Dislike the loud, arrogant, or pedantic? Cringe around self-importance or conceit? Annoyed by dogmatic self-proclaimed experts or vexing braggers?

Embracing your Phoenix's ability to soar may trigger your dislike for these narcissistic traits. However, trying to avoid being grandiose may inhibit your efforts to spiritually expand. Fears of being great, may keep you small. How to allow the unfolding of your self-expansion without triggering these loathsome images may come down to one word: Love.

Meditation One

Water, Air, Fluid Fullness of Love and

Personal Fullness

Imagine swimming in an Olympic-sized pool, surrounded by water. Dive deeply for a moment, experiencing water yielding to your movements and swirling around your skin. Come up for a much needed breadth and gasp in the refreshing air shared by all. Suck in that air deeply, and feel your expanding lungs and pounding heart work in unison. Oxygen rapidly spreads throughout each of your personal body's cells.

Now imagine Love as this ever present water and air. Consider air and water--Universal Love--available to every human. Then imagine Love moving with you, around you, inside you, and enlivening your existence. Allow yourself to swim inside Love. Take deep gulps of this Love feeding every part of you: body, soul, and spirit. Next, consider this Love as the fuel which supports your Phoenix-Self, fuels your spiritual expansion.

Notice, this Love is accessible to all. Also, this Love is a gift you can share as if giving out emergency oxygen tanks or teaching Pranic healing breaths. Imagine next this Love begging you earnestly to become your all: your fullest and natural potential.

Being your huge, free, expanding spiritual self does not result in arrogance or self-centeredness when fueled by this Universal Love-energy, air or water. Stop praising your smallness. Also, there is no need to be smug: spiritual expansion awaits everyone if they so choose. Everyone can be their Phoenix-Self.

Meditation Two

Oceanic Powers of Love and Personal Greatness

Once again, employ your imagination and contemplate the grand oceans. Sense their immensity in size, their depths unfathomable, and their powers both massively destructive and amazingly life-supporting. Their grandness is in their essence not in their self-proclaimed importance. Oceanic power is a given, not a pretense. Innumerable lives are supported in and by oceanic resources because that is the nature of oceans.

Similarly, your spiritual nature is immense, deep, powerful, life-supporting and vaster than the oceans. Yes, your spiritual nature could be destructive too, and spiritual cults do exist which exploit spiritual tools. You being small does not make this planet safer. Trying to make others smaller, even if they are cruel or destructive, also does not make any place safer.

Recognize that being meek contradicts your natural inclination to expand. You staying small surrenders you to others who opt to be more powerfully themselves than you are choosing to be.

Recognize daily any urges to remain small. When those urges peek out, close your eyes. Then, imagine swimming in the oceanic power of Love. Imagine breathing in deeply, and being refueled by Universal Love. Hear the beckoning of Love asking you to be your full potential. Love longs for your hugeness to embrace your universe. Embark on your adventure of being your naturally huge Phoenix-Self, soaring in the air of Love.

About Dr. Carol Francis

In addition to her spiritual counseling and intuitive work with metaphysically inclined seekers, Dr. Carol Francis has practiced for 37 years as a Clinical Psychologist, Life Coach, Clinical Hypnotherapist, and Marriage, Family & Child Counselor. She assists individuals, couples and children who seek to optimize their current situation and overcome complications of daily living. These individuals seek deep relief and growth for depression, anxiety, stress, career moves, family discord, child and parenting issues, relationship dissatisfaction, habit control, and the psychology of financial success. Practicing and licensed in Southern California for over 37 years, Dr. Carol Francis can be reached at drcarolfrancis.com or 310-543-1824.

Publications by Dr. Carol Francis

Study Skills for Successful High School and College Students
Helping Children with Divorce

Schizoid Anxiety

Helping Children with Natural and Manmade Disasters

"Horrific Parental Imaginings"

"Therapist's Countertransference with Abuse Couples"

KISS Method for Stop Smoking and KISS Cigarettes Goodbye

If You Can't Stop Eating, Maybe You're Hungry: Reset Your Cravings

Re-Uniting Soldiers with Families

Evolving Women's Consciousness: Dialogue with 21st Century Women.

Spiritual Paths, Spiritual Gurus: Your Choice

Spiritual Journeys: Astral Projection, Shamanism, Akashic

Your Akashic Records

CHAPTER 4

THE CRAFT OF COMPASSION
BY MICHAEL ORTIZ HILL

In my work, *The Craft of Compassion (1)* four steps of love's development emerge – from self-compassion to *living* compassion. In living compassion, one sets the self to the side so compassion can move with its radiant intelligence.

Living-compassion is unimpeded.

Living-compassion is in fact the liberation of the soul.

How does one come to such freedom?

With each step the opportunity to love is always now.

Not a new and improved "now" but merely this very moment is love's now.

As the Zen teacher Cheri Huber puts it, "love as much as you can from wherever you are with what you have got. That's the best you can ever do." (2)

Step One
Self-Compassion and How the Light Gets In

How do we accept our radiant imperfection? How does humiliation transform into humble acceptance and tenderness for ourselves?

Latin offers the phrase *amor fati,* to "love ones fate," which I would argue describes the foundational stratum of self-love. Self-love includes embracing *one's fate* – not what you have chosen but what has been chosen for you: these parents, siblings, ancestors, this body and gender, the delights and terrors of your childhood, and the hard wiring of your character.

What awakens love of one's fate and the sustaining of self-compassion? A spontaneous song of gratitude comes from recognizing that waking or sleeping we forever bask in gifts. Everything, every moment presents as gift – from the vastness of the universe to this very small life, to your very next breath.

In the call and response between one's self and the world, one perceives the gift of everything and responsively sings "thank you." This simple thank you makes it possible to love one's fate and provides the most reliable source of self-compassion. It is gratitude that allows one to love the gamut of one's self without judgment, unfettered.

In the years I was recovering from homelessness, I kept a "GRATITUDE JOURNAL" in which I wrote ten things at the end of each day for which I was grateful: my little girl's laughter, the striations of red and magenta in a sunset, the small ways I was learning to be a human being. As I continued, learning gratitude became a spiritual practice in its own right. As I advanced into the complexities of living an adult life off the street, learning to love my fate became the key to broadening and deepening gratitude and self-compassion.

So which came first – the chicken (gratitude) – or the egg (self-compassion)? Well gratitude does give birth to self-compassion. There is no self-compassion until one can say "thank you" for being alive. In a circular fashion, self-compassion undeniably gives birth to gratitude, truly and profoundly. Our ideas of causality are confused by the radiant truth of love.

Emphatically both self-compassion and gratitude makes the love of one's fate vibrant and durable. Whether one enters the door of *gratitude* or *self-compassion,* one arrives in the same place.

The authenticity of loving one's fate arises in any circumstance where one is undone by the unforeseen. You have lost your job. The father of your children has left you for another man. Your grandmother who you thought would live forever has suddenly died.

Your doctor has just informed you that you have multiple sclerosis, my fate.

I have sometimes asked friends or patients "what have you learned from your heart condition (or cancer or AIDS or addiction and recovery, etc.) that you could not have learned any other way?" A pregnant question, to be sure, which invites the ethos of loving one's fate. When I was diagnosed with multiple sclerosis five years ago it was my turn to ask that question of myself and ask it fully and completely. Time to walk my walk.

MS found me a stubbornly young and arrogant man when a range of "symptoms," which I had seen as a nurse, now took my body. Falling down in public and unable to get up, incontinent of urine and shit, an unreliable set of legs, sleepless and out of my mind on steroid therapy, losing my eyesight and not knowing if it was mine to be blind. Et cetera.

Early on, not yet recovered from my first exacerbation, I hiked to my refuge on the Big Sur coast to spend two weeks alone in prayer and reflection. It took eight hours to hike what I knew to be an hour walk; I did not know if I would be able to walk back out. This was *amor fati* proper.

"Let go and let God." I had to give up the fetish of certainty. For twenty years I assumed it would be mine to see my older wife through the end of her life but that was suddenly far from certain. Everything – everything – was far from certain.

Now, these years later, only gratitude remains of my passage through MS. Indeed the medicine of gratitude, of embracing my fate, seems tied up with my healing. It has been two years since my last exacerbation, and I do not anticipate another. As I wrote this essay, my neurologist, Dr. Russ Shimizu, was shocked at my recent MRI.

I am free of MS, the MRI revealed. Few would recognize me as someone with an "incurable" neuromuscular disease.

The transformation of humiliation to humility was, like with so many, a passage through dis-ease.   The catalyst of that transformation was gratitude. That is how the light of self-compassion gets in.

Nick Vujicic exemplifies *amor fati* and by his very being, he demonstrates how self-compassion is contiguous with compassion for others. Nick was born without arms or legs and learned as a child that he had to live by gratitude or simply sink into the despair of what he could not do.   Watch his video, weep with gratitude, humbly.

http://www.youtube.com/watch?
v=H8ZuKF3dxCY&feature=related

Step Two

Compassion for Others

The Buddha defines compassion with clarity. Compassion, he says, is sympathetic joy and sympathetic sorrow: sorrow over another's sorrow and delight over another's delight. This is the stuff of profound teaching. It is sacred for its homey truth. These ancient understandings can seem abstract but when we live by them, they are vivid, warm, and sometimes intimate.   "How far you go in this life," writes George Washington Carver, "depends on you being tender with the young, compassionate with the aged, sympathetic with the striving, and tolerant of the weak and the strong, because one day you will have been all of these." (3)

Sympathy is grounded in the fact that we, or someone we love, did or will experience the same thing as those whom we help. It is just a matter of time before you or a loved one is ill, perhaps hospitalized. One out of two men and one in three women will die of cancer. We know it is just a matter of time before you or someone you dearly love dies. We diminish our own hearts if we deny the jeopardy that is the common truth of being human and mortal.

Sorrow and joy are the fabric of the everyday, renewed with each new life experience. "Joy and woe are woven fine: A clothing for the soul divine" writes William Blake. (4) They are the raw material out of which a compassionate life is discovered and lived. If we live our lives consciously – that is to say with the intent of extending compassion to ourselves and everyone we meet – then all that we are and do is the act of weaving.

This weaving is an act of joy as is opening to another's sorrow. By meeting sorrow we are freed from our self-preoccupation which is where our suffering renews itself.

Compassion is, in fact, joy. We hold our experiences of sorrow and joy as stories, and these stories instruct our souls in the range of experiences which make every human life a common and blessed thing. The work of anyone who seeks to awaken compassion involves gathering his or her own stories like seeds. They hold the possibility of sprouting, and in time perhaps, bear fruit for nourishment or flowers for beauty.

We all know sympathetic joy. Your friend's HIV test comes back clean. Your sister had her first child, and she's a doll. The lump in your aunt's breast turns out to be benign. Your cousin finally got out of a very bad marriage and she's starting to smile again. We share these moments with sympathetic joy. Relief, peace, and happiness: we all share in such uplifting moments.

I emphasize suffering not to deny the sheer blessed fact of being alive, but because we would rather deny suffering. But the denial of suffering is a machine which generates suffering!

Joy that relies on the denial of suffering is a superficial and fragile fiction. Eventually it will be undone. Misery can be hidden away in the shadow of an overly optimistic culture; when misery is brought out into the open into the common ground of suffering, it can awaken compassion. In this sense, linking your personal suffering to that suffering of others becomes a gift to you and through you, a gift to them. Below are a few examples.

Roland has AIDS, and will likely die soon. He is only thirty-five. I lost my friend Charlie, a Vietnam vet who worked with the criminally insane; Charlie died from AIDS when he was the same age. My friend Alberto had AIDS, too. A month before Alberto died, I did a Tarot reading for him and of course he picked up the Death card. He was so relieved to talk about Death openly. All of his friends in his large gay community had lost loved ones, and it was unbearable to them that it was Alberto's turn. "It's time," he said. When I bathe Roland, I think of Charlie and Alberto.

My youngest brother, Paul, was psychotic. Mad, he wandered off into the New Mexico Mountains and died there. Every young psychotic could be my brother. Carl is homeless, in his early thirties, an addict and diabetic, cellulitis oozing on his left foot, soon to be an amputee. What broke him? I was homeless for three years as a teenager. I know how to love him remembering how fierce and cold it can get.

Each of these stories of my friends and loved ones is intimately real to me, but when linked to another's suffering, it is no longer mine. They are now not a burden but an opportunity for connection, which offers a kind of freedom. Naïve individualism infects the Western world, so much so that we imagine freedom to be a lonely, even alienated state. The kind of freedom I speak of here is not independence but interdependence. Interdependence is the vibrant community of we who sustain one another;

sometimes we set one another free beyond the edge of our own precious but small life.

Clutching at personal suffering amplifies and distorts it. Sympathetic joy and sorrow delivers us into a lived understanding of living in the human community. We walk through the life that we have lived even as we walk through whatever comes our way: the two meeting each other in a field of sympathetic sorrow and joy. Here we can see sorrow and joy as the possibility of compassion that lives within the stories of our lives and the lives to which we bear witness.

The spirit of kindness is deathless. Perhaps you have met it in moments, but it existed long before your birth and will persist long after you are gone. It is the bedrock from which we all spring, the God that is love and the love that is God.

Those who can meet another's joy with joy, and those who have transformed a portion of their suffering into compassion, are walking a very old path. Many have walked this way.

Below is a video of sympathetic joy, a common story of the reconciliation between loved ones after a long separation. All of us have experienced this and because of that we participate in the joy of compassion.

http://www.youtube.com/watch?v=FZ-bJFVJ2P0

Step Three

Radical Empathy

John Howard Griffin's book, *Black Like Me (5)* exemplifies what Tibetans call *dakshen nyamje*: "equalizing and exchanging self and other." I call *dakshen nyamje* radical empathy. Griffin, a white man, had his skin color pharmaceutically changed, then shaved his head and arms, and traveled through the deep south as a black man during the height of the civil rights movement. I write of Griffin as metaphor. There is a profound education of the heart when one slides from one's own point-of-view to the perspective of another.

In my early twenties, a passionate and earnest feminist, I became a housewife. My first wife, Marsha, was a speech therapist with elementary school children, and I was a high school dropout. When we had our daughter it was most sensible that I stay at home with Nicole and learn the arts of bottle feeding, diapers, potty training, the terrible twos, cleaning house, and getting a meal on the table. While Nicole napped I would read feminist literature and was disciplined in my efforts to understand the mind of the "other half."

Dakshen nyamje rhymes with the Cherokee proverb that 'you cannot understand another until you have walked three moons in their moccasins.' Radical empathy follows through on the question, "What if it were I or someone close to me who is suffering so?"

Amber is twenty-five and has leukemia. She loves the theater and at her bedside there is a photo of her in *A Midsummer Night's Dream*. For the moment she is undone by a stem cell transplant; her gums bleeding and asleep on Ativan. "My daughter is Amber's age," I whisper to her father when I bring him a cup of coffee. There comes a swift, silent understanding. Nothing more need be said. This is radical empathy.

Mrs. Brown just had a mastectomy, as did my wife. She is painfully self-conscious of her flat left side. Such was the rapport between us that I borrowed from my love of my wife's beauty. I laughed, "The running joke with my wife is that women with two breasts have come to look a little unnatural to me." Mrs. Brown confessed that she seemed to have more trouble with her mastectomy than her husband. "Borrowing from my wife's beauty" was radical empathy. Radical empathy: equalizing and exchanging self and other. One's own story is not privileged over another's.

Professor Glen Hougan of the Nova Scotia College of Art and Design, created an "empathy suit" that vividly allows the wearer the experience of radical empathy with the elderly. The wearer's movement, sight, hearing and breathing become impaired. While watching this video. I could not help remembering walking the streets with my 90 year old friend, John Seeley. Those years I was gifted with the tailor made empathy suit of multiple sclerosis. I recall being the 'gimp,' crazed with steroids and walking slowly to a counter to rent a video. There were half a dozen people behind me and the teller was most impatient, rude actually, as I slowly, slowly looked for my ID and more slowly counted my change. The spirit of radical empathy was with me – for those debilitated as I was - but also for the teller. I recall many times as a hospital nurse tending to a person newly diagnosed with a stroke and suffering from expressive aphasia.   I was then the 'teller' – impatient, suffering not to 'appear' rude, having half a dozen other patients to attend to – I easily understood the teller, the patrons, these patients, my friend John Seeley, and myself.

http://www.youtube.com/watch?v=z-sx_e8_Q-U

Step Four

Living Compassion

"No self and no other" is how Glaser explains the mysterium, the (non) vision that is living compassion. I will try to describe Living compassion, however, although the lived truth is outside of language. Glaser merely says, "The self-other axis cannot be separated from the no-self–no-other axis if our compassion is to achieve full expression. Both are equally true, but taken alone, each is false. Self and other, and no-self and no-other, must be understood as co-existing and interdependent realities if we hope to find the grail of compassion." (6)

Authentic self-compassion slips into compassion for others. Likewise, radical empathy can give way into the spaciousness and clarity of living compassion. "To study Zen is to study the self. To study the self is to forget the self. To forget the self is to be enlightened by all things," says Dogen Zenji. (7)

Across cultures, living compassion reverberates: "Not I but Christ in me," and the Muslim *fatiya* of forgetting one's self in God's will. The "I and Thou" dichotomy momentarily drops away, and one is amidst the forever unifying truth of living beings, loving them unconditionally.

Unconditional love is another way of expressing living compassion. In this, one is enlightened by all things. You are no longer self-consciously kind towards another; you step forth *as* compassion, un-self-consciously. You are fully identified with the process of compassionate activity. You know when you have entered into living compassion when the profound "gift nature" of the loving act reveals itself. You are not living compassion if you are expecting anything in return.

Living compassion is the essential nature of human freedom. Living compassion is itself pure gift. Zadie Smith describes it precisely: "The moment when the ego disappears and you're able to offer up your love as a gift without expectation of reward. At this moment the gift hangs, between the one who sends and the one who receives, and reveals itself as belonging to neither." (8)

Compassion as a presence – as *presence* – is most relevant here. The person who meets this or that situation compassionately is a vehicle for this quality that the bottom line of which is not personal. The spiritual practice of living compassion requires that the self simply step aside. It is radically and blessedly simple, and its experience is extraordinarily ordinary. Compassion is the environment that one is in. One is alert to its presence, available to being its vehicle but one does not for a moment *possess* compassion.

When I met Lewis I was not well. I had just returned from Africa, and my body and soul were in the African time of my

African friends – which is to say slowness not at all compatible with what is required to endure a twelve-hour shift as a hospital nurse. I took to the poison of course – half a dozen cups of coffee – thinking it would help me meet the tasks at hand.   No go.

I was in a dream, agitated, the other staff members spinning around me like so many drunken dervishes. So, when I was told at 3 a.m. that I had an admit, I was less than enthused. Nonetheless, when I came to the door of his room, I took a deep breath and sighed a hopeless, exhausted prayer, "Make use of me."

Lewis was fifty-five years old with Down's syndrome. His head was a lopsided melon bulging in front, his hands and feet curled up with a wheelchair at his bedside because he could not walk. His elderly mother had brought him to the hospital because he had a nasty infected abscess in his left foot.

Admitting Lewis, I got a little of his story – very little, very sparse. His father had died recently and it was not altogether clear how long his mother would live.   What would happen to Lewis then? An institution, I suppose.   It was not the content of his story that touched me as much as his inscrutable manner. The lack of self-pity or melodrama could certainly be read as "cognitive deficiency." But the indefinable nature of our interaction left me stranded between interpretations.   An imbecile? A holy one? Neither or both? I simply could not read him.

"You are a remarkable man," I told Lewis later as I cleaned his wound, laid strips of wet saline gauze across it, and wrapped it in Kerlix dressing. "Thank you," he replied.   Did he understand what I meant? I left his room feeling put back together again, grateful, and humbled by a humble soul.

Where was the spirit of kindness with Lewis? In him? In me? Or hovering between us in the neon glare as he told of his father's death while I tended his wound? It was my meeting with Lewis that convinced me that the spirit of kindness is indeed a spirit; I could not locate it, but I was nonetheless healed by it. The closest I can explain this experience is to say that the meeting itself healed me of my fragmentation. Lewis's story carries light: gentle and lucid radiance. Through the simplicity of two men meeting across worlds, I learned that compassionate activity itself is medicine. I was incoherent before we met, and was rendered whole. I could not find the thread until we received one another. Lewis drew something out of me which proved new and unanticipated.

I have tried to fold the lessons of day-to-day life while living *compassion* which I have experienced both inside and outside my hospital work. I try to approach each interaction with others with quiet intent to be hopeful while available to kindness. Yes – to keep the faith with the intent. And there we meet – I to Thou, yet as One.

In this life the spirit of kindness "bloweth where it listeth." One can be responsive to its presence but cannot control it. One can only be hospitable to it, alert to its movement in oneself and others in whatever situation. One can be attentive to the crazy discipline of being available as its vehicle. This is a fierce and glorious path. Fortunately, there are many moments which become teachers; and, as they say, "a teacher touches infinity." It is for us to recognize those teachers, discern their teachings, and live by what we learn.

With Lewis the self-other axis was illuminated up by a third – the spirit of kindness; and, with that, there was an aware self-forgetting. The thought of me being compassionate toward him would be simply false. He and I met in the environment of compassion: radiant and fresh. My time with Lewis extends beyond Shakespeare's injunction through Portia (9):

> The quality of mercy is not strained.
>
> It droppeth as the gentle rain from heaven
>
> Upon the place beneath, it is twice bless'd

It blesses him that gives and him that takes.

Lewis and I were thrice blessed because the spirit of kindness allowed us for a few moments to extend and receive mercy from each other. "Self and other" are not abolished by living compassion. They are contained within selflessness, but they also lend body and ground to selflessness. They are necessary to one another, interdependent truths.

When the sacred nature of plurality is honored in the meeting of two, the Hasidic Jews say, then an angel is born.

The *mysterium* of living compassion is in this light of *presence* which I tried to express with the story of Lewis. In this light, love is made visible. Living compassion *is* loving the self and the other selflessly. The opportunity to love is always now. The place for love is always in this place, here. From now and from exactly where you are, withhold nothing.

Follow the contours of this arc (of your heart) -- loving yourself and daring to love all you meet. Dare even to *live* compassion; then the craft of generosity will become the vibrant truth that you live for.

T.S. Eliot (10) writes:

> *We shall never cease from exploration*
> *And the end of all our exploring*
> *Will be to arrive where we started*
> *And know the place for the first time.*

http://www.wimp.com/doanything/

37

References

1. Ortiz Hill, Michael (2010) *Conspiracies of Kindness: The Craft of Compassion at the Bedside of the Ill.* Hand to Hand Publishing: Topanga, California.

2. Huber, Cheryl (2001) *There Is Nothing Wrong With You: Going Beyond Self-Hate. What You Practice Is What You Have.* US: Keep It Simple Books.

3. Carver, George Washington. *http://www.brainyquote.com/quotes/authors/g/george_washington_carve r.html*

4. Blake, William. Poem: "Auguries of Innocence" from *The Selected Poems of William Blake.* Great Britain:Woodsworth Limited Edition, 1994, Page 139.

5. Griffin, John Howard (1977). *Black Like Me.* New York: Bucaneer Books, Inc.

6. Glaser, Aura (2005). *A Call to Compassion: Bringing Buddhist Practices of the Heart into the Soul of Psychology.* Berwick, ME: Nicolas-Hays, Inc., Chapter 5.

7. Port, Dosho. (2008) *Keep Me In Your Heart a While: The Haunting Zen of Dainin Katagiri.* Wisdom Publication.

8. Zadie, Smith (2009). "Always Another World," *Readings, Harper's Magazine,* January 2009.

9. Shakespeare, William. *Merchant of Venice.* Act IV, Scene I; Portia's statement.

10. Elliott, T.S. The Waste Land. From "Little Gidding" the last portion of his *Four Quartets*

About Michael Ortiz Hill

As a nurse and patient, Michael Ortiz Hill embodies the essence of the progressive learning of *The Crafts of Compassion*. Prolific writer of profoundly moving realities, Michael Ortiz Hill speaks to the heart of readers with the raw verve of compassion's magic. He embodies what he writes as mentor and student.

A few of Michael Ortiz Hill's books are:

Twin from Another Tribe: The Story of Two Shamanic Healers in Africa and North America by Michael Ortiz Hill and Mandaza Augustine Kandemwa

The Village of the Water Spirits: The Dreams of African Americans by Michael Ortiz Hill and Mandaza Augustine Kandemwa

Dreaming the End of the World: Apocalypse as a Rite of Passage by Michael Ortiz Hill

Conspiracies of Kindness: The Craft of Compassion at the Bedside of the Ill by Ortiz Hill, Michael

FRANCIS & O'MALEY

CHAPTER 5

LOVE - GREATER THAN

ALL SPIRITUAL GIFTS

MAKE LIFE HAPPEN NEW TESTATMENT PARAPHRASE EDITION

I CORINTHIANS 13

IF I channel, perform psychic readings, or communicate with spiritual beings, spiritual guides, or even teach profound wisdom gained from angels, gurus, swamis, or theologians, but do not speak from Love, experience Love, or radiate Love, all my "spiritual" words are obnoxious, noisy clangs, and meaningless bongs of gibberish. Dwelling in Love is the beginning and end of all connections, gifts, and communications.

2. Even if I utter God's exact words, or understand all mystical or spiritual mysteries, or possess infinite knowledge, or perform miracles such as moving mountains or healings, if I do not embody Love, I am meaningless. I am nothing. Why? Because Love is the Essential Source from which all else springs.

3. If I give everything I can including my body, but am not in Love's essential stream, there will be no benefit to me.

41

4. What is Love like? Love is expressed through patience, kindness, compassion. Love provides freedom from jealousy about someone's wonderful life or possessions, and freedom from being boastful or arrogant about one's life, possessions, talents, skills, or looks.

5. Love avoids all cruelty, avoids selfish choices or thoughts, avoids anger, avoids revenge, or retaliation for selfish reasons. Love is power. Love is the Source of ultimate corrective actions. Love is the clarity that sees beyond stupid meanness. Love is the fuel raising up the beaten, oppressed, and demeaned. Love is also the Source of energy and power that can stop the beater, oppressor or demeanor. Love of true-self, love of the true-others, love of right, love of growth, love of all there is reflects the recognition that we are all from the same Source and flow in the same fluid of life. That Source, that Fluid is Love.

6. Love enjoys the good people are and do, and does not gain pleasure in wrongdoing. Love does not excuse or justify cruelty, abuse, destructiveness but does look beyond these inhumane actions for remedy, protection, and ascension. Love may outrage against wrongdoing out of love for both the victim and the perpetrator. Love provides the vision which enables us to see that ultimately Love, as the form of power, is the source of healing and change for both those hurt and those harming.

7. Love forgives everything ultimately. Love always trusts not in the liar, abuser, or seducer but in the ultimate deep power that Love can inspire change in everyone, and in these ways, Love fuels hope persistently.

8. Love never ends. No need to worry about running short of Love. Also, remember always to begin all and end all in the wonderful presence of Love. All the spiritual skills,

mystical tools, or divine knowledge will end. But Love will never end.

9. Even with all our learning, experience, and spiritual expansion, we still know so little about our universe, the All, the Source, the Divine.

10. Ultimately, our limited knowing will give way to perfect clarity and understanding.

11. Yes, we will continue to mature from being spiritual babes into more mature and spiritually awakened if we choose.

However, even with this exciting evolving spiritual maturity, we still will see so dimly, so partially. Our understanding is foggy and filled with guessing and experimentation and wonderment. But at one point, each of us will know fully and understand from the Divine point-of-view. We will understand ourselves, each other, all realms of existence, and the ultimate Source.

And when we see fully, we will know that Love is the greatest and the ultimate knowing, the beginning and the end. Yes, now we have faith, hope, even love, but at that point, hope and faith will be unnecessary. Love will be known as the essence of All, the Fuel of all that Is, the Fluid in which all swims, the egg and the sperm out of which all has become. In like manner, Love is the ultimate Mystery of sincere mystics, the ultimate energy of healers, the conduit of worthy psychics, mediums, channelers, sages, gurus, swamis, theologians of all persuasions. Love is the energy inherent in all spiritual powers and tools. Begin, move within, and end always in the fluid flow and presence of Love no matter what you do, seek or be. Love will be your power. Love will be your magic. Love will be your spiritual awakening tools.

12. We have our belief systems, our profound hopes, and our personal ability to love, but always know the greatest is always Divine Love as the Source, Fuel, Reason, and Connection.

*Excerpt above is from the Bible's New Testament, I Corinthians 13:1-12, *Make Life Happen Now Bible Paraphrase Version.* Rancho Palos Verdes: Make Life Happen Publishing, 2014.

CHAPTER 6

GALACTIC FAIRY TALE

BY MICHAEL LIGHTWEAVER

Introduction to A Galactic Fairy Tale: Often we need imaginative tales to describe deep mystical truths. Face it, the realms of metaphysics often surpass ordinary reality and its limited beliefs.   To transcend these limits, sometimes science fiction, fantasy, poetry, or fairy tales help us reach deep inside and reach way above. We grasp inconceivable truths which are otherwise indescribable with the help of fiction and prose. **Michael Lightweaver's A Galactic Fairy Tale** *helps us reach these other realms of our truth so we can be Love and Light in our ordinary lives.   Enjoy and be enlightened by this Fairy Tale about your spiritual ascension living within this era of the Heart, of Love.*

A long, long time ago in a galaxy far, far away there were all of these little light beings just hanging out enjoying life in that joyful and timeless dimension. And then one day a very large, magnificent angel came to them. He had a very serious look on his face. He was looking for volunteers for a very important cosmic mission.

We have this small - but very special - planet out at the edge of the Alcyon galaxy called Gaia. It is quite unique like a beautiful garden and it is teeming with hundreds of thousands of different life forms. It has been something of an experimental station in the galaxy and it has a most interesting humanoid life form that incorporates the very highest and lowest frequencies known in the cosmos. It is in fact the very epitome of dualism. On the one hand it is an incredibly beautiful life form and is capable of carrying the highest frequencies of love, light, and joy known throughout the whole Universe. On the other hand it is capable of carrying the densest and darkest frequencies the cosmos has ever experienced - frequencies which the rest of creation evolved beyond eons ago.

Here is the current situation. Within the domain of time, this planet goes through periodic cosmic cycles. It is now coming to the end of two major cycles - a 2,000 year long age of Pisces and the 25,000 year long cosmic year in its journey around Alcyon, the central sun of the Milky Way galaxy.

With the completion of this cycle, many things are coming to an end and many things are about to begin. But most importantly, the planet is experiencing an infusion of light that is dramatically increasing its frequency. As during any major time of transition, there will be a certain amount of turbulence. Some of this will be geological, for Gaia herself is a living planet and is also evolving. But much of it also involves the hominoid species that dominates the planet.

This will not be a particularly easy time for the species - especially for those who are sleeping and those who are vibrating at the lowest frequencies. As the frequency changes, it will create insecurity, which in turn will create fear.

The first era of evolution on this planet was the physical era and the key word was survival. The second era, which is now ending, was the mental era and the key word was logic. The third era, which is now beginning, is the era of the heart and the key word is love. This is the highest frequency.

46

Those who currently hold the reign of power on the planet are of the old order of the physical and mental. To the extent that they can make a graceful transition to a heart centered and divinely guided life, it will be an easy transition. To the extent that they are unable to do this, they will experience much turmoil.

So this is the current situation of Gaia. The reason I am here is to seek volunteers who would be willing to incarnate in humanoid form on the planet at this time to help make this an easy and smooth transition. We have sent prophets and teachers in the past. Very often they were brutally persecuted or killed. In other instances they were set up as "gods" to be worshiped and these humanoids built elaborate religions and rituals around them and used these religions to control each other. They did everything except follow the simple teachings that were offered.

So this time we are trying a different approach. No more prophets, saviors, and avatars that they can use to create religions. This time we are sending in thousands - actually hundreds of thousands - of ordinary light beings with only two assignments:

* Stay in your heart. Regardless of what happens, stay in your heart.

* Remember who you are, why you are here, and what this is all about.

Now that seems easy enough, right? Unfortunately, No! As I have said, duality has reached its peak on this planet. This species has perfected the illusion of good and evil. The greatest challenge you will experience is to remember Who You Really Are, Why You Are Here, and What This Is Really All About. When you remember, you will be able to stay in your heart, regardless of external events.

So how will you know when you are forgetting? It is easy. Watch your judgments. The moment you notice that you are in a place of judgment you will know that you have forgotten Who You

Really Are, Why You Are Here, and What This Is Really All About. That will be your signal.

Now here is the challenge. Life on this planet will require a great deal of discernment - wise evaluation of what is true, what is appropriate, and what is for the highest good, both for you and for the planet. In many ways discernment is similar to judgment. However, you will know when you are in judgment and when you have moved out of your heart when you are in a place of blame.

We know how challenging that this planet can be. We know how very real the illusions on this planet appear to be. We understand the incredible density of this dimension and the pressure you will face. But if you survive this mission - and it is a voluntary one - you will evolve at hyper speed.

We also should say that we know that some of you who will go to this planet as star seeds, will never germinate - never awaken to the remembrance of who you really are. Some of you will awaken and begin to shine, only to be choked down by the opinions and prevailing thought forms around you. Others will awaken and remain awake and your light will become a source of inspiration and remembrance for many.

You will incarnate all over the planet; in every culture, every race, every country, every religion. But you will be different. You will never quite fit in. As you awaken, you will realize that your true family isn't those of your own race, culture, religion, county, or even your biological family. It is your cosmic family - those who have come as you have come - on assignment to assist in ways large and small in the current transition.

True brotherhood and globalization in its highest form will come only in remembering Who You Really Are, Why You Are Here, and What This Is Really All About. It will come as you return to the true temple of Divine Presence, your heart, where this remembrance takes place and from which you are called to serve the world.

So, are you ready? Good!

Oh, and by the way, there are a couple of other minor things I should mention...

Because of the density, you can't operate in that dimension without a space suit. This is a biological suit that actually changes over time. There are many things we could tell you about this, but our orientation time is short so I think you can just jump in and experience it. You should be forewarned, however. There will be a danger that if you forget who you really are, you may think you ARE your space suit instead of the fact that it is simply your vehicle in that dimension. Once there, you will notice that there is an infinite variety of space suits and a great deal of attention given to these. However, in spite of the infinite variety, because this a planet of duality, they all fall into two basic categories called 'genders.' Again, we really don't have time to go into this now. But you will find your relationship with your own space suit to be most instructive and interesting.

The other little thing is this. In order to operate in that dimension, you will also receive a microchip called a 'personality.' This is like an identity imprint that, along with your space suit, will essentially make you different from everyone else. This will allow you to participate in the hologram there - something they call 'consensus reality.' Once again, there will be a real danger that you will become so engrossed in the holographic personality dramas that you will forget who you really are and actually think that you ARE your personality. I know it sounds rather unbelievable right now, but once you get there...

Again, there is so much more we could tell you by way of orientation, but we think you can learn the rest experientially 'on site.' The only thing that is important is to remember Who You Really Are, Why You Are Here, and What This Is Really All About. If you can do that, everything else will work out fine. But take note: So few really DO remember this they stand out as 'different' and others call them 'Enlightened" or 'Awakened" and similar terms. Strange isn't it?

Well, Good Luck and Bon Voyage!!!

About Michael Lightweaver

Michael gave permission to copy this from his website: http://www.n2012.com/n2012/lightweave_writings/Galactic_Fairy_Tale.htm.

Michael's fairy tale has virally traveled the world wide web inspiring millions to consider their true origins, purpose, and position in history as transcendent beings. Michael can be reached at P.O. Box 18909, Asheville, NC 28814 (USA). His beautiful location is often used for meditation, transcending workshops and respites. His prime investment is to inspire a worldwide awakening.

YOUR SOARING PHOENIX

FRANCIS & O'MALEY

SECTION II

HEALING POWERS

ANCIENT TO POST-MODERN

FRANCIS & O'MALEY

INTRODUCTION

HEALING POWERS: ANCIENT TO POST-MODERN

BY MARY O'MALEY

When it comes to healing practices it looks as though we may be coming full circle. We know that healing in ancient times always included the spiritual aspects. A little more than one hundred years ago practical, provable science took hold in the Western nations as the best way, and perhaps the only way, to heal the body. Today, largely due to public intervention, spiritual healing has found its way back and is often found walking hand in hand with Western medicine.

Clearly, of course, if everything is energy, then healing must be energy, too. So in Section II, spiritual healing arts and energy work are revealed as spiritual partners.

Reiki Energy and Western Medicine, by Raven Keyes, bestselling author of *The Healing Power of Reiki*, introduces us to the power of energy healing when combined with surgery. The addition of Reiki Energy not only lessens the trauma of surgery, but also facilitates faster healing. Raven Keyes journeys into the surgery rooms, Ground Zero of 911 and private lives of cancer and cardiac victims touching our hearts as Raven Keyes's Reiki Energizes their bodies.

Kathi Wolfrum, DC, generously shares with us her personal journey into becoming a spiritual healer who performs the mechanical and intuitive aspects of Chiropractic care in **A Healer's Journey to Mastery.**

Another Chiropractor, **Dr. Andrew Cort,** reminds us that we also learn valuable lessons from our patients. **Lessons from the Patient,** reminds us to live more fully and with more kindness by remembering that we too, will die.

Reiki Master, **Alberto Amura** eloquently reminds us that it is our personal responsibility to both heal ourselves and heal Earth in **Healing the Individual and Humanity**. He reminds us that environmental transgressions need our attention and that the human effects of subtle energies impact our environment as well.

We have all heard the wisdom of only needing faith the size of a mustard seed. **Jane Sibbett's, All You Need is One Percent**, tells the story of a miraculous healing journey with Braco, whose healing gaze worked with the one percent possibility of healing a courageous woman's stage four cancer.

Michael Almaraz, CHt., uses the art of Hypnosis to reach the thought, spirituality, and healing process of body, mind, and spirit through one's Higher Consciousness in his chapter, **Harnessing the Light**.

Belinda Farrell, CHt., illustrates the absolute power of our thoughts in the healing of the body and the world in **Explaining the Unexplainable**, from her book, *Find Your Friggin Joy.* She shares the unique process of thought forms learned from the Hawaiian Huna shamanic practices.

Dr. Marjorie Miles, DCH, tells her personal story of healing by commanding her body to heal using poetry extending from her heart. **Spirituality, Cancer and Poetic Healing** will inspire you with the elegant simplicity of Haiku healing energies.

The blueprint that is uniquely you can be found in your chakras. **Dr. Carolyn White** explains the concept of energy in color, sound, and movement and gives us the steps to know and to heal ourselves through our chakra centers in **Chakra Energy Healing**.

Mary O'Maley, MSHN, CHtI, demonstrates how using the energy of colors and nature can empower us to change the way we feel and respond to life stressors while having a great deal of fun in **Playing with Energy.**

CHAPTER 7

REIKI ENERGY DURING SURGERY: ALL PATIENTS DESERVE IT
BY RAVEN KEYES, REIKI MASTER

As the Reiki master who brought the ancient practice of Reiki into operating rooms, I have a unique perspective on the healing it brings to patients during surgery. Reiki is pure unconditional love that heals. Through Reiki training, a practitioner is taught how to welcome this healing energy into their own body and to share it with clients through gentle hand placements.

Reiki is slowly being incorporated into medicine as doctors come to realize the benefits it brings to their patients. Although we are still waiting for a major study to be conducted, clinical evidence is mounting to prove that Reiki truly is a healing power that deserves further investigation. For example, in some cases, Reiki sessions were able to shrink cancerous tumors even before standard allopathic treatment was administered, and patients receiving Reiki during chemotherapy have had much better results without the debilitating side effects normally experienced.

In my book, "The Healing Power of Reiki" I discuss my work at New York-Presbyterian/Columbia University Medical Center, which began when one of my clients discovered she needed open-heart surgery. Her process of interviewing surgeons led her to choose Dr. Mehmet Oz, who at the time was the premier thoracic surgeon in the world. She chose him not just because of his stellar reputation, but because he would allow me to assist her during the surgery by administering Reiki to her in the operating room. This occurred in November of 2000.

The experience with Dr. Oz opened doors to other surgeons and my work in this area of medicine has continued. Although heart surgery is still one of the most violent procedures performed in the medical world today, no matter what type of surgery a patient may require, Reiki during the operation has a huge impact on the outcome. Blood pressure remains steady while the patient is on the operating table, much less pain medication is needed afterward, and healing is much faster in the days following any procedure, no matter how drastic it may have been.

I've borne witness to what patients must endure during surgery, which has made me passionate about Reiki being available to every patient in every operating room throughout the world. Although it may be a long time before this is standard operating procedure, this passion has led me to wholeheartedly commit myself to educating doctors about the benefits Reiki can bring. This dedication has made it possible for many medical professionals to witness that the patients just "do better" when they receive Reiki as part of their protocol.

I am most grateful to the doctors at New York Presbyterian/Columbia University Medical Center for leading the way in bringing Integrative Medicine to the forefront, not just in words but also in their actions by allowing their patients to have Reiki as they endure the terrors of the operating room. I have worked alongside world-renowned breast cancer surgeon Dr. Sheldon Marc Feldman, who has pointed out that all the doctors and technicians in an operating room *must* concentrate their full attention on their specific crucial task in order for the surgery to be a success, so without a Reiki master present, there really is no one there to take care of the *patient*!

It's true that at this writing most doctors have never heard of Reiki, and therefore have no idea that Reiki can bring healing to their patients, even while surgery is underway. How can more doctors be positively inspired to bring this healing modality into their operating rooms? I believe the most effective movement toward change will come from the patients themselves as they remind doctors during interviews that *as* patients, they do in fact have power. This is because like it or not, money talks. Every hospital makes the most amount of money from their operating rooms. Doctors are assigned certain days for their surgeries. For example, a busy lead cancer or heart surgeon might have Tuesdays and Thursdays assigned to them, which means they go from operating room to operating room, performing surgery on patients, one right after the other. These operating rooms must be full to capacity in order to bring in the money that the hospital needs to keep its doors open. If patients start demanding Reiki and choosing to go to a hospital where they can receive it during their surgeries, the whole of medicine will be forced to change, because taking care of patients in this way will become the most financially sound decision.

I have personally attended many kinds of surgeries and have trained a team of Reiki masters who also share in this work. Because the hospital we work in is a teaching hospital, more and more young doctors are being introduced to Reiki. This is a great blessing for future patients, since some of the surgery residents exude great enthusiasm for Reiki. In a recent open heart surgery, I was sitting on a stool in the front of the OR while the patient was being prepped – I never watch any of this, because it's only when I'm actually *administering* Reiki that I am inured of my natural squeamishness. One of the young surgeons came in before he was scrubbed up and asked me to give Reiki to his hands. He explained that the eczema on his hands never healed because he was constantly in rubber gloves. I was stunned! This had never happened before.

The patient was elderly and was already risking her life by having a heart valve replacement, but her doctors had assured her that without the surgery she would soon die. It was only after the procedure was a complete success, and the patient had recovered faster than anyone could believe, that it hit me. I had actually given Reiki to two of the hands that saved the patient's life, and her children had experienced less worry, knowing a Reiki master was caring for their precious mother while the doctors performed their miracles.

Reference
Keyes, Raven (2012).   The Healing Power of Reiki: A Modern Master's Approach to Emotional, Spiritual & Physical Wellness - Foreword by Dr. Oz. Woodbury: Llewellyn Worldwide.

About the Raven Keyes
Raven Keyes is a Reiki master, teacher, certified hypnotherapist, and a guided meditation instructor. She was part of the original Complementary Alternative Medicine Program at Columbia Presbyterian Hospital led by Dr. Mehmet Oz. In the world of professional sports, Raven brought Reiki to athletes in the NFL and NBA. Featured in national magazines such as Vogue and W, she was named "Best Reiki Master in New York" by New York Magazine and was televised as "New Yorker of the Week" on NY-1 for providing volunteer Reiki services for eight and a half months after 9/11.   Raven lives in New York City with her musician/composer husband Michael Pestalozzi, and their dog, Murphy.

CHAPTER 8

BECOMING A MASTER HEALER

BY KATHI WOLFRUM, D.C.

If you have outdated, unnecessary memories running your body, you cannot fully express your highest potential of health.

We are all born with unique talents to share, and I believe mine is healing. I came in with the purpose of sharing knowledge regarding health. I also believe I am gifted with a healing touch that attracts me to body work. In my 20's I discovered chiropractic techniques and this approach to healing. It allows me to help others rediscover their own ability to heal. I say "rediscover" because I believe many lose their ability to listen to their bodies' needs. Reflecting back on my journey, I realize I have always been a seeker, and more times than not, was able to listen to my soul for guidance.

The more I study, the more I become aware that true healing comes from within. Even in chiropractic practice, we do not heal, rather we assist or facilitate. Unlearning is a challenge, relinquishing control is also difficult. My journey taught me to use less force, to be still, present, listen, and allow.

I started helping others by listening to my own intuition and acting upon it. Later, I moved into the scientific realms, studying human biology. Much later I discovered the wonderful world of

Quantum. Quantum scientific information helps elevate me in my ability to transmit energy. Energy medicine is what gave birth to my mastery in my field.

By sharing some of my experiences and lessons, I can help you understand better what I consider mastery as a healer. My search for knowledge and truth has created the opportunity to have a successful chiropractic business during the last 25 years. Truly the best part for me is that I am excited to go to work. My work is filled with, and fills me with, love and joy. Sometimes it feels timeless and effortless. But before I got to this point, I had much to learn and experience.

In Chiropractic College, I was introduced to the concept that our innate intelligence runs our bodies. Automatically, the healing comes from the inside out. This was monumental for me. I believe it was something I already knew deep inside. Where do I fit in as a Doctor? How can I assist others to heal themselves? I wanted to learn how to tap into that intelligence and work with it. With this information in my consciousness, new doors started opening.

Much later in my career, spirituality became an essential component, and I began consciously connecting with a higher power. I was seeking something much greater than myself. I invited the divine to flow through me with the desire to become one with it. I now visualize myself as a conduit for the energy flow. Yet, my concern was how I could use this to make each treatment more efficacious, allowing for faster healing?

Along the way not everyone understood or appreciated my approach. I had to release my need to defend myself. I really began listening and allowing. The many lessons seemed to come as a natural progression, building upon themselves and strengthening my core beliefs. One of my mentors, Dr. M.T. Morter, inventor of Bio Energetic Synchronization Technique (B.E.S.T.), urged us to merely get out of the way and let the body do the healing. It took me many years to fully understand what that meant and to practice it.

Looking back, I began doing body work as a child. I recall letting the body do the healing and getting out of the way of such. For example, I remember vividly working on my father's back when I was less than 10 years old. He would come home from work, flop on the floor, and I would massage his neck and shoulders. I would even walk on his back, deliberately "cracking his spine" with my feet. Not until later did I understand what I was doing. Surely, at some point my ego began to govern my life, and I moved away from doing what once felt so natural. I am, however, thankful that I explored at a young age what I now feel is a gift that I was meant to share.

In middle school, high school and even into college, I was very athletic. I did ballet and gymnastics from a young age. Many feats we did required me to go internally and really explore my physical capabilities. One of the best practices I learned from that period was proper body alignment and posture. I refer back to lessons learned from ballet to help my patients today. Ballet's many repetitions enhanced my teaching because I understood the body at a visceral level. If we are willing to pay attention, many hidden gifts from our development help us later.

The next step in my career advancement was opening my own aerobics gym in Florence, Italy, of all places. I had gone there to study in my third year of college and decided to stay after my year was up. To get the gym up and running, I began teaching way too many classes. Although I was young, the result was physical burn out. Someone suggested that I go see the chiropractor that many of the professional ballerinas were using to keep themselves healthy. I probably heard the word "chiropractor" before, but I had no idea what it meant or what they did. I was desperate, so I decided to give it a chance, whatever "it" was. It was love at first adjustment. I knew in my gut that this was what I wanted to become: My "ah-ha" moment. I felt this was a profession in which I could combine my knowledge and experience as well as this deeper urge to be a healer.

The choice to become a chiropractor meant moving back to the United States. I left Italy with a two-year-old son, very little money, and a burning desire to go back to school. Of course, there were obstacles, but my desire was so laser focused that nothing seemed insurmountable. Once I made that decision I never wavered from my path.

Even though I had only experienced a few treatments, when I started Chiropractic College, I was already adjusting as many people as I could get my hands on. When I started studying, they planted fear in me that I could potentially hurt someone. Thus began the journey away from my creative right brain into my left brain search of knowledge. School was my life. I became so cerebral. I was studying long hours, taking an extraordinary amount of units so I could finish early. It was intense and stressful and exhilarating. I passed my state exams, first try, and hung my shingle out in my home town.

Failure never occurred to me. That initial period was magical as I grew my practice. I even have some of my original patients from 24 years ago. It was also a period of experimentation. I sought and learned new techniques. As serendipity goes, the only two chiropractors I knew at the time were learning B.E.S.T., Bio Energetic Synchronization Technique. This gentle technique nudges the nervous system instead of bombarding or forcing the body to shift. Deeper emotional issues stored in the subconscious mind could additionally be addressed through B.E.S.T.

I learned that the subconscious runs the body, and 90% of your day is memory driven. *If you have outdated, unnecessary memories running your body, you cannot fully express your highest potential of health.* Although I did not fully understand what these new concepts meant, I was intrigued. My gut feels at ease with this information and B.E.S.T. has become second nature to me. This is my "niche," and I now find that my patients seek my care because they have heard it is gentle yet powerful.

While working with patients, I intentionally slow down. I remind myself to release any tension in my body, using my breath. I ground myself, open my crown chakra, and allow energy to flow through me. Importantly, during each treatment, I create an energetic bond with my patients. I remind myself to shift out of my head and into my heart. I try not to have preconceptions so that I do not interfere with the process. I allow the process to unfold naturally, letting their bodies speak to me.

This is an energetic dance of sorts. I am in a moving, meditative state, often treating with my eyes closed. I find the lighter my touch the better, so I can feel their bodies respond to my questions. Communication is elevated to that higher level, and the answers become clear. It is like following a path to its ends.

My goal is to uncover the core of the person's interference with health and where the problem began in their bodies. Symptoms disguise or symbolize what is really creating the disturbance. "Where your attention goes, energy flows." We are energetic beings; energy is our life force. Therefore, I aim to create an energetic synchronization between the patient's mind and his/her body. I aim to create harmony between the conscious and the subconscious mind. Thoughts and emotions have energy as well and are part of this bigger picture.

Different experiences guided me to relinquish my need to control the outcome. That meant learning the lesson that my happiness could not depend on whether or not the patient got well. I did my job and they had to do theirs. Health is a personal responsibility, and I could not do it all for them. Raising my children has helped me learn this lesson as well. The patients have to participate and do their homework, whether that means learning to forgive, eating right, or changing their negative mind chatter. Patients need to make healthy choices and use thoughts to create a healing environment. Mastery in my technique really began to blossom with my efforts to help others release unhealthy patterns. Educating people became an integral part of my treatment protocol.

We are all in different places, and each one of us needs to come into our awareness in our time and in our own way. An example of this is when people show up for care. Often times, patients will ask me, "Why didn't I come in earlier?" I respond, "You were not ready. It is perfect timing now and as it is meant to be." When the student is ready, the teacher will appear.

Learning to "let go and let God" was one of the most freeing experiences. This attitude alleviates the pressure of trying to take total responsibility for another's health. Those shifts allow more joy and love to flow freely from my heart space. My intentions are pure; my attention is in the now. I forever strive to be non-judgmental and compassionate. When I am able to accomplish that, I am able to stand in my power and express my hard-earned mastery. This is my gift to share with humanity, and for that, I am immensely grateful. I am excited and passionate about my future options in the healing profession.

I pray this information was helpful to you in some way. I feel it is important to support one another and to encourage the next generation of health care providers. I wish you well on your journey to discovering your own mastery in whatever your particular area of interest that is. May your journey be as satisfying as mine has been. Together we can create a healthier world.

About Dr. Kathi Wolfrum

A Chiropractor for 23 years, Dr. Wolfrum specializes in the Bio Energetic Synchronization Technique, or B.E.S.T., and has personally studied with both Dr. MT Morter and his daughter, Dr. Sue Morter. Kathi practices a system of healthcare that is truly state of the art in balancing Body/Mind memory energy fields. Over the last 5 years, Dr. Wolfrum has expanded her practice through teaching and writing. Dr. Wolfrum is the co-creator with Mary O'Maley of Soul Cruise Retreat. – She can be reached at (310) 833-3795 and www.southshoreschirpractic.com

FRANCIS & O'MALEY

CHAPTER 9

LESSONS FROM THE PATIENT

BY ANDREW CORT, D.C.

I am of the opinion that of all the many things I have learned about my spiritual path, nothing is more urgent, nothing is more potentially life-changing and potentially world-changing, than learning to remember one's "death."

In the late 1980's, while I was living in New York City and practicing chiropractic interventions, I was asked to join the Executive Board of an organization that was working with the AIDS epidemic. It was called H.E.A.L. (for "Health Education AIDS Liaison"). Basically, our mission was to have supportive meetings, and to encourage more research into possible treatments, holistic or otherwise. There was little available in traditional medicine at the time besides AZT, a very toxic drug. Other possible avenues of research, medical and alternative, were often being systematically discouraged.

Over the coming months, I met a great many people who were HIV positive, a large number who had contracted AIDS. I watched a great many of these new friends die. It was a heartbreaking time. I hasten to add that not all people with HIV or AIDS died. H.E.A.L. tried very hard to get people to see that not all people die from HIV or AIDS. The relentless media propaganda proclaimed that "AIDS = DEATH." This propaganda produced fear and terror causing the mind to become a deadly force of negativity and despondency. As a result, many people gave up the fight and spiraled into sickness and death merely because they were convinced they were supposed to. We tried to counter this with facts – not everyone who contracted AIDS died! So here is a good piece of general advice: Do not let the world's negativity, sensationalism, and propaganda kill you!

I certainly did not treat AIDS with chiropractic interventions, but it was an adjunct treatment. I also employed nutrition, herbs, and some acupressure as part of my practice. Sometimes some coincidentally would hurt their neck or back. I fairly frequently had patients in my office that had AIDS. I remember how hard it was, especially early on, to hear that some young friend had just gotten back his or her lab results and discovered Kaposi's sarcoma or PCP. They were confronting the looming possibility of death. I often left the room on some pretense or other and found it so hard not to cry or scream.

Then one day, one of my patients told me to stop being so sad. He said that AIDS was the best thing that had ever happened to him! I did not know what on earth he was talking about. He explained that once he came to grips with the realization that he (like all of us) was going to die, he stopped wasting all his time being moody, cynical, lazy, or mean. Every second became a great joy. He said he felt sorry for me, and all the people like me, who act as if they are going to live forever and waste time indulging in negativity.

Both Gurdjieff and Castaneda emphasize that the most important thing we can learn is to remember, at every moment, that we are all going to die. This patient, and many remarkable people who I was privileged to know through H.E.A.L., made this teaching meaningful, made it real. So now, I try really hard, and so should you, to remember that we are going to die. I could die in the next moment. That person we are talking with, or ignoring, or even just thinking about, could die in the next moment. There will never be another chance to say something kind, or helpful, or friendly, or loving.

Of course, this is really hard! Someone annoys me, someone cuts me off in traffic, or maybe I am just tired, and I completely forget! I try to remember what my patient said to me that day. I try to think in a new and better way about the beauty, wonder, and fragility of my life, and the precious life that surrounds me. I try to live with appreciation and gratitude. I try to remember to not let opportunities for love and decency pass by unattended because I am too busy or in a bad mood. I do not always succeed, but when I realize later what I missed, I make a new commitment to try again next time.

The spirit, of course, never dies. But the personality that I identify with as 'me' here in this material realm, the personality that feels and experiences and acts in this world, is going to die just as this body is going to die. To callously ignore the human reality and suffering is a cop-out, and does nothing for one's spiritual growth. As Marianne Williamson once said, "I don't feel there is any spiritual or metaphysical justification for turning our backs on human suffering."

So I am of the opinion that of all the many things I have learned about my spiritual path, nothing is more urgent, nothing is more potentially life-changing and potentially world-changing, than learning to remember one's "death."

About the Author

Andrew Cort is an author, speaker, attorney, teacher, and doctor of chiropractic. He is an ordained Interfaith Minister. He has authored many books including The Door is Open.

Dr. Cort can be reached at Andrew@AndrewCort.com, or by writing or visiting INTERFAITH AWAKENING, 9 Rock City Road, Woodstock, NY 12498.

FRANCIS & O'MALEY

CHAPTER 10

HEALING THE INDIVIDUAL AND HUMANITY

BY ALBERTO AMURA

"There are numberless energy rays in the Universe...All rays... come from the subtle nature of the Universe...The interwoven energy net influences the lives of individual human beings, whole societies and entire races...A virtuous individual who responds to the high, pure, harmonious Subtle Energy rays and integrates them with the positive elements of his own inner being may strengthen his life, enhance his health and power and lengthen his years."

-Lao Tzu, Hua Hu Ching, 500 B.C.

I consider Lao Tzu's statement, written 2500 years ago, one of the simplest and clearest descriptions of our subtle reality and the mechanism involved in healing. As an energy healer with a background in science and education, I deeply appreciate both meaningful and motivating explanations about the mysterious forces that affect our human reality. These forces are so little understood, ridiculed by the media, and ostracized in mainstream science. Moreover, within the mysterious realms of these subtle interwoven energies exists the answers and tools which help us understand and effectively resolve our individual and collective challenges and diseases.

Our species, in its great majority, still aims and strives in the wrong direction to access a higher state of evolution and wellbeing through a limited concept of the Universe. We can keep trying to clean our polluted planet through empty bureaucratic discussions and expensive energy efficient devices. We can use lucratively formulated, yet deceptive, new medical drugs. We can use faster, wide-reaching media technologies. Yet, such approaches to evolving humankind will never reach the objective of truly "Healing" our unstable nature. Such will not help us become a truly evolved and beneficial race for the Universe.

Nothing will effectively do the job in the long term if we do not realize that the worst contaminant and infectious disease on our Planet is brewing constantly inside us. These internal infectious contaminants include noxious thoughts, fear, anxiety, extreme emotions and, above all, a chronic lack of awareness of our Self and our environment in our daily life. The vast majority of humanity re-creates in itself a pattern of everyday unnecessary self-inflicted suffering and illness. We systematically cause terrible loss, trauma, and pain to others. The worst aspect of this condition is the morbid capacity to systematically justify and deny such destructive behavior.

These patterns, which are programmed in our semi-conscious minds, are directed and sustained by our drama-attached egos which become easily hooked into fear and anger. Such patterns are fed by traumatic experiences and wrong past actions. These patterns can arise from inherited familial, societal, and educational systems which program self-limiting and alienating beliefs. Clearly, mental programming by the media is continuous as well.

As a Reiki practitioner, I witness over and over the truth in Master Usui's creed about the damaging power that fear and anger have over our bodies and over our ability to cope with life's challenges. In addition, working with the subtle energies of our environment, I witness the strong and crystalizing effect that our thoughts and emotions have. These crystalizing effects can stay a long time in a space, silently and steadily, affecting those residing in it, including animals and plants.

Recently, studies in Japan and Russia used advanced technologies to detect subtle vibrational forces in organisms, spaces, and water, measuring subtle influences and effects. We now know through these recent studies, that water holds a memory structure. Water remembers the subtle emotional vibrational energy gathered from the environment. Therefore, our water can be contaminated by noxious emotional energy. Consequently, water can contaminate the human body. Through this vector, any negative emotional field subtly spreads.

In the process of Healing, we pay attention to subtle noxious energies. These noxious energies are produced by the physical environment and created by our thoughts and emotional fields. In the case of emotional energies, most of the exchange is unconscious. However, the human perception has been for millennia effectively manipulated with fear and anxiety to create needs and repulsions. The more divided and psychologically weakened is our mind-body structure, the more susceptible we are to harmful energies and subconscious influences.

I see in all methods of healing a common procedure of re-tuning and harmonizing the body and mind. Healing seems to release, neutralize, and/or transmute the original noxious energetic roots. These roots are the ultimate cause of physical or mental challenges. During healing, the organs are exposed to a tuning energy that pushes them back into their healthy vibrational pattern. Moreover, the full healing will be directly related to the individual's conscious and subconscious will to heal and evolve, as well as related to his/her karmic protocol of learning experiences. Only the highest good is the outcome.

Our service as healers and spiritual counselors is to help open the doors to awareness. We help raise the individual to a clearer view of life. We help them notice the subtle forces that govern and maintain their true wellness and sanity as humans. It is a process of becoming aware of low energies, self-depleting attitudes, and harmful chronic emotional responses which create unbalance and illness.

At the same time, it is a process of releasing and neutralizing those noxious energies through the specific subtle methods applied, in my case using Reiki. Accordingly, each individual does the necessary life changes to reach inner harmony and outer balance. Our subtle energy work done with individuals also includes his/her willingness to make the healthy changes and utilize the compassionate and truly caring interventions of mainstream medicine. These combined efforts can bring a true definitive resolution to physical and mental challenges.

I consider it very important to clarify the concepts of curing and healing. An individual could become deceptively cured of the symptoms of an illness or trauma. However, perhaps what was virtually cured or ameliorated might be the expression of the problem, not its ultimate cause. The root or origin of physical and psychological traumas and illnesses may still be active. It might likely express itself later in the body in the same, or other related manifestation. Particularly, I look for this in the cases of immune related challenges and functional disorders. There is enough scientific evidence which proves that our emotional-mental patterns and outer environmental conditions, including noxious subtle energies, influence the immune system and our genetic re-building processes, both positively and adversely. For example, in psychological traumas, the apparently resolved emotional issues could be triggered again by a casual situation. Such casual situations might resonate with and activate the inner old wounds and extreme emotions. These wounds and emotions could be deeply stored inside the cellular memory of the emotional energy body, and may not be fully released by traditional therapy.

When we apply the methods and subtle techniques of Healing arts, it does not necessarily imply that the cure of a physical illness will occur. Though the physical expression of a challenge might remain in the body, an inner clearing and awakening process may occur. This awakening process can restore the inner balance, and release the accumulated noxious energies and emotional blockages. Such a process aims to bring a deeply positive change in the life of the individual. However, it might not always create an instantaneous or rapid physical cure.

During the majority of healing sessions I perform, feedback from individuals reveals a deep feeling of peace, emotional release, sensations of less weight, or lightness affecting them mentally and physically. Additionally, individuals often view their challenges differently after making necessary changes to their inner and outer lives. The more the individual surrenders, and at the same time strengthens their awareness and inner will, the more effective and thorough the process becomes. In addition, change occurs when they are not focusing only on the actual physical or psychological challenge. Meditating, creating periods of inner silence and peace, as well as overcoming drama, despair, and self-pity helps considerably. Through the two-way healing process of the healer's help and the individual's willingness to do the necessary adjustments in life, the individual can transform him or herself into their higher nature and heal.

With an open heart and mind, every human can become a healer to himself and to others. It is a gift inherent to our human nature. However, if we have not been born with that skill, we need to bring our consciousness and understanding to such healing reality, and learn methods which awaken its flow. From there, we need to realize that we become conscious instruments of such healing forces. Some individuals have the gift of healing and discover it later in life. Others dedicate their life as healers, as a service and as a profession. Each mainstream, health-related practitioner and scientist can deeply incorporate into his/her understanding and practice our human reality in all its aspects, and then open his/her heart and mind beyond old rigid views, and then become in touch with how to activate his/her own Healing capacities.

When expansive views are embraced fully and without prejudice at the academic level, I believe medicine will finally achieve its highest contributions to our wellbeing. The drug industry will be re-directed to become an instrument for healing. We need the physical and the metaphysical sciences to combine. As physical and spiritual understandings combine we can effectively and safely help, heal and evolve our human plane of existence.

From ancient shamanic rituals to contemporary alternative energy techniques, Healing is the path of becoming conscious from being unconscious. It implies that we can reach a state of balance instead of mental alienation. Eventually, we can become fully aware of our-Self. Then, proactively we become aware of others not divided, not humanly alienated. As healers, we are willing instruments of the Universe to help others and ourselves to become conscious and harmonize with the interwoven, beneficial energies. Above all, as the wise sages and saints of all spiritual paths have stated, the ultimate Healing is the healing of the human race into a mental, spiritual, and physical state of wholeness and harmony with others and the Universe, as well as being fully awakened and fully aware of Its wonders.

References

1. Korotkov, Konstantin (2014). *The Energy of Consciousness, Volume 1.* (No publishing information available on book - Book information available on Amazon.com.)

2. http://www.bibliotecapleyades.net/ciencia/ciencia_agua07.htm

3. http://korotkov.org/what-is-the-structure-of-water/

4. Emoto, Masaru (2004). *The Hidden Messages in Water.* Hillsboro: Beyond Words.

5. http://www.masaru-emoto.net/english/hado.html

6. Lipton, Bruce H. (2012). *The Biology of Belief: Unleashing the Power of Consciousness, Matter, & Miracles.* Hay House.

7. Oschman, James L. (2000). *Energy Medicine: The Scientific Basis.* Edinburough: Churchill Livingstone.

8. Ravitz, Leonard J. (2002). *Electrodynamic Man.* Rutledge Books, Incorporated.

9. Diaz, Luis Angel (2010). *Memory in the Cells.* Bloomington: iUniverse.

About Alberto Aura

Alberto Amura originally from Argentina, lives currently in Brazil after residing 25 years in the US. He holds a Master of Science in Metaphysics, and a certification on Biogeometry®, which is the science of space energy balancing, from the Biogeometry Institute of Cairo, Egypt. He completed advanced training on Quantum Healing Hypnotherapy with the internationally renowned hypnotherapist Dolores Canon. His formal instruction in Argentina includes a Professorship in Natural Sciences with specialization in Biology and Ecology, and studies in Industrial Chemistry, Psychology, and Arts.

Besides his intuitive energy healing gifts he trained and developed his skills with shamans and healers during the 9 years in Taos, New Mexico. He is an experienced certified Reiki Master-Teacher, with students that include medical doctors and therapist from a variety of fields.

Alberto Aura's healing practice extends also to animals, working specially with horses. He is a former member of the faculty at the University of New Mexico Holistic Health and Human Services Program, where he introduced students to the field of energy healing methods. In addition to his intuitive healing and Reiki practice, he is a professional radiesthesist specializing in the identification and neutralization of adverse subtle energies in living and working spaces. As an instructor and speaker, he leads seminars and retreats on metaphysics, energy healing and Reiki, Radiesthesia, integrated wellness, and inner development.

Alberto Aura is associated with Integrated Healing-Cura Energética Integrada Terapeuta Intuitivo e Mestre em Reiki (Associação Internacional de Profissionais de Reiki), Mestre em Metafisica (Instituto Americano de Teologia Holística), Cura e Reforço Sutil de Residências, Estabelecimentos e Terrenos. He can be reached at albetojoy4@yahoo.com and www.lighttide.com.

CHAPTER 11

ALL YOU NEED IS ONE PERCENT

BY JANE SIBBETT

As once the winged energy of delight
carried you over childhood's dark abysses,
now beyond your own life build the great
arch of unimagined bridges.
Wonders happen if we can succeed
in passing through the harshest danger;
but only in a bright and purely granted
achievement can we realize the wonder.
To work with the Things in the indescribable
Relationship is not too hard for us;
the pattern grows more intricate and subtle,
and being swept along is not enough.
Take your practiced powers and stretch them out
until they span the chasm between the two
contradictions . . . For the god
wants to know himself in you.

Rainer Maria Rilke

Meet four people who have changed my world: Braco, Mas Sajady, Machelle, and Mary. Braco has an unusual gift; he gazes silently into people's eyes and their lives transpire. Braco gazes and illnesses heal and circumstances change with startlingly positive outcomes. Mas

Sajady died twice which resulted in his intuitive and healing abilities being activated and demonstrated in ways that have resulted in international significance. Machelle and Mary were seriously ill with one percent chance of getting better. This is their stories which changed my life.

One percent was all the nurse said she needed to get one foot in the door; to kick it wide open for the light of possibility to shine.

"Jane, there is a 99% chance she won't make it." Braco looked grave. There was no time to negotiate. I had to be back in the ballroom to introduce Braco to the 500 or so people assembled and I had less than three minutes.

"Okay. Well, I really think you need to make a miracle." He looked at me, surprised I was so matter-of-fact. The woman, Machelle, was dying. I suppose I was a little bold, but 99% that she would not make it left 1% of possibility that she *would*. "Can you try?" I asked. "It would be great if she could live. Please? Try?"

He, the man known for his healing gaze, makes no promises. He looked deeply into my eyes as if the measurement between reality and the miraculous was behind my pupils not his. Then Braco shrugged his shoulders before smiling with a sigh, "I'll try."

I patted his arm with a "Good. Thanks. Gotta go" and I headed back into the ballroom, my heart freshly ablaze knowing this was paradigm-shifting time – at least for me. I was lit with anticipation. As I presented Braco's gazing gift hourly for the next 7 hours to a steady stream of hundreds and hundreds of people, I watched that woman's 1% improbability grow incrementally and steadily better. Throughout that day and into the next, she improved. On the next day, she was standing on her own, out of her wheelchair for the first time in a year. At the end of the event, just a day later she was even speaking to the audience stating she was sure she was going to be "a miracle" and "healing other folks."

The assembled people cheered, and I quietly hoped this would be true.

Ten days later, back in Hawaii, I received a text from her friend that the tumor of Machelle's Stage 4 cancer was amazingly 80% smaller. Before her trip to our event she had been told by her doctor that she had two weeks tops to live, and it was time to say goodbye to her kids and write her obituary. Now, her doctors were shaking their heads. It seemed she was going to make it. Four years later, Machelle is still making it and inspiring an international audience through the documentary, *"Braco – The Golden Bridge."* Her healing encourages others to have faith and believe they also can join her with their own stories of miraculous odds-breaking recoveries.

Two years before I had ever heard of Braco ("The healer who does not call himself a healer"), I was entranced listening to Mary Manin Morrissey at the Agape International Spiritual Center. She shared her tale about being a pregnant teenager; she was a despondent social outcast, and so sick she was literally dying in the hospital. Worse, she was too depressed to care.

Mary explained that had a nurse who asked her if there was something anywhere inside of her that believed she could, and maybe wanted to live. Sullenly, Mary said, "Maybe one percent." The nurse replied, "I'll take it. I just need one!" That one percent was all the nurse said she needed to get one foot in the door to kick it wide open for the light of possibility to shine. One percent was all that was needed to open Mary to the possibility of a new and much better life: a life which Mary had never dared to believe she could enjoy. So, this nurse prayed and prayed for her through that little one percent, and Mary experienced the first of many miracles to come. She was given a new lease on life, and this lease apparently had some spectacular divine plans for Mary to kick other doors open. Since the 1990's Mary Manin Morrissey has been a best-selling author and a popular voice of New Thought

Wisdom, touring the world many months a year and inspiring audiences everywhere.

For me, it was this reminder from Mary, this light-filled room to which Mary's nurse alluded, that was the great gift which propelled me forward to ask Braco to save Machelle that day and to ask others to dare to believe, too.

When Braco asked me to help him share his gaze with the world, I had no experience with healers, or with public speaking. I was not even well versed in the healing modalities of this New Age. I was an actress, writer, and producer – a beginner here who was also a student of life, craving only to help where I could. Mary's story of her brave angel-nurse coupled with Braco's vision that I could help him help others, kept that door of possibility unlocked. I was not ever sure, but I had hope and a feeling of "Wouldn't it be cool? Wouldn't it be great? What if all this were true?"

I know there has been no harm in asking everyone since Machelle's healing to try a little harder and to tap into their own gifts for healing. I encourage us all to reach a little higher or love more freely.

I know more of this sweet stuff is possible than most of us remember. Every time I have tested such, healing emerges. Sometimes it is little. Sometimes it is just a ray of allowing, or a gentle joy. Perhaps a break in depression occurs from an all too big, too much, and too rigidly held perspective. Other times, I have witnessed the big bang, pinch-me-I'm-dreaming-miraculous-moments such as a man walking for the first time in years or cancer gone as with Machelle or Mrs. Schwartz. Even love – true love inexplicably blooming in a war zone of fear - breaks through. In the last few years, I have been a tsunami of tears of joy and consumed with wonder about it all.

Mary and Machelle's stories, combined with others of surprising delight and significance, kicked the door open for me like a screen door slammed open by the summer winds. These experiences over and over help me invite others to have faith, to courageously open up their hearts. Health or happiness or both many times poured into folks who previously did not believe they wanted healing or who did not feel they deserved happiness.

Now, beyond my work with Braco and the tour of years on the road, I finally learned to be truly present to this work. I, too, have to do the work of healing. I quite humbly and sometimes publicly also dumped out the contents of my own worn out old baggage which keeps me in lack and limitation. I have donated it all to Goodwill and C'est La Vie. Fresh and spare have opened my heart up anew. I explore dynamic new ways to continue working with others hoping they will also tap into their own inherent gifts more intimately, personally, and even radically.

Recently, I have met and have been touring with Mas Sajady. Mas Sajady moves beyond kicking all the doors open. His powerful and kind soul's gift is an all-out-roof-raising-light possibility for us. His two near death experiences offer an all-access-pass to a super-highway flow of Pure Source Energy. Little delights him more than sharing this 24/7 beauty of our being. He is equally eager for us all to take up all our tools to finally and fully attain, claim, and most generously and graciously share our best, brightest gifts.

Heaven has always been on Earth if we have the eyes to see and know. At long last, with all these doors, windows, and roofs opening, with healers and masters awakened, with all awakening together, we have now the healthiest, happiest Collective Spirit with which to freely dance in the full-flush of it all, too. We have the eyes, the tools, the hands, and the heart to embody the gifts. Shoulder to shoulder, we go forth now realizing the wonder is right here. The wonder of it all is with you, and you, and you, and you, and me. As Rilke shared, the god wants to know himself in you ... unfolding, enfolding, 100%.

About Jane Sibbett

Jane Sibbett is a well-known actress who simultaneously supports the international exposure of deep spiritual teachers and healers, such as Braco and Mas Sajady, through her publicity business and skills. Her first book will be published 2014 by Hay House International.

The Golden Bridge DVD and other DVDs were produced by Jane Sibbett and Wild Aloha Studios which can be viewed at http://bit.ly/1glScS1. These DVDs share the events, people and healings described in this article.

Jane Sibbett can be reached at Jane Sibbett at PO Box 1380 Kamuela, HI 96743 or at Janesibbett.com, Massajady.com, BracoAmerica.com.

CHAPTER 12

HARNESSING THE LIGHT
BY MICHAEL ALMAREZ

Hypnotherapy and spirituality tend to cross paths due to everything being energy whether it is physical, mental, or spiritual energy that seemingly permeates everything. Native American Indians have used energy and spirituality for good and bad: leading their nations into peace and tranquility as well as war and brutality. Huna, a spiritual discipline derived from ancient Hawaiian traditions, teaches that "energy flows where the attention goes." This Huna concept helps us understand the connection between hypnosis and spirituality. There is a direct connection between so called mental energy (stated plainly our "drive") and the esoteric spiritual or metaphysical energy that ancient cultures and eastern medicine have long since acknowledged as being the source of great personal power.

The very first time I came in contact with a true clean unadulterated form of metaphysical energy was while mourning my mother's passing. There are times in life where our mettle is tested and we must overcome the challenges that threaten to tear us asunder. Losing my mother was it for me: the epitome of one of these occurrences. If I had not had such a firm foundation in spirituality, I can say that I would be lost to this day. Being the last child born into a family of five gave me a connectedness to my mother that very few experience.

She was the first spiritual energy with whom I came into contact after the beautiful but nonetheless traumatic experience of leaving the secure warmness of the womb. You are placed in your mother's arms and placed on her chest allowing that love and unadulterated energy to bond with yours, creating an inseparable energetic connection. This ritual creates a timeless bond that every mother and child has during the period of beginning stages of life.

While my mother was on her death bed, I began to explore the connection between the physical and mental energy. She spoke to beings and relatives who had already transitioned to the other side. At one point she started seeing and communicating with the woman who lived in her house prior to my father purchasing it. My neighbor who had lived there half her life confirmed my mother's described apparition as valid. From my exposure to my mother's abilities, I started learning and understanding the movement of inanimate energy as well as spiritual energy and the mental creative energy that flows in any direction you push.

Just as physical energy influences physical objects, mental or psychic energy (in this context "psychic" purely means relating to the psyche) influences psychological entities, thoughts, and emotions. Carl Jung's seminal essay, *On Psychic Energy,* illustrates this point perfectly. Drawing a parallel to Newton's laws of physics, Jung attempted to formulate a precise scientific formula about which psychological phenomena would be evident. Similar to Freud's concept of libido, Jung's psychic energy is an instinctive force which drives us. Some modern neuroscientists equate the body's physical energy level to the concept of psychic energy. Numerous studies have shown that mental energy is directly related to increased metabolism in the neurons of the brain, also validating Jung's hypothesis.

Vital energy derived from the philosophical concept of vitalism, is a concept with which most are intimately familiar. Vital energy is thought to be the immaterial "spark" that distinguishes inanimate matter from animate matter or the continuum that unites the mind and body. Similar concepts are found world-wide. For example, in traditional Chinese cultures the concept of vital energy is called *qi* or *chi*. Vital energy is *prana* in the Hindu religion and *mana* in Hawaiian culture. Interestingly, all three words are linguistically derived from their cultures word for "breathe," associating this form of energy with the metaphor of life as breath.

Breath is perhaps one of the clearest connections between these three cultural terms for energy. Our breath not only regulates our biological functions within our body, but it also helps us control our mental energy, as neurological cellular metabolism is regulated by our oxygen consumption. The yogic practice of *pranayama,* meaning "the extension of the breath" energizes both the body and the mind. Although the concept of vital energy has yet to be proven scientifically (science being the study of what we can directly observe with our five senses), it is obvious that there is some form of energy that flows through each and every living thing.

Now, I fully understand that there is so much more to learn about the energies that surround us which will benefit my clients and myself as well. This energy work is done directly or indirectly in my office depending on my clients' beliefs and needs. You see, I learned that for many people, including myself, that during life changing events such as a traumatic situations, we tend to open up to the full potential of spiritual energy. Similarly, many people find religion during difficult times. Human beings are more open during stressful times because we are seeking change. The eagerness to find relief and solutions is a perfect opportunity to explore spiritual or vital energy. As a hypnotherapist, I too have found ways to communicate deeply when I am moved by my clients' deep needs. In essence, calling upon energy or my spiritual energy helps me open channels and allow spiritual, or god-like energy to flow in order to help people create new behaviors. At times, small changes in people's beliefs help them find their true selves.   The true self helps each rise above their stress, circumstances, or bewilderment and embrace a higher way of using their power to create change and increase strength and endurance while moving forward.

Also, keep in mind that the energy works or flows when a person is in movement, or mental, emotional, or physical action, even during stress, loss, or trauma. For example, losing my mother was a catalyst for me to understand how this spiritual energy can create solutions and increase our capacities to rise up to our greater selves. Realize first, spirituality is something we all have in us, dormant or active. Second, spirituality is a way to harness the energy of your mind and activate your physical form. Then, physical movement can harnesses spiritual energy and push you into achieving your highest potential.

My spirituality started only at the time when I felt that I was at the lowest point in my life.   I learned that it was easy to be religious being raised Catholic, but at the same time I learned it was very difficult to understand what spirituality really was. I had to look past the fire and brimstone of religious dogma, though. I remember meeting a preacher who stated to me that being spiritual was always going to be much more difficult than being religious. That statement will live with me for the rest of my life. I believe that merely releasing, letting go, and becoming one with your inner energy helps motivate studying, understanding, and feeling the true meaning of spirituality. Your inner self is the only way you find true spirituality.

The earth, plants, humans, and animals all have a rhythm. Even the Earth as it rotates has a rhythm of its own. Spirituality is also achieved when you can become one with these rhythms, with everything, nature and mankind. Loving each other unconditionally and assisting others helps connect us to our higher self as well.   When you can become connected to the rhythms of life and free of judgment, spirituality is deeply experienced as full, free, and loving.

One more way to reach into your spiritual light is to calm your mind. Go deep inside your soul and open your mind to understand. Be one with yourself and with the energy of silence. Such still meditation, prayer, or dreams, have one thing in common and that is silencing the mind and opening it to your higher self.

All the best to you,

Michael Almaraz CHT, NLP, RP

Deeper States Mind and Wellness

www.deeperstate.com

About Michael Almaraz CHT, NLP, RP

Michael Almarez is a Master Certified Clinical Hypnotherapist and Neuro-Linguistic Programmer who helps people overcome problems with alcoholism, smoking, other addictions, depression, anxiety, panic attacks, weight loss, sexual dysfunctions, athletic excellence, exam taking and past life regressions.

CHAPTER 13

EXPLAINING THE UNEXPLAINABLE

BY BELINDA FERRELL

This Chapter is a reprint from Belinda Ferrerll's book "Find Your Friggin' Joy" with author's permission.

As a civilization we're moving forward faster than ever before. If you don't prepare yourself on the inside, you will likely be caught up in a whirlpool of fear and unresolved emotion. The news is filled with disasters in our outer world: earthquakes, floods, military uprisings, government breakdowns, corporations crumbling, real estate devaluation, oil spills, gas prices, water shortages and on and on. We are tenants living on Mother Earth temporarily. She will right the wrongs done to Her over time. How you handle what is happening in the world will reveal how SECURE you feel inside yourself. It is said that we are living in the DREAM we have made by our COLLECTIVE THOUGHTS. When we stop believing in the dream it will change its structure. When people stopped believing in Communism in East Berlin, the Berlin Wall fell. The majority of people now seem to be freeing themselves from conventional ideas that don't work any longer. If it doesn't feel good at the truth level, you need not participate. No one wants to be ruled by a dictator, and now the people are standing up and saying "no more." As things change in our outside world, we begin to see how it is possible to change our inner world, especially if our ideas are somewhat outdated.

For example, take the way we've been conditioned to think about healing. The general consensus tells us to go to a doctor when we have an illness. But I'll bet when we were young, the majority of you had your "boo-boo's" kissed away by a well-meaning adult. We knew the boo-boo would heal by itself in just a few days. How many of us will know with conviction that we will be fine again when illness strikes.

As we grow older and develop more conscious skepticism, we lose touch with our connection to our UNCONSCIOUS MIND ... the part of us that RUNS OUR BODY. We already talked about how our unconscious mind serves as the computer to our conscious mind's commands. So if you really want to communicate with the unconscious and change the negative patterns you've been accumulating, and then begin to listen to what you're saying to yourself. Are these things you would want anyone to hear? What's your inner script? When you are aware enough to be able to write those phrases down, you'll see what direction your unconscious mind is taking and why your body has been doing what it's been doing.

Eric, 58, in a wheelchair, came to me for a healing session. At 19 he broke his neck in a car accident. He told me he knew he had set up this accident long before it happened. Unconsciously, he wanted to know what it felt like to be paralyzed. Whatever the unconscious believes to be true becomes your reality. Now Eric was ready to heal himself from feeling like a victim. He has been able to unplug from the burden of "victim thinking" thus freeing himself to be lighter. Now, he invited his Higher Self to begin the healing.

Martha had cancer when she came to see me years ago. At the time I was doing only hypnosis and past-life regression. At five years of age, Martha's mother died suddenly. As a child unable to understand death, Martha decided that she was to blame for her mother's death. Developing cancer was her way of punishing herself and ultimately joining her mother. In the regression, Martha's mother revealed herself and the reason for her death, which had nothing to do with Martha. Finally getting the closure she needed, Martha's body began to respond to the medication given to her to stop the cancer. Martha recovered from the cancer. Our unconscious desires are running our body. Getting in touch with the way they have been programmed will open our eyes to how we want to proceed. The unconscious also holds the key to reach the Higher Self, which ultimately knows how to heal our illness.

As a Huna Practitioner of ancient Hawaiian healing, I learned about the three Selves of Man and the role that the Higher Self (which is in all of us) plays to change our DNA and heal the physical body. For the ancient Hawaiians, the ultimate goal was to reach the Higher Self. Clearing the unconscious mind of the negative thought-forms from the past, you can then send your "desires" up the pipeline to the Higher Self for activation.

I experienced this myself 16 years ago, when my spine collapsed with nerve damage. My son Brian was living with me in Tiburon and carried me to bed when I could no longer walk. I was told by medical doctors that I wouldn't walk again without surgery. Brian and another well-meaning friend urged me to go the "safer surgical route." Not wanting to be cut, I decided to put the Huna recipe into action. Within four days of actively doing these processes, my back recovered completely ... even healing my scoliosis I had since birth. Shocked that I could walk again and feel normal, Brian was more fearful of his own "inner cleansing process" which he was not ready to comprehend. Personally, it felt like I had won the lottery, only better. I could heal myself together with my Higher Self. These Huna practices really worked! That brought me lots of friggin' joy! I decided to devote my life to teaching others how they could do the same.

So how do you explain the unexplainable? How do you explain calculus to a 3-year-old? Reaching our Higher Self is what some of us aspire to in hopes of receiving Divine Truth, yet it can belong to the realm of the unfathomable, to our limited conscious mind. Healing my back was nothing short of a miracle to me. Yet, the recipe was available and I followed it, as I clearly believed in it.

And now, if you are ready, if you make the choice to believe, we have for you the cleansing and the ancient cleansing practices and techniques that can bring back to you – if you are willing – your friggin' joy.

Reference

Ferrell, Belinda (2013). *Find Your Friggin' Joy.* Bloomington: Balboa Press.

About the Belinda Ferrell, Huna and Reconnect Healing Practices

As a Certified Master Hypnotherapist, NLP Master Practitioner, Huna Practitioner, and Reconnective Healing Practitioner, Belinda is effective at getting results and enhancing performance in people's lives. She graduated from the University of California at Berkeley with a B.A. in English and Spanish. After obtaining a Lifetime Elementary Teaching Credential at Cal State at LA, she taught third grade for five years in Puerto Rico and Los Angeles. She played the character Snow White at Disneyland, was a TV News Reporter for KABC Channel 7 in Hollywood, and was on staff for Senator Charles H. Percy (Illinois) in Washington, D.C.

Belinda trained with Anthony Robbins (author of *Unlimited Power* and *Awaken the Giant Within*), and has effectively used these skills in her own life. In addition to fire-walking (18 times), Belinda was a professional Precision Stunt Car Driver for TV commercials and films. Her credits include ads for Buick, Cadillac, BMW, Volvo, Nintendo, Audi, Toyota, Lexus, AC Delco

Spark Plugs and many more. She was a film and stage actress, having co-starred on the television series Midnight Caller, dozens of industrial films, commercials, and voice-overs. Belinda is the mother of two grown children, loves to "workout," bicycle, rollerblade, snow ski, and just be healthy and have fun.

Belinda received her training in Huna on the Big Island of Hawaii. Huna means "secret," and the secrets were hidden in the chants. The ancient Hawaiian chants became part of her life. They bring down the Higher Self (Aumakua/5th Dimension) that is in all of us. These ancient healing techniques flourished at a time when there was no mental illness on the islands, before the missionaries arrived. "As a Huna Practitioner, I've been ordained to bring back these ancient healing secrets. Inner empowerment is our birthright. We are all powerful spiritual beings, connected as one," declares Ferrell.

Fifteen years ago, Belinda collapsed with herniated discs, spinal nerve damage and paralysis. She was told by medical doctors that she would not walk again without surgery. Instead, she utilized the ancient Hawaiian healing techniques and completely recovered within days. Even the scoliosis she had since birth disappeared. She retired from stunt car driving and began teaching these healing modalities full time.

Overcoming a lifelong fear of water, Belinda guided groups for 10 years to the Big Island of Hawaii to teach Huna and swim with wild spinner dolphins. Swimming with the wild dolphins of Hawaii reconfirmed the connection to the 5th Dimension, the Higher Self in each of us. The dolphins remind us how we must work together harmoniously if we are to co-exist together and build a New World of peace and harmony living in the 5th Dimension.

Between 2007-2009 several personal events altered her destiny. After moving to Santa Cruz in March 2009, a friend took her to see the movie "The Living Matrix" featuring Dr. Eric Pearl of The Reconnection. There was an instant attraction to the

Reconnective Healing work and within a few weeks, Belinda was attending the seminar in Chicago and completed Levels 1, 2, and 3 in Reconnective Healing and The Reconnection. "This new Light and Information beckoned me to climb higher, leaving behind old modalities and stepping into a multidimensional frequency. This is the frequency of the 5th Dimension combining color, sound and information that can regenerate the functions of the human body on all levels. I am humbled to be a part of this shift in time and honored to share this healing experience with you." You can contact Belinda Ferrell at her new office in Santa Cruz, Ca. Toll Free (866) 583-8370 or e-mail: belindafarrell44@yahoo.com

CHAPTER 14

SPIRITUALITY, CANCER, AND POETIC HEALING

BY DR. MARJORIE MILES, DCHT

The holiest day of the year in Jewish tradition is Yom Kippur. This Day of Atonement is an opportunity to resolve to "do better." I was sitting alone at the service feeling restless and distracted. I love tradition and ritual, and I am proud of my cultural heritage, but something was wrong.

I was tuning out. First, I found myself admiring the pretty red hat on the woman in the pew in front of me. Then I thumbed through the responsive reading section of the prayer book. *This is going to take a long time,* I sighed.

"Forgive me for . . ." I recited the words written on the page in cadence with the congregation. *These words don't fit me. They don't describe my life and what I want to amend in the upcoming year.*

I felt disconnected and separate from those around me. Instead of reading, I longed for direct communion with the God-Source. That was *not* happening. I felt like a hypocrite. I rose, closed my prayer book and left the synagogue in the middle of the service.

That decision was a turning point in my spiritual journey.

Trained as a psychotherapist, I had always searched for deeper meaning within life's experiences. Eventually, I became a dream worker who loves to explore symbols and images, and the Dreaming Mind's innate wisdom and guidance. On my spiritual quest, I have learned to trust my intuition, to embrace the simple premise that Love is at the heart of everything, and that each of us is a *spiritual being having a human experience.*

Unfortunately, I felt extremely human the day I heard the words, "its cancer." This life threatening diagnosis precipitated an identity crisis and more spiritual questioning.

Even if you are "cured" of cancer, how do you become whole again? Medicine may fix the body, but it does not put your life back together. How do you pick up the pieces of your former self and weave them into a new tapestry of life?

What helped me answer those questions was *writing* about it.

After surgery, removal of the lower lobe of my left lung, followed by chemotherapy, I began radiation treatments. I never expected a "spiritual awakening" during one of my visits to the oncology radiologist. I was waiting for the doctor to arrive for my appointment. I wanted to be outdoors in nature, whole and healthy again. Instinctively, I took some deep, cleansing breaths and relaxed into a daydream. While in that state of consciousness —between waking and sleeping—I heard a Voice tell me to write a poem, specifically a Haiku poem.

Haiku, I recalled, is a Japanese poetic form—consisting of three lines, the first containing 5 syllables, the second 7 syllables, and the third 5 syllables for a total of seventeen syllables.

Cancer treatment is NOT poetic! I thought angrily.

Yet, inexplicably, I picked up my pen and began writing a poem. The Haiku seemed to emanate from a long-forgotten place within me. I wrote:

Radiation...Zap

Search and find the mutant cells

Glowing...going...GONE!

Something powerful, mysterious and incomprehensible just happened.

Why did the Voice tell me to write a Haiku?

Upon reflection, I realized that Haiku captures the heart of your experience with life. Haiku penetrates the essence of the moment. Haiku offers surprising insights and wisdom. In my case, this Haiku was a prescription for living life which was even larger than the single chapter of my life on which I was focused.

When the doctor arrived, I said, "I just wrote a poem...about radiation...and I would love to read it you."

He listened while I read my poem for the very first time.

Surprisingly, I found myself performing my Haiku with hand gestures—including a loud clap on the last syllable and the last word, GONE! In that moment, I *knew* I was cancer free.

For what seemed like a long time, the doctor and I just stared at one another. Finally, he broke the silence and said, "May I have a copy? I want to share this with my other patients?"

It was during that exchange that I realized the spiritual and healing power of poetry. Writing this poem was more than scribbling seventeen syllables on a blank sheet of paper. Haiku could transform itself into a container for the essence of the human spirit—despite the vulnerability of the body—and communicate that core to another human being.

The next day, I began a *daily* Haiku journal. I did not realize it at the time, but through writing Haikus, I was building an interior place within myself where I could rest, find comfort, hear my intuitive voice—and recover my creative expression.

As John Fox, a certified poetry therapist reminds us in his book, *Poetic Medicine,* poetry helps you remember that you are more than your physical body and your suffering and your fears. There is something within each of us that remains untouched and transcendent; it is your spiritual essence, and poetry is one of its voices.

In times of crisis, finding meaning is strength, and the deepest meaning is carried by the unconscious mind and the language of dreams and symbols. Poetry speaks this same language and helps us hear the meaning in illness, the meaning in the events of our lives, and our soul's Voice.

Recovering my own artistic voice and helping others through creative Self-expression has been transformative. It has been the guiding spiritual force for facilitating an ongoing expressive writer's group "Writing with Your Dream Muse." It has inspired my book, *Healing Haikus—A Poetic Prescription for Surviving Cancer* and co-authoring, *Cancer: From Tears to Triumph* (release date 11/2014).

Can someone really be "saved" by a poem? According to author, Kim Rosen, the answer is a resounding, "Yes!" She states that poetry, the most ancient form of prayer, is a necessary medicine for our times. Poetry is a companion through difficult times. Poetry is a guide when you are lost. Poetry is a salve when you are wounded, and a conduit to an inner source of joy, freedom, and insight.

References

Miles, Marjorie (2013). *Healing Haikus—A Poetic Prescription for Surviving Cancer.* North Charleston: CreateSpace Independent Publishing Platform.

Miles, Marjorie and Co-author unnamed (anticipated publication date 11-2014). *Cancer: From Tears to Triumph.*

Fox, John (1997). *Poetic Medicine: The Healing Art of Poem-Making.* New York: Penguin Putman, Inc.

Rosen, Kim (2009). *Saved by a Poem.* United States: Hay House.

About Dr. Marjorie Miles

Marjorie Miles, DCH, MFT, a former psychology professor and psychotherapist, earned a doctorate in clinical hypnotherapy. She is a Dream Expert, Creativity Coach and author of *Healing Haikus-A Poetic Prescription for Surviving Cancer.* She can be reached at drmarjorie@journeyofyourdreams.com and her classes "Writing with Your Dream Muse" are scheduled on that site as well.

FRANCIS & O'MALEY

CHAPTER 15

CHAKRAS:
YOUR PERSONAL BLUEPRINT
BY DR. CAROLYN WHITE, DCHT

You are a spiritual being having a human experience. What is "Spirit" and how does it manifest its "human" experience?

You live in a sea of energy—the Universal Energy Field (UEF). Quantum physics refers to this field of possibilities as the "Quantum Soup." Ancients called this life-force energy "chi" or "qi." Western mystics talked about Cosmic Consciousness, Infinite Spirit and "The All." Contemporary philosophers discuss the "Divine Matrix of Creation."

No matter what you call it, energy is energy and it is the "stuff" of the Universe. Energy is neither good nor bad—it just "is." Energy only realizes its potential when in motion.

"Nothing rests; everything moves; everything vibrates." - *Third Law of Hermetic Wisdom.(1)*

The Law of Vibration is an ancient concept that forms the basis for many contemporary scientific observations and theories. Everything that exists in the universe has its own natural frequency of vibration. Light, heat, magnetism, and electricity exist because of vibration. According to John W. Keely's first law of Sympathetic Vibratory Physics, published in 1893, vibration is the beginning of all matter (2).

The frequency of the vibration determines its form: the lower the frequency, the more physically dense the form. A form that is more refined and subtle has a higher or faster vibratory rate. If you change the frequency of the vibration, you will alter the form.

Without frequency, which is the repetitive rate of vibration, your brain would have nothing to process. You would not have a basis for discriminating between elements in your time-space reality.   Color and sound rely on specific frequencies for their uniqueness.

What creates your "uniqueness?" You are aware of the body-mind-spirit connection which is the concept which points your way to wellness and wholeness. So, what are you connected to?

The body is a collective of cells which forms a tangible, three dimensional being that is "you."   The mind is a complex maze of cognitive processes that enables consciousness, perception, thinking, learning, reasoning, and judgment.   The mind is intangible.   So is spirit. Throughout history, philosophers and scientists have offered their various takes on what the mind and spirit are and where they are located.

The body-mind-spirit connection compartmentalizes what you really are: energy vibrating at different frequencies. It is another way of expressing the human energy experience. This holy trinity defines the range of energy along the electromagnetic spectrum. Think of the body being a denser, lower frequency, the mind a mid-range frequency, and the spirit a higher frequency.   This is analogous to the frequency of the Earth at about 13 Hz, humanly audible sound between 20 and 20,000 Hz and visible light, which ranges between 4×10^{14} Hz (red) and 8×10^{14} Hz (violet). You are energy, vibrating energy. Your body vibrates at a range of frequencies that gives it solidity. Your mind vibrates at different ranges of frequencies. This is measured via brainwave activity.

Given this analysis, is spirit a higher frequency? Many gurus propose that you are a being of light. Is this why spiritual seekers strive for en-lighten-ment? If spirit is light, then how can you best connect with this frequency of energy?

During the 40+ years of my personal quest, my mentors, from Jack Schwartz to Doreen Virtue, taught that clearing and balancing your Chakras was the most important thing to do on a daily basis.

What are Chakras? "Chakra" is a Sanskrit word which means "a spinning wheel or disk." In this context, the chakras are a series of wheel-like energy vortices that form the human energy field. This is an ancient concept embraced by Hindu philosophy over 5000 years ago.

Collectively, the Chakras process your incoming energy (chi, life force). Chakras act as transformers that tap the sea of energy around you and condition it for your use. A Chakra is the interface point between physical aspects of your body and the subtle, non-physical, non-local, UEF, i.e. the Quantum Soup.

When daylight passes through a prism, it is refracted into the seven spectral colors—Red, Orange, Yellow, Green, Blue, Indigo, and Violet —the Rainbow. Think of your spirit as a "crystal" or prism, an interface that refracts the living light of the UEF to manifests your essence. Your physical body is stepped down energy of light, filtered through a system of interfaces which are these seven major Chakras. Your Chakras act as lenses that focus your unique pattern and expression in this incarnation.

Chakras serve as your structural blueprint, a conduit for energy. This information is stepped down through the Matrix of Creation into a physical expression of that energy—you. Chakras are what feed you the parameters for your 3-dimensional reality.

Chakras link you to the Divine Matrix. Each of the seven major Chakras optimally vibrates within a certain frequency range that corresponds with a spectral color. Just as a radio frequency carries information, each of the seven spectral colors broadcasts data. Consider each color as an archetype of your space-time reality, carrying a range of human experiences, qualities, and characteristics. Just as with a radio, if you tune into this broadcast and have a clear channel, you will receive the information you need, without interference, to actualize the power of your life's purpose.

Besides receiving energy from the UEF, the Chakras store energy patterns and broadcast this information "back" to the UEF. As such, the Chakras act as transceivers, constantly exchanging information with the UEF. This is how information is "written" into the Akashic records. Chakras are portals to the collective consciousness.

The amplitude and frequency of each Chakra's "output" determines the "look" of your Aura. Think of your Aura as representing the exhaust-fumes of all the Chakras' output. The filters that you develop in your human experience can alter the frequency, size, and shape of the Chakras.

When all of your Chakras are understood, cleared, balanced, and interconnected with the UEF, you become the bridge between matter and consciousness. The Chakras are gateways between various dimensions as they link all aspects of your body to non-physical, non-local counterparts within the energy of the Creation Matrix. Through the interface of the Chakras, you can access the entire range of creation and fully realize the potential of your body/mind/spirit connection.

What can you do to tend to the health of your vibratory interfacing links, the Chakras, to the UEF? Explore these common themes to keep the channels clear and open:

1) Intention

First and foremost, declare that you intend to honor the connection of your Chakras with the UEF. Stating to the Universe that this will happen will make it so. This is the first connection.

2) Know Thyself – Learn What Works for You

You are made out of the same stuff as the Universe and you are also unique. Discover what methods work for you. Are you a highly visual person? Do you see pictures in your mind? If so, initially work with colors and related images, i.e. a strawberry equals red. Does sound move you? Perhaps listening to chanted mantras, toning or singing will connect you. If you love motion and respond to touch, incorporate movement or bodywork into your practice.

As you resonate and connect with the Chakras, you may want to vary your practice. If you have been working with color, perhaps experiment with adding movement. Remember, there is no "cookie cutter" technique for clearing and balancing the Chakras. Become aware of other's techniques and then make them your own. Before you embrace another's methods, ask, "Is this for my highest good?" Always question and listen to your inner-tuition. Having an inside-out viewpoint allows you to trust your inner guidance.

3) Maintain the Energy Flow and Rhythm

Remember, you are in a constant energetic communication between your Chakras and the UEF. The only constant in life is change. Traditional Chinese Medicine (TCM) suggests that your energy blueprint—your Chakras—is perfectly aligned only at your birth and the time of your passing.

Realize the ebb and flow of this energy exchange. Think of a figure eight (∞). Physically or mentally, trace this image above each Chakra. Imagine you are connecting that Chakra with what it needs in the UEF. Notice what you experience. The infinity sign energetically symbolizes the flow of the life-force, the taking in and letting go, the giving and receiving and the yin/yang balance of the UEF. Embracing the equilibrium of this flow keeps you in tune with your energetic blueprint. Adopt a method that adapts to the vibratory motion of the UEF.

4) Learn Mindful Breathing Techniques

The breath carries the life-force energy — Qi — of the UEF. Without your breath, you would not have life. Breathing is one of the few autonomic functions that you can consciously regulate. Learn diaphragmatic, or belly breathing. Use your breath to connect your Chakras with the UEF.

5) Explore Energy Psychology Techniques (EPT)

Unresolved emotional issues inhibit the functioning of the Chakras. If you believe you have such issues, EPT, such as Emotional Freedom Technique (EFT), can gently and swiftly release traumatic events frozen within the body-mind-spirit connection. EFT is also an effective way to rapidly balance the Chakras on a daily basis. Check out the May 11, 2011 video posted on www.ChakraCoach.com, which demonstrates just how quickly EFT brings the Chakras into balance.

Learn self-hypnosis to provide skills with which to access your inner wisdom. Remember that your words and thoughts create energy packets, sending information to the UEF. Learn to make your thoughts and words congruent.

6) Discover the Meaning of Colors

Discover the archetypal meaning of the seven spectral Chakra colors. Over the centuries, color psychology evolved from observing the biological, visual, psychic, emotional and aesthetic responses to color. Understanding the energies inherent in each color enhances the awareness of your potential. Although each Chakra corresponds to a spectral color, let your Chakras emit the color vibration most beneficial to them in present-time. Play with color and integrate it into your life.

7) Practice – Have Fun – Keep It Simple

Using the Aura and Chakra Imaging System, I have observed that hearty laughter and radiant, unconditional love are the fastest ways to balance the Chakras and connect with the UEF. Keeping the channels clear and open is a dynamic, ongoing process. Enjoy the journey and travel light.

References

(1) For a more detailed explanation of these very important Laws of Hermetic Wisdom go to this website: http://www.mind-your-reality.com/seven_universal_laws.html#Part_2- *Third Law of Hermetic Wisdom.*

(2) For an introduction to Physicist John W. Keeleys 1893 work go to this website initially: http://www.svpvril.com/fortylaw.html.

White, Carolyn (2013). *Think It, Say It, Be It: Use Your Words to Change Your Life.* Bloomington: Balboa Press.

About Dr. Carolyn White

Carolyn White, Ph.D., DCH, is a metaphysical educator, energy therapist, Reiki Master, and author of *Think It, Say It, Be It: Use Your Words to Change Your Life.* Learn more at www.ChakraCoach.com.

FRANCIS & O'MALEY

CHAPTER 16

PLAYING WITH ENERGY
BY MARY O'MALEY, MSHN, CHTI

Everything is made of energy, and, energy can be manipulated into anything we can imagine or desire. So, for these next few minutes, we are going to play with aspects of energy.

Using energy to change the way we feel physically, spiritually, and emotionally is fun and relaxing. To demonstrate this, take a moment to think about the color red. Imagine it swirling around you, then in and all through every cell in your body. See if you can feel the vibration of the color red or maybe hear the frequency of it. Does it make your body feel energized, relaxed, agitated, tingled, or something else? How are your emotions effected? How does your spirit respond to the color red?

Now, try this again with the color blue. But this time, experiment with different shades of blue. How does the light blue of the sky feel differently than the deeper blue of a sapphire? Try it again with green, yellow, purple, gold, and silver. Then try mixing different colors . Try pink tinged with gold. I love that one!

Find a place on your body that is tense or in some pain. Ask yourself what color would relax the tension or wash away the pain? Give it a try right now by directing that color directly into that spot, like a laser. Flood it with your color for a few minutes and notice what happens. Do not worry if nothing happens right away. Allow yourself to relax into the idea and the experience. The more you relax into it, the faster it can work.

I have noticed that people will often suggest surrounding one's self with a white light for healing, relaxation, and protection. Sometimes that works just fine for me, but most of the time it feels like something is missing from it. I often instruct a client during hypnotherapy to allow whatever color feels right to them for healing and relaxation to enter at the top of their head and slowly move down their body. When I ask them what color they chose, it is rarely white. Sometimes it is a very pleasant shade of blue or green, but just as often it is red or yellow. Each of us can and will respond to the energy of colors differently and even respond differently to colors at different times. When it comes to feeling protected, the color black feels the most comfortable to me. I find that white works best for cleansing.

If you are feeling sad, ask yourself what color you could use to lift your spirits. If you are feeling anxious, ask yourself what colors you could use to calm and soothe yourself. Now that you have practiced playing with the energy of colors, how can you use this to your benefit?

Let's play with the energy of nature. Imagine bringing the energy of a rock into you. How does it feel to be a rock? Could you use that slow, calm energy of a rock to slow down your heart beat?

How does it feel to be water? Can you feel the power of being water in a waterfall, or water flowing gently in a brook? What would it mean to be a drop of water in the ocean making your way around the world? How is it to be water absorbed into the sky and becoming part of a cloud, then to be released back as a drop of rain feeding the earth in a garden?

What would it be like to be fire? Can you change your body temperature by imagining the heat of a fire place warming your body on the outside; or can you imagine spreading a fire from within your body to warm and relax your muscles?

Feel the wind. Can you feel it caressing your skin and gently blowing through your hair? Or, maybe wind is blowing away the cobwebs in your mind?

Years ago, I was on my way to an interview and I was so anxious about it I could barely focus on driving my car. I realized I needed to calm down or I could endanger myself, not only while driving, but also ruin my experience during the interview. When I asked myself what I needed in order to calm down, a picture of a grand mountain came to me. I allowed the energy of this mountain to seep into my body, mind, emotions, and spirit. Suddenly, I felt strong, grounded, calm, timeless, and powerful. I was so happy to be me and knew that all would be well. During the interview, I was relaxed and confident and all went very well for me. I believe that was the first time I used the experience of an outside energy to influence and change the way I felt. I have used the energy of being an ancient tree with deep roots and tall branches with a strong trunk that has collected the wisdom of the ages, to access my own higher wisdom. It has been an extraordinary tool for me and one I pass along to my clients. Even though I am certified in four different energy therapies, I will generally open up and ask the Universe for whatever energy the client needs. That energy then flows through me and into them or into them directly.

Another aspect of energy work unfolded when I become familiar with the healing energies of Archangels Ariel, Michael, and Rafael. One day a beautiful energy came through me that felt light, full of love, and with a childlike sense of fun and wonder. I asked who this was and heard, "Hi! This is Jesus!" This particular client was deeply connected to her Catholic faith and while working with her, I got to experience the energy of Jesus and his mother, Mary. It was incredibly beautiful and moving for me, and of course, for my client! I have felt the powerful energy of Celtic,

Egyptian, Roman, Greek, and Hindu gods run through me. I have called on the saints and angels for their healing energy.

Who do you relate to? Call on their energy and send them yours in return.

Everything is energy and made from energy. Energy is an ever flowing inexhaustible resource. Energy never runs out! This also means that you can never be "sucked dry" by an energy vampire. The next time you feel you are being drained by someone, face them and open up your heart and let the energy of the Universe run through you and straight into their heart. They do not really want your energy; they want to control you or they feel woefully empty themselves. When you funnel energy to them this way, they likely will suddenly become more peaceful, and you will see and feel them back away from you.

I often send energy from my heart, mixed with white light, to cleanse a room before I begin to work in it. After doing this, I have seen people walk up to the doorway and then back away and not come in. The results of this very quick room cleansing can be astonishing.

So, feel free to play with energy! You cannot break it nor ruin it nor ever run out of it. You are never stuck with it. If you do not like an energy which you have conjured, simply choose another. If you do not like where your life choices have taken you, be the energy of your soaring phoenix. Feel the burn at the end of that life experience and the joy and power and renewal of being reborn from the ashes and rising again. Above all, have fun!

About Mary O'Maley, MSHN, CHtI

Mary O'Maley holds a MS in Holistic Nutritional Health Science and is a Certified Hypnotherapist and Hypnotherapy Instructor with International Hypnosis Federation. She is recipient of the prestigious IHF Award of Excellence & Chapter Woman of the Year from American Business Woman's

Association. Mary specializes in Past Life Regression, Intuitive Nutritional Counseling, Life Coaching, five energy healing modalities, psychic and medium readings, and hosts various programs and events.

Mary O'Maley, as Life Coach, created the Retreat-Reconnect-Recharge-ReEmerge Coaching. This R4 Coaching provides in-depth, personal-retreat experiences which help you access, trust, and follow your inner wisdom.

Certified in Reiki, Access Energy Clearing, Matrix Energetics and Reconnective Healing, Mary O'Maley also developed and provides Crystal Chakra Balancing. Crystal Chakra Balancing was discovered through Mary O'Maley's Akashic Records work.

Mary O'Maley teaches basic and intermediate hypnotherapy through IHF, nutritional approaches to health at various medical facilities, and metaphysical information at various international conferences and local venues.

Mary O'Maley's metaphysical studies allowed her to reignite her psychic and mediumship gifts which she uses for home, gallery and individual readings, given since 1997. She is certified and tested as a member of Best American Psychics. Mary O'Maley hosts and produces The Merry Medium Show. On The Merry Medium Show, Mary interviews many wonderful spiritual explorers from the metaphysical and holistic communities. Podcasts of The Merry Medium Show are available at blogtalkradio.com/the-merry-medium. She also hosts live events in the Los Angeles area: **The Merry Medium and Friends – Where Science and Spirit Meet Live Events.**

To reach Mary O'Maley for her alternative health services, psychic and mediumship readings, radio programs, live events, materials, workbooks and books, contact her at http://www.maryomaley.com or call 424-234-9260.

FRANCIS & O'MALEY

SECTION III

BEYOND THE VEIL

PSYCHIC TOOLS MEDIUMSHIP, AND BEYOND

FRANCIS & O'MALEY

INTRODUCTION

PSYCHIC TOOLS, MEDIUMSHIP AND SEEING INTO THE BEYOND
BY MARY O'MALEY, MSHN, CHTI

In this section we share many experiences and applications of psychic work from those who use these gifts in their daily practice. Psychics routinely are consulted by people from all walks of life and religious practices. Celebrities and government officials use the services of psychics as do many of us, seeking practical advice on love, finances, business, and health. Psychics are no longer relegated to the archetype of the turbaned-mystic who reads palms or crystal balls at the carnival.

Mike Rogalski's Remote Viewing chapter provides exercises for honing remote viewing skills. These skills are akin to those which help develop many aspects of ESP, PSI, or the Sixth Sense. He also reveals some fascinating history of the U.S. Government's Remote Viewing programs, including scientific confirmation of psychic spying using remote viewing.

Dennie Gooding's chapter, **Psychic from Birth,** flows through her childhood and adult experiences as a psychic and a medium. Her unique perceptions were sometimes judged and silenced. Yet, Dennie persevered providing a worthy template for others developing their psychic proclivities. Dennie Gooding's work with the government, law enforcement agencies, and private clientele is well known and proven to date.

Mary O'Maley's chapter, **I'm A Medium, Too**, treats readers to the joy and work of a medium who facilitates the spiritual journeys of the living and the dead. Animals too can telepathically communicate with their human friends, if only someone will listen. Since 1997, Mary has heard and conveyed messages verified by the living and shared by those beyond the thin veil.

Dr. Carol Francis's chapter **Channeling: How, Who, Why?,** examines the steps, experiences and task of channeling spiritual guides. To illustrate the process of interfacing with channeled guides, Dr. Francis details four discourses and the personal characteristics of four channeled guides to help others understand the process and results of spiritual channeling.

Changing of the Guides by **Mary O'Maley** playfully illustrates the ebb and flow of human relationships with spiritual guides and the progressive, ever-changing interactions with various spiritual assistants and angels.

In **Tarot Meditations for Soulful Connections**, world-renowned **Brigit Esselmont** o f *biddytarot.com* a n d tarotfoundations.com urges readers to expand their meditative spiritual growth using the art and mystical messages of the Tarot Cards. Consider here how to use this oracular tool to access the mysteries of your own extraordinary awareness.

CHAPTER 17

REMOTE VIEWING TOOLS
BY MIKE ROGALSKI

History of Remote Viewing

Remote Viewing was developed as a method of teaching psychic spying by the CIA. Remote Viewing received unprecedented governmental funding for 17 years once researchers proved that psychic energy could not be stopped by any conventional tricks of physics such as shielding, immersion in salt water, distance, etc. This was related to the Stargate Project.

Dr. Russel Targ, previously chief scientist at Lockheed-Martin, with Dr. Hal Putoff were tasked with disputing the veracity of Remote Viewing. They were unsuccessful. Eventually, they developed counter-measures to massive Russian Cold War PSI efforts which also included Remote Viewing.

Ingo Swann, a certified psychic, was hired for testing. The work with Swann proceeded to discover many ancient vedic, shamanic, and mystical writings which lent an understanding to the process of psychic vision. These practices were subjected to standardized scientific methods of research. Government funding, of course, required that this division organize a scientifically based method of training people to remote view with measurable degrees of reliability and validity. Such training procedures worked far better than anyone imagined at that time.

Training Procedures for Remote Viewing

Remote Viewing involves brain functions or brain pattern profiles. First, alpha-brainwave inducement is initiated and maintained. Next, a suspension of "left brain" judgment and critical thinking is practiced. This "left brain" critical thinking is a euphemism for the cognitive capacity to 1) draw conclusions, 2) organize data bits into recognizable patterns, 3) make logical or inferential sense of information, or 4) accept or dismiss a perception as factual.

During remote viewing sessions, it is essential to maintain this absence of "naming" or refrain from "assigning a function to" anything perceived. This abstinence maintains an aperture within the thinking functions or the perceptual functions. In this way, an aperture within the subliminal arena, somewhere between the subconscious and conscious, is maintained so remote viewing is unimpeded. By staying in this mindset, the signal-line of the remotely viewed target will not abate quickly. This structure of perception, sans critical thinking, supports an attitude of observation without the interference from critical judgment or from premature conclusions.

During Stargate, the teams focused on objectively established rigid protocols which ensured there would be no "cueing" or body language which might give away a target during a remote viewing session. No one in the room would know what the target was. The double-blind research model was carefully organized.

The next step of remote viewing is to establish a psychic intent to remote view. One method used during training is to nail down the psychic intent of the target by using an eight-digit identification number to specify the target established for the brain or mind to perceive. Often a computer-generated number of no significance is attached to the envelope containing a photograph of the target. This numbering system also serves to keep the accounting of the target-session organized and maintains the double-blind model as well.

During formal remote viewing sessions, the viewer is next given assistance to start *perceiving* the target, *not thinking* about the target. The first step of this protocol involves ideograms. Ideograms are the first human kinesthetic physiological response drawn by the viewer. Ideograms are gestalt forms. Often these forms are simple, crude and quick depictions of the target as human, environmental, energetic, geographical, man-made structure, water, et cetera. Much like Jungian archetypal objects, these ideograms are common, simple depictions which researchers determined were generically evident in the human subconscious.

Procedurally, when the eight-digit "Target Reference Number" is provided during a session, it creates a psychic "trigger event." Then, at this very moment the viewer draws one of these ideograms which are provided on a chart. This drawing becomes a reflection of the perceptual subconscious representation of the target. It is the first spontaneous reaction to the target. Such a quick response also helps steer the brain process into perceptual representations as opposed to critical thinking, guessing, or analysis.

The one-second, unfocused scribble of the ideogram is followed by "receiving" sensory related dated such as colors, textures, smells, shapes, and emotional variables, which are quickly written down on a form provided to the remote viewer. This collection of quick notations is written by the remote viewer quickly, much like a "To Do List." Consider your everyday "To Do List" and notice how writing down your chores simultaneously focuses your mind and also frees your thoughts for other contemplations. Similarly, quick notations free the remote viewers to record and then open their minds to collect additional impressions, without keeping cluttered and active thoughts. Also, the act of trying to remember a perception might unhelpfully stifle the viewer when the viewer needs to remain free-floating and available for the target's next input.

To avoid imagination creeping into the process, a list of descriptive words is provided for each category of sensory and dimensional information. All one has to do is go through the list for each sensory and dimensional description, then pick the words which seem to "pop up" into one's primary awareness. For example, is the object smooth, furry, bumpy, or cool, hot, warm, hard, pliable, or penetrable. In later stages of development, remote viewers examine significant words and elaborate on them, creating a link to other thoughts, impressions, and objects.

These word associations draw upon previously developed neuronal constructions. Such words then trigger the conscious mind to recognize or select which descriptive words most adequately apply to the target content. This loose-association process brings a coherent assembly of impressions into tangible form to be easily recorded. By emphasizing significant impressions, and eliminating those of lesser impact, the target takes shape.

Applicable emotional impressions are selected in the same manner. Experience has shown that emotions contribute to visual perceptions pertinent to target sites at a specified time—either past, present, or future. It should also be noted here, that remote viewers contend that the mind functions outside time. Hence it is capable of perceptions in any time frame. The mind is thus devoid of the necessity for time-proximity.

So far in the 15-30 minute session, the remote viewer 1) has meditated to produce alpha-brainwaves, 2) has been given a target introduced with a TRN, Target Reference Number, 3) has drawn the spontaneous ideogram, and 4) then has selected key words associated to any perceptions which have been received that relate to sensory data and emotional data. The fifth step is when the remote viewer begins to draw.

The viewer draws what is being perceived without referencing memories and without drawing any thoughtful conclusions. To help avoid drawing conclusions with the critical, logical brain functions, there is an AOL section ("analytical overlay" or AOLs) on the remote viewer's paper. This AOL space allows for alternate images or thoughts to be written which are too related to memories or related to trying to "figure out" what the image in the target is. These AOLs include any ideas, thoughts or images which seem to be interrupting perceptions or seem to be prematurely organizing the images. This is a type of cognitive trashcan for ideas which may prove to be or not be helpful for the viewer during the session.

Well into the session, remote viewers note that all of their sensory abilities, and creative aspects of their mind have been tapped. Free expression of all input which was sensed has been accessed. They may also use clay to shape objects that reference tactile or 3-D messages about the target. During the later stages of the session, remote viewers also jump in and out of pure psychic processing as well. Importantly, the entire process is re-iterative which allows development of nuanced information to flow progressively. This re-iterative process when the remote viewer cycles through each of the steps over and over again spontaneously also enables other processes or data to be collected, too.

At the end of these input-collection procedures, a left-brain analysis is finally allowed. The viewer writes summary notes including all impressions and conclusions in a grammatically connected fashion. Probable features are factored in by their strength, impact, and number of times encountered. Above all, any impressions, no matter how far-fetched they seem, are included in this final written analysis. This procedure adds to the credibility of the work being done. Critical thinking, logical reasoning and conclusions might also be included during this last writing phase of the session. The end of session time is noted. Fifteen minutes is an average session length.

Only at this point in the session can anyone in the room see the photograph or object. In an intelligence gathering mode, however, no one in the room would know what the ultimate target is in order to maintain objectivity of sorts. This is to preclude the possibility of what is called "telepathic overlay"--reading the nature of the target from the monitor's mind.

Many narratives from remote viewing participants now mark modern history, worthy of your consideration and referenced below. Contemplate that remote viewing may be the most durable means of psychic training available to you as you expand your spiritual awareness and tools.

I have remote viewed or "seen" designated targets on the other side of the world with uncanny accuracy, under strict scientific conditions. I have generated images of real-time targets created by remote computers and programs designed to avoid experimenter-error (body-language, clues, or nuances about the targets). You too are welcome to experiment with these tools and can participate in my remote-viewing training sessions as listed below. No charge; my gift to you as a fellow-explorer.

Remember, training enhances target scores, and thusly enhances your psychic reading skills. Remote viewing improves with practice which strongly implies that remote viewing is a skill-set which you can learn. Remote viewing is a tool to be honed which increases your appreciation of your mind's vast abilities to travel outside of time and space.

Recommended Reading List:

The Psychic Battlefield by M.H. Mandelbaum This is a history of Psychic Spying down through the ages.

Remote Viewing by David Morehouse, PhD -- This is the most concise collection of remote viewing instructions.

Limitless Mind by Dr. Russell Targ -- This is a survey of the practical research results about remote viewing.

The Seventh Sense by Lyn Buchanan -- This is a practical application of remote viewing techniques and its history.

<u>Mind Trek: Exploring Consciousness, Time and Space</u> by Joe McMoneagle -- This includes incredible stories about the application of remote viewing to spying, criminology, etc., and how it applies to time-space perception.

About the Author:

Mike Rogalski is a retired audio engineer living in the Mojave Desert. He teaches Remote Viewing Lessons in Lancaster, El Segundo, and Pasadena, California through Meetup.com and offers these courses free-of-charge. Mike Rogalski also has written two novels, an autobiography, Remote Viewing Manual, and many articles on remote viewing as well.

His real name is actually "Dr. Dimension, Trans-navigator of the Quantum Universe(s) and Chronic Violator of the Time-Space Continuum". He also has an overblown sense of humor.

FRANCIS & O'MALEY

CHAPTER 18

PSYCHIC FROM BIRTH
BY DENNIE GOODING, M.A.

People like me are commonly described as "psychic." I have never cared for the word as I feel it limits the understanding of its meaning. Negative connotations come from media advertisements. I wish to clarify these misconceptions by describing my life experience as a psychic.

Commonly, I introduce myself as a clairvoyant. "Clairvoyant" is a French word meaning clear sight, and a psychic clairvoyant is one who sees other beings, times, dimensions, and so forth. Also, I am a "sensate," or "sensitive." I often smell, taste and hear, as well as physically and emotionally feel what I am both consciously and unconsciously focused upon.

This has been my life since I was a baby. I would embarrass my mother as a toddler by trying to save a being I could see who was already sitting on the chair my mother had directed a guest to occupy. A mother can laugh this off for only so long and she would explain it away by stating "that's one of Dennie's little friends." I learned to run over quickly, grab the being, and take it with me to salvage the situation. This too was hazardous as sometimes the guest would find themselves sitting on my hand because I was not quick enough. My mother was often quite annoyed with my manners. I could not understand why it was rude for me to save someone from being sat on, while it seemed perfectly fine for an adult to sit on them. I did not understand that others could not see or hear these beings.

Many people believe that some alternative skill-sets are gifts. I can write another thousand words on that idea alone. For now, let's just agree that it is a mixed bag. I strongly believe that every person can learn to use psychic skills. I recommend they look into skills with which they are comfortable. All people are born with differing skills or various talents. For example, my mother was a singer. No one in their right mind would wish me to sing no matter how hard or long I practiced. It is not one of my gifts.

In 1946, when I was about two years old, my mother moved to a ranch in the Black Hills of South Dakota. Working from sun up to sun down, with no electricity or running water, the days were long and hard. My mother and stepfather would leave the house slightly after sunrise, and breakfast was left on the table for me to eat when I awoke. Since early mornings have always been the best times for what is now called meditation, it worked well for me. I called it "going." My body would be in bed, but my spirit and mind then was out of body.

My playground at home was the barnyard and some glorious large rock formations which were as old as the earth itself. It was especially fun in the spring because there was nothing more fun than playing with the baby lambs and goats. The four-legged mothers generally accepted me as either a welcome distraction or one of their own. While I played, the animals, as well as beings that other people could not see, would communicate with me. I did not need my voice. Communication could be integrated in my mind with all species.

As a baby and to this day, I hear voices all the time. There is a constant group that I have labeled "The Gang," who consistently provides information. The nature of the group can fluctuate depending on the information sought. Most of the information is useful or interesting and even funny at times, but also sad on occasion.

I could gather solace from the rocks if I felt sad. The animals were also always my friends. However, the most magical and wonderful part was my walk into the Black Hills to visit My Tree. She was an old tree under which lived a family of porcupines. For at least three years, I would visit this family nearly every day. Generations came and went. During my visits, the adult male looked carefully around to protect his family. When there was no obvious threat, his mate came out with her four curious babies behind her. It was delightful. Most people do not know or even realize it but baby porcupines are soft. Often I would put one in my shirt pocket and we would explore together, find wild strawberries, and then bring it back to the tree. I strongly advise not trying this unless you already have a good relationship with such a family. However, because of the wonder of the earth and the tree, the porcupines and I were family. These animals are a large part of my early memories and taught me respect for and communication with all beings.

Growing older and later living in towns or cities, I lost these friends who were then replaced by other entities who I could see, hear, feel, smell et cetera. My mother hated for me to talk about these. For a long time I thought everyone saw and felt these beings, but that it was rude to discuss them, rather like bathroom habits. I was in college when I found someone like me who explained all the differences which helped considerably.

My first profession was teaching. I taught first graders. Being a sensate is an extremely handy tool for such a job. I was and am a good teacher. I love it. Regardless of whether or not I am formally in a classroom setting, I believe my purpose on this earth this time is to teach others. When people receive psychic readings from me or when I oversee a classroom, the point is always about teaching people to creatively solve problems for themselves.

I was also the first female manager for a Fortune 500 company. Certainly, I kept my unusual skill-set to myself, but I became known as a troubleshooter. I loved to anticipate (The Gang helped) and solve problems. I was able to survive what was still in those times a man's world, and put my son through private school as well as college by listening to my Gang.

In 1991, I opened an office to do psychic readings in Massachusetts, very near where the actual punishment for the Salem Witch Trials occurred. Here, I discovered that I could work with energies and do readings anywhere. Many clients came to me in secret. This is how I learned that telephone readings are very similar to face-to-face readings. Energy is energy. While working in Massachusetts, a well-intentioned Christian woman screamed at me about the work I was doing and then proceeded to douse me with holy water. I was very tempted to mimic the Wicked Witch from the *Wizard of OZ* and slowly weave down saying "I'm melting! I'm melting!" I thought it would be wasted on someone who had little sense of humor.

Now living in California, I am learning more on a daily basis about alternative skills. I attempt to practice all I have learned, finding I am better at some skills than others. I very much love my work, but it is not always easy. So many people are so sad, and I not only hear their words, but literally feel their pain. The resulting physical demands require mandatory recovery time for me, a lesson I have learned the hard way. I can only deal with a limited amount of readings a day.

A bargain has been made with The Gang not to provide me information that is of no use or will not be helpful in some way. This request limits but does not prevent interruptions throughout my day in the form of news about children in trouble, car accidents, airplanes going down, or the neighbor dreaming of murder. Sometimes, I need to get paper towels at the grocery store like anyone else, but pick up many pieces of information about others in line or from those around me. I have learned to be pretty good at isolating myself when I go out using an energy field, but sometimes things still penetrate through. For example, one particularly bad day, I touched the man I loved and knew he was done loving me. This is what it is like to be someone like me which I would not change even if I could. I would miss The Gang and the information even when the message is painful.

Every now and then I go to a pre-school where it is natural for the young souls to throw out their joy with abandon. I play too, and once again find myself back with the lambs, baby goats, and baby porcupines. Share happiness when you can. It helps us all.

About Dennie Gooding

Dennie Gooding is an intuitive reader and spiritual counselor. She provides precise guidance and gentle clarity in the midst of seemingly challenging life paths, personal, business, and relationship concerns. She uses her degrees in psychology and sociology to help her clients find solutions. A clairvoyant, clairaudient, and clairsentient, Dennie Gooding reveals wisdom from her own and her clients' guides which offers assistance and individualized solutions to integrate into your life. To reach Dennie Gooding e-mail www.denniegooding.com or call 310-699 8818.

FRANCIS & O'MALEY

CHAPTER 19

I'M A MEDIUM, TOO?

BY MARY O'MALEY, MSHN, CHTI

Discovering I am a medium was something that literally sneaked up on me. I was barely getting comfortable with some of my psychic abilities when I began to notice that there were other beings in the room with my clients and me. It is a very odd juxtaposition to see nothing in the room with open eyes, yet simultaneously have a mental vision of a being occupying the same space. This ability is like having an additional set of eyes right behind your eyebrows.

I tried to ignore it, but one day during a session, one of the beings became persistent and seemed to be yelling at me stating he did not like some of the things which were going on with his sister. I finally asked this client if she had a brother. She confirmed he had died the year before. When I asked if he were very controlling of her, she stated emphatically, "Yes!"

As her older brother, he raised her after their mother died. Clearly, he took his job as surrogate parent very seriously. She felt guilty about letting go of her need for his guidance and continued to ask him for help. Instead of moving on, he was still around, parenting personality intact, causing problems, and trying to control her from the other side. With the help of my guides and hers, she was able to let go of him, trust in her guides, and begin to follow her own heart. I could see the change in her smile, attitude, and body language—she stood taller and was more confident and relaxed when she left that session.

That was the last time I ignored another presence that came in with a client. I began to understand that Mediumship is a true gift that can greatly help people. People who are alive and dead can heal from loss and move forward with their lives when a medium hears and communicates messages on behalf of each person.

As a general rule, our loved-ones can be called upon for comfort and information, but human beings also have higher wisdom, guides, and guardian angels which help us in our day-to-day lives. After all, if dear old Aunt Meg was not very good at relationships in life, you would not want her helping you from the other side to find your soul mate.

So, how did I know this woman's brother was in the room? In addition to my inner eye awareness, I felt his presence. For me, the atmosphere in a certain area of the room becomes heavier and takes a shape. All mediums perceive the dead in different and unique ways. Likely, we perceive them with our dominant senses. Clairvoyants see, clairaudients hear, clairsentients feel, and claircognizants know. My dominant senses are feeling and knowing; however, I can also see and hear.

The gift of Mediumship is for the living, on both sides of death's veil. Grief is a complicated emotion comprised of many diverse and even conflicting feelings. When we lose a person with whom we have been intimately involved, whether positively or negatively, the part of our personality that was defined by that relationship may become lost right along with the person who died. Alongside our grief and conflicting feelings, there is a sense that a part of us has also died. In order to fully move on, that part of us eventually has to be redefined, which sometimes requires that we completely recreate ourselves.

You may have questions for the person who has passed over, or you may need to say things you were not able to share while the person was alive. You may just need to know if they are all right now and happy. If it was a negative or abusive relationship, the dead may want to apologize or explain their behavior. Communicate clearly, without holding on to the old pictures of who they were on Earth or who you were with them. Both can evolve, move forward in their realms and both of you can continue to connect in these evolving forms. However, if you never wish to connect with that person again, know that there is no obligation. You are in charge. Disrespectful beings can, and should, be sent away.

A good medium can help you gain closure so that you can re-engage with life. I have never met a deceased spouse that wished for the living spouse to follow him or her immediately. Without fail, the deceased partner wants you to experience joy and love while you are still alive. The same is true for children who pass over. I often find them playing at the feet of a client, and they will tell me when they knew their parent in a past life and when they will be together again. The love that pours forth from these children is so pure and bright that I can only encourage the parents to nudge aside their grief just a little and feel the beautiful presence playing at their feet. Many parents understandably feel guilty about experiencing joy after the loss of a child, and so choose to carry the tragedy in their hearts. This is not what your child wants for you. While you may continue to feel grief and loss throughout the years, make sure you also allow yourself to experience peace and joy.

While I know this will cause some controversy, I find the same to be true with children that were aborted. I never feel judgment from them, only sadness sometimes that it was not the right time for that parent to have the child. They either hang around until the parent is ready, or they just move on to another situation that meets the needs for their life's path.

When your loved-ones who have passed are present, they will often create a sign to let you know. Some signs I have heard people share include butterflies, hummingbirds, dragonflies, feathers, and coins. Sometimes people will feel a touch on their head, face, or shoulder. Sometimes it is a smell like a favorite perfume or cigar smoke. When my father is around, I feel him as a pressure in my right eye. Sometimes he gives me a hug and all the hairs on my skin stand up! Many times they come to us in dreams.

Ask the deceased for a sign if you are not sure. Pay attention after you ask, as the sign may present itself in subtle ways over the next days or weeks. Reach out and ask them to touch or hold your hand, then notice what you feel. Send them love; they can feel it. However, if it were a negative or abusive relationship, feel free to send them away. You are completely in charge.

Do not be afraid to see a medium. If, after two or three years, you are still feeling traumatized and suffering from a loss, the results of working with a good medium can be miraculous.

How do you find a good medium? Ask your friends! More of them than you can imagine have probably sought help from that realm. You can also go to reputable websites like bestamericanpsychics.com, lisawilliams.com, johnholland.com, and of course myself, at maryomaley.com or TheMerryMedium.com. These websites require their psychics and mediums be tested, ensuring they are the real thing. While a Mediumship session may be emotional, it should ultimately be a positive experience, and a good medium will make it a safe and wholesome experience for you.

About Mary O'Maley, MSHN, CHtI

Mary O'Maley holds a MS in Holistic Nutritional Health Science and is a Certified Hypnotherapist and Hypnotherapy Instructor with International Hypnosis Federation. She is recipient of the prestigious IHF Award of Excellence & Chapter Woman of the Year from American Business Woman's Association. Mary specializes in Past Life Regression, Intuitive

Nutritional Counseling, Life Coaching, five energy healing modalities, psychic and medium readings, and hosts various programs and events.

Mary O'Maley, as Life Coach, created the Retreat-Reconnect-Recharge-ReEmerge Coaching. This R4 Coaching provides in-depth, personal-retreat experiences which help you access, trust, and follow your inner wisdom.

Certified in Reiki, Access Energy Clearing, Matrix Energetics and Reconnective Healing, Mary O'Maley also developed and provides Crystal Chakra Balancing. Crystal Chakra Balancing was discovered through Mary O'Maley's Akashic Records work.

Mary O'Maley teaches basic and intermediate hypnotherapy through IHF, nutritional approaches to health at various medical facilities, and metaphysical information at various international conferences and local venues.

Mary O'Maley's metaphysical studies allowed her to reignite her psychic and mediumship gifts which she uses for home, gallery and individual readings given since 1997. She is certified and tested as a member of Best American Psychics. Mary O'Maley hosts and produces The Merry Medium Show. On The Merry Medium Show, Mary interviews many wonderful spiritual explorers from the metaphysical and holistic communities. Podcasts of The Merry Medium Show are available at blogtalkradio.com/the-merry-medium. She also hosts live events in the Los Angeles area: **The Merry Medium and Friends – Where Science and Spirit Meet Live Events.**

To reach Mary O'Maley for her alternative health services, psychic and mediumship readings, radio programs, live events, materials, workbooks and books, contact her at http://www.maryomaley.com or call 424-234-9260.

FRANCIS & O'MALEY

CHAPTER 20

CHANNELING TOWARD ADVANCED SPIRITUAL ENLIGHTENMENT

BY DR. CAROL FRANCIS

Spontaneous or scheduled information-downloads from invisible sources is one way to describe *channeling*. Almost without fail, spiritually advanced individuals admit that they channeled information while speaking, counseling, meditating, or writing. Curiously, almost every progressive scientist who explains the way they discovered their pivotal ideas also include a reference to channeling. Often these scientists report sensing that their information came as if inspired through dreams, informal meditations, deep contemplations, and the odd feeling that ideas where spewing forth from some unknown source outside themselves. Authors, lyricists, music composers, poets and artists express this sense of being inspired and informed from some source other than their own training and consciousness. By definition, one could easily consider these forms of *Channeling*.

Channeling is a tool used for spiritual advancement. So, consider grooming your ability to consciously and easily channel if you have not already done so. Secondly, deliberately test the validity of the materials channeled. These two practices are both essential for spiritual advancement. Channeling expands spiritual knowledge and resources since much of the information that advances our spiritual awareness must come from sources other than the typical, every day teachings. Some examples below will illustrate this expansion in a moment.

Of course, test, test, and test the trustworthiness of the channeled information. Verification is essential. Untrustworthy information gathered during a channeling session can erupt from our misguided imagination. Our limiting memes and prejudices can twist the information. Our current paradigms or our slanted perspectives on truth can limit channeled messages too. Our fears and judgments or our misinterpretation of experiences can obscure gifted knowledge. Additionally, there exists the possibility of connecting with an unreliable channeled source. Never enslave yourself to a channeled source or its information. You are never subordinate to your guides, angels, or spirits. Never stop analyzing and do not mindlessly accept any information. Shrewdly require that your guides are respectful of you and your understandings even if they are teaching you contradictory or confusing materials. You are an equal member of spiritual teams even if you are a student of a master or less informed or less evolved.

Hypnosis, trancelike meditations, automatic writing, group channeling meetings, or recordings of messages during channeling meditations can easily be a part of your spiritual practices. Right now for instance, select a writing device. Breathe deeply. Pray for white-light-protection and deep guidance. Ask a very important question. Then listen and do not edit what you hear. Listen and write down. Again, listen and write down. Next, listen more deeply and more freely without censorship. Next, place your writing to the side and begin to dialogue with that voice or messenger you were transcribing moments ago. Ask your question, debate, even ponder your thoughts with that messenger and then listen to all the responses that come from visions, words, explanations, or by bodily sensations. Let your imagination be open to any and all types of information. Be aware that any information that violates or contradicts your previous perspectives will not be "heard" by you as easily as that information which fits what you already believe. So be open and savvy. Then, write down what you learned even if you disagree with it. You can only learn new, eye-opening information if you are ready for new information.

Write your dreams daily. Write what you think a guide or angel is telling you in a moment. Dialogue together – using the speak, listen, then write ... speak, listen, then write cycle. As you do so daily, the messenger will be clearer along with the messages. Also, you will be able to test the veracity of the messages more fluidly. Remember, you are not relinquishing your wisdom to another entity. You will need validation in the same way that one of your students will need validation about your teachings.

For those of you, who already have a channeling practice; expand the interaction with guides using the following. Ask harder questions. Speak and listen more frequently. Use your wisdom to test and validate in many Earth bound circumstances. Also, request spiritual manipulations of physical materials. Know your true spiritual guides are quite comfortable with such vetting. They know there are deceivers in their realms and in all of ours too; vetting is welcomed by secure spiritual guides.

Additionally, expand your channeling by increasing the communication tools available to your spiritual guides. Allow your guides to use your dreams, synchronistic signs, day dreams, time travels, astral projections, remote viewing, group channeling circles, automatic writing, recordings, bodily sensations, tarot decks, drawings, and various brain or cerebral sensations. Hear their voice whisper in your ear. Feel their energy interface with your bodily triggers.

One more way to expand spiritually through Channeling is to increase your circle of entities or guides. Many dimensions, many domains of consciousness, and many universes occupy only a portion of the Infinite-All within which we dwell. So, as a consequence, having more entities with diverse backgrounds can help you explore more, too. Yes, you will be exposed to extraordinary startling information and experiences. You will need to remain grounded in your Earthly physical life and its demands.

To illustrate all of these ideas about how *Channeling* progresses one's spiritual awareness, the following four examples are channeled from four different entities from very different "walks of life." The question I posed to each entity was "How can spiritually expanding humans be more available to receive more dynamic information from teachers from different parts of the cosmic reality?" Each entity will be briefly described after the channeled communication; this helps demonstrate that--yes-- spirit guides have their own points-of-view or perspectives as do humans.

Ryan

Question: Ryan, how do you and I connect when we are in the midst of a Channeling session and what can I do to increase the ease of receiving your information?

Answer: *Carol, accessing the human comprehension center is quite fun actually. To describe to you or those in our groups what I mean to share requires that I first read everyone's needs and their points-of-views on a topic. To do so, I experience their vibrational signature in that moment on that topic. If you wish to know what I experience, I would show you colorful waves of energy woven with other colorful waves creating a tapestry radiating from each individual. I decode the meanings on many levels of their tapestry. Then I can understand their current experiences or knowings based on their design of colors.*

Said differently, I listen to the sound of their colorful wave patterns and how the sound vibrations are fluidly woven into tunes. I can hear their tunes or songs on a topic and can evaluate how what I share helps their tune become more harmonious or lively.

As I speak an answer, I note how their tapestry moves as a unit and how their tapestry begins to develop into different patterns. Their tapestry of colorful waves of energy typically do not change drastically until they have what you would call an "ah-ha" moment. Their musical vibrations will become harmonious and dynamic during these "ah-ha" moments too.

So actually, it is I who bares the effort to communicate in a way that will facilitate a different musical or colorful pattern. If a human wishes to help me communicate better with them, they can pay close attention to how they hear or see themselves as an energetic expression of vibrational patterns. Also, they could note when their patterns are open, dystonic, empty, pleasant or unpleasant. Then, they can establish an openness or a willingness to be listened to or seen by me so I can more easily discern their true music or their true vibrational colored tapestry.

Description of Ryan

Ryan is an entity who is moving energy. "He" manifests to me as colors flashing which are constantly shifty as if I am watching electrons swirl purposefully but without apparent pattern. There is no sense of definition from my point-of-view. Ryan has no guile, no judgmentalness, nor sense of good or bad. Ryan explores and assists with an attitude of kindness and helpfulness throughout his cosmos. Earth is part of his cosmos. Ryan is a collector of wisdom and experiences and views all as if each moment and entity is a delightful encounter to be understood and enjoyed. Ryan does not function in any form and has no sense of time or space as we do on Earth. He can "go" elsewhere but wherever he "goes" is in the here or now of his awareness. He can delineate a sequence of events where events come before, next and after, but has no sense of time passing or being short or long as is associated with the human experience of waiting or being worried or anxious. Ryan has a

---

sense of beginnings but not death. Ryan's reverence for the Divine is deep and filled with reverential awe.

Petite Angel

Question: Angel, how do we connect during Channeling and how can I be more mindful of increasing my availability to being taught your information?

Answer: *To hear me, Carol, you always need to turn on certain senses inside of you which have to do with feeling Love. Haven't you noticed that when you call on me, your body's heart, midriff, and abdomen become simultaneously quieted, warm, and humbled by the emotions of Love, as well as emotionally appreciative of the All-Encompassing sensations of Love. Then you passage through a moment of feeling undeserving of being in Love's humongous presence and next accept or push away the powerful gifts of compassionate kindness that begin to flood into your core. If you choose to accept this presence, your physical core feels as if it is infinitely expanding as if your emotional core correlating with your physical core becomes a black hole or worm hole which spirals or connects into the infinitude of Love. If you allow that process to continue you move to the next level of feeling humbly exuberant as you resonate as one with Love. Love and you become one; you temporarily disappear without any discomfort into Love. Then, if you choose, you can remember to be yourself separately, conscious of your identity within this arena of Love, and that's when you call for me. From that vantage point, I can enter into your presence and begin our work or answer your questions.*

Description of Petite Angel

Petite Angel presents as having immaterial form that is white, organized, fluid light. Petite Angel appears to fly or float and never interfaces with a sense of up or down unless orienting to my body's gravitational sensitivity. Angel possesses a profound innocence and burden-free lightness and yet is aware of how entities can be sinister or evil in intent. Her demeanor seems female. When she interfaces with sinister or evil, there is no judgmentalness, only savvy. Her savvy is a type of profound knowing about the intent and power and negative destructive possibilities that might impact certain domains if the evil is set loose. Petite Angel sets or responds to the boundaries that are established in order to keep the evil contained until the evil opts to become clean. Angel does not have limits to time, space or dimensionality and traverses any definitions of reality. "Now" is always now with all that is existing within that now. To Petite Angel, Love is the air, water, life energy, essence of all that is and the fluid in which everything flows; this is Petite Angel's experience of the Divine. Healing and pure heartedness are Angel's resonate ways of interfacing with other entities.

Pepe

Question: Pepe, how do I enter into the Akashic Records and find you and then receive the information?

Answer: *Carol, when you call me or decide to enter the Akashic Center, instantly a series of functions begin to open in your various cells or selves. Notably, your visual cortex activates associated to your ground center (ground chakra) which then triangulates to your solar plexus and then to your heart chakra, then throat. While these systems sync-up, messages or questions arise from either your heart, curiosity or throat. The nature of your visit is etched into the movement you begin as you move consciousness with these chakra centers into the Akashic Center.*

151

Your third eye (Ankara) sends a signal about 3 inches outside your forehead and then that signal receives mass energy from your crown chakra. These two sources of signals converge at this spot about three inches in front of your third eye and then transmit together pointing toward the Akashic Records Center. With these transmission centers all wired and ready to go, your cells/selves are all represented and present. You then flow into one of the Halls of the Akashic Center and you go to the location where I am in attendance. We commune, since this is a familiar re-uniting; we chat, explore the information you are seeking, and then I might show you something you might be curious about such as when we explored Hitler's Akashic work in the Golden Room. This information is downloaded into your cells along your arms extending from your neck and head. Next, you begin to extend this information toward the individual asking the questions, either yourself or another soulful explorer.

Description of Pepe

Pepe is one of many keepers of the Akashic Center and has certain domains within that Center to attend. He is like a guardian, organizer, librarian, gentle overseer. Additionally, Pepe can pray for the well-being of the souls he oversees like a gentle but attentive grandfather who helps spiritually, energetically and informationally. Of course, he does not interfere, only informs. Pepe also has various life journeys and is more humanoid-like than the other two guides discussed so far. His perspectives are oriented to time-space dimensions and time-lines enacted in reference to a bigger series of dimensions and cast of characters and lessons to be learned. His roles include education, record keeping, making the records accessible when requested, and care taking over the souls when complications interfere with progression or the sensations of hope. He is able to see events in terms of time-lines, yet he does not live within time-space lines unless engaging in some personal lesson to be learned for his own evolution. He has been material and physical and even Earth-bound for lives but is consciously able to access all other time-space lines while serving in the Akashic Center. Thus, he has a very different perspective on time-space associated to one's life than we do when we are myopically experiencing only one human life.

Red Fox

Question: How does our work together related to Channeling for myself or others actually create messages?

Answer from Red Fox:

Red Fox answers the above questions by first listening attentively. Resting. Then, he encourages me to follow him to discover the answers the Red Fox way. I follow through fields of low grass and small wild pastille flowers. The skies are blue, clear and laced with clouds. I feel the freedom of running or walking behind Red Fox. We happen upon a cliff, of sorts, and look down to see a medium sized waterfall cascading down to a rocky pond. When the water smashes into the pond, the rest of the sitting water overflows the edge of the rocks and begins to pour down and breaks into various streams in the surrounding valleys below. Those valleys are equally beautiful with trees, low grass, butterflies and lilting flowers. Red Fox and I jump into the waterfall, and during that fall, we become the water so no harm is done to our "bodies." Becoming water is like losing any sense of identity and only movement and gravity are "sensed" in this experience of being water. Cleanness, as water, is water's general attitude which I experience as joyful. The water, we have shape-shifted into, flows into one stream in particular and then moves up one bank into the hands of a little child standing beside the stream. This girl exudes so much peacefulness and a deep sense of appreciation toward the water as she anticipates quenching her thirst. Her thirst is overpowering her mouth and organs. She takes in the water as if it is an ecstatic moment and deep appreciation pours forth from her as she receives the gift and messages of the water. She experiences a moment of perfect satiation, an answer to her deep and necessary thirst.

Then Red Fox is done showing me my answer. I sit and mull over each aspect of his message until I glean as much as I can related to my question. In this case, I am clear on many details. Let me explain a few. The water is the flow of spirit guides wishing to inform and communicate with us. Spirit guides wish to address our thirst and dehydration. Receiving or listening to the information requires deciding to listen to the guides' message first; this is a free-will moment of choice. Then, it requires listening, watching, and observing all the signs along the path and noting the essential beauty in all of the paths presented. Next, we become the water or we become the energetic water droplets that lose separate identity while receiving the downloads of information. We have nonetheless a sense of being refreshed while in unity with Divine. The next step is again to follow the stream which breaks away from the Unity. That stream has a mission: to answer my question. The message becomes important to receive, like the little girl scooping water from the stream. This is especially true if the receiver recognizes the wonderful gift of the water and how it is the answer to needs and desires. The message can be a relief that quenches, and there is joy in receiving the water. When the child takes the water innocently, there is a moment of being at one with the message. In that moment there is reverence, respect and thankfulness for the message and messenger. This latter part reflects how the All loves to flow information and answers to all seekers who desire answers. *Messages are more fluidly delivered to receivers who are eager and excited to enjoy the answers.* Respect and joy keeps the conduits open and clear.

Description of Red Fox

Red Fox is an animal spirit guide in line with the Shamanic traditions. There is a type of telepathic communication that does not limit itself to words or thoughts. Shamanic Journeys involving animal spirits can be filled with details symbolic with meaning on all emotional, psychological, mythical, and energetic levels. The entire scenario often becomes the message. The animal spirit becomes your tour guide to safely move you through the details and the activities which will address the moment. Decoding the message becomes part of the channeling process. If channeling for another person, describing the events and images in detail is first. Thereafter, the recipient and the Shaman team-up to decipher various aspects of the journey.

Conclusion

Yes, Spirit Guides channeled or Spirit Guides communed with teach from many perspectives. They have limits. For example, they diversely view the Divine, Good and Evil, Time-Space

Therefore, be open to many spirit guides collectively being part of your spiritual training. Remain savvy, maintain equality and respect for them and yourself during each communication and afterwards. Be open to many types of communication styles and types of information conveyed.

References

Francis, Carol A. (2010). Spiritual Gurus, Spiritual Paths: Your Choice. Rancho Palos Verdes: Make Life Happen Publishing.

About Dr. Carol Francis

In addition to her spiritual counseling and intuitive work with metaphysically inclined seekers, Dr. Carol Francis has practiced for 37 years as a Clinical Psychologist, Life Coach, Clinical

Hypnotherapist, and Marriage, Family & Child Counselor. She assists individuals, couples and children who seek to optimize their current situation and overcome complications of daily living. These individuals seek deep relief and growth for depression, anxiety, stress, career moves, family discord, child and parenting issues, relationship dissatisfaction, habit control, and the psychology of financial success. Practicing and licensed in Southern California for over 37 years, Dr. Carol Francis can be reached at drcarolfrancis.com or 310-543-1824.

Publications by Dr. Carol Francis

Re-Uniting Soldiers with Families

Evolving Women's Consciousness: Dialogue with 21st Century Women.

Spiritual Paths, Spiritual Gurus: Your Choice

Spiritual Journeys: Astral Projection, Shamanism, Akashic

Your Akashic Records

CHAPTER 21

CHANGING OF THE GUIDES
BY MARY O'MALEY, MSHN, CHTI

While working with people, I often find that they are going through a change of guides and/or gathering many new guides around them. Whenever I find that happening, I know that it usually precedes big life changes for the client. Sometimes the guides are there to help with changes in earthly life circumstances and sometimes they are there to help with changes in the client's spiritual perceptions and growth. I find that there are usually one to three guides that are consistent, but it is not unusual for the number of guides to greatly fluctuate.

My dear friend and co-author of this book, Dr. Carol Francis, called me one day and announced that she had just fired all of her guides. She had been working with them on a personal issue and was not progressing; a new type of assistance and advice was needed. So she fired them all and demanded new guides who could really help her. I remember responding with something like, "WTF? You can do that?" Well, she did and it worked!

Yes, relationships with guides can be funny things. Years ago, as I was adding new healing therapies to my practice, I was told by a marketer that I would have trouble with my marketing until I settled on one main therapy. At the time, I was working with a handful of guides that I called "The Five." So, I asked my guides how I should choose a therapy to market. They responded, "We don't care what you do as long as you can get them (the clients) in front of you for five minutes so we can do our own healing on them." Thanks, guys.

A couple of years ago I met a lady that channels a group of nine archangels. One day I was playing with channeling her archangels when a very whiny part of me said, "I want some archangels of my own to channel."

Some months later I began hosting my own radio show, The Merry Medium (http://www.blogtalkradio.com/the-merry-medium). Before the first show, I was very nervous and went into a meditation beforehand to ask for help from my guides. About five feet behind me, I noticed a trio of beings whom I had never before encountered. I asked them who they were, and why they were there? They told me they were the archangels I had asked for, and that they were there for the radio show. Okaaay...I tuned into The Five, and it seemed as though they had left the room. Not only was this my first time hosting a radio show but I would be doing it with brand new guides that I did not know. Sheesh! The program was more dynamic than I could have imagined.

Over the next few weeks I noticed they moved closer and closer to me until I could feel them as part of me. They told me their collective name is Anantha. "Anantha" is the Greek word for flower, or a type of flower. They told me that they are my connection to all of the archangels.

When I am doing readings, particularly gallery readings, I can feel various angels and guides stepping forward for different individuals. Individuals' archangels are distinctly different from Anantha. During these readings, it seems as though Anantha is working like an old fashioned switchboard operator, directing "calls" to the appropriate archangel.

Anantha has also changed the way I approach a reading. Anantha insists that my clients ask specific questions, which cause the client to be much more engaged and focused on the important issues in their lives. Also, Anantha will not let me use psychic tools such as tarot cards. In fact, when I asked them what I was supposed to do with the oracle cards which I literally no longer seemed able to read, the cards were knocked out of my hand. (Yes, I have a witness.) The information exchange with Anantha is extremely fast and clearer than the tarot cards were.

Guides and archangels and other beings come forward anytime we call on them. They are there to serve us. I have worked closely with Archangel Michael and learned that in his army, I carry a light and a sword. Ariel consistently comes forward in my energy work. Raphael has intervened with healings, especially with distance healing.

Being raised Irish Catholic and around Catholics of many nationalities, I can tell you we love our Saints, many of whom are simply transformations from the Old Gods. The Goddess Brigid, becomes Saint Brigit. We call on them to keep us safe, healthy, to find lost items, bless our homes, and transform lost causes. From my studies of Druidic practices and other earth-science-spirit-based religions, I understand that many of them are based on the premise of one supreme being or Source, but honor the different gods as physical, material, emotional, and mental representations, or personalities, of the One Source.

We may not consider our saints and gods as guides, and yet, we call on them all of the time, just like we do with our guides and guardian angels. We have statues and pictures and sculptures in our homes, cars and offices. We hang pictures of guardian angels over the cribs of our children. We have Buddha and Quan Yin statues on our dressers; maybe sitting beneath the crucifix on our wall. We wear them as jewelry and hang them from our rear view mirrors. We create altars in our homes. Yes, our guides are everywhere; both those that are intimately linked with us throughout our life and those we call on for favors.

Anantha tells me that one of the best ways to become comfortable with the communication process of your guides is to write down five questions, and then write down how you received the answers. In this exercise it is not the answer that is important; it is how you receive the answer. Do not be surprised if you receive the answers in five different ways. The point is you will know your guides voice and know that they are listening. And, if they are not, don't be shy about giving them a pink slip!

About Mary O'Maley, MSHN, CHtI

Mary O'Maley holds a MS in Holistic Nutritional Health Science and is a Certified Hypnotherapist and Hypnotherapy Instructor with International Hypnosis Federation. She is recipient of the prestigious IHF Award of Excellence & Chapter Woman of the Year from American Business Woman's Association. Mary specializes in Past Life Regression, Intuitive Nutritional Counseling, Life Coaching, five energy healing modalities, psychic and medium readings, and hosts various programs and events.

Mary O'Maley, as Life Coach, created the Retreat-Reconnect-Recharge-ReEmerge Coaching. This R4 Coaching provides in-depth, personal-retreat experiences which help you access, trust, and follow your inner wisdom.

Certified in Reiki, Access Energy Clearing, Matrix Energetics and Reconnective Healing, Mary O'Maley also developed and provides Crystal Chakra Balancing. Crystal Chakra Balancing was discovered through Mary O'Maley's Akashic Records work.

Mary O'Maley teaches basic and intermediate hypnotherapy through IHF, nutritional approaches to health at various medical facilities, and metaphysical information at various international conferences and local venues.

Mary O'Maley's metaphysical studies allows her to reignite her psychic and mediumship gifts which she uses for home, gallery and individual readings given since 1997. She is certified and tested as a member of Best American Psychics. Mary O'Maley hosts and produces The Merry Medium Show. On The Merry Medium Show, Mary interviews many wonderful spiritual explorers from the metaphysical and holistic communities. Podcasts of The Merry Medium Show are available at blogtalkradio.com/the-merry-medium. She also hosts live events in the Los Angeles area: **The Merry Medium and Friends – Where Science and Spirit Meet Live Events.**

To reach Mary O'Maley for her alternative health services, psychic and mediumship readings, radio programs, live events, materials, workbooks and books, contact her at http://www.maryomaley.com or call 424-234-9260.

FRANCIS & O'MALEY

CHAPTER 22

PSYCHIC ANIMAL INTERVENTIONS
BY MARY O'MALEY, MSHN, CHTI

Some of my most amazing experiences as a psychic is psychically reading animals. My first reading happened with a race horse, JJ, which belonged to a friend of mine. She and her business partner had recently moved JJ 200 miles away to work with a new trainer and he was having some trouble adjusting. My friend asked me to do a reading to find out what was troubling her horse. I had never worked with animals before this, and it was a long distance, but she encouraged me to give it a try.

Tuning in psychically resulted in JJ informing me was that he was all alone. He had been removed from his siblings and the other horse companions. He was without his herd and very lonely and feeling lost.

Before JJ's next race, my friend and her business partner spent some time talking with him. They assured him that he belonged to them as a family member, and that they were here for him. Additionally, his new trainer and the other horses with which he now lived were also his new companions to enjoy. Their communication with their horse seemed to work as he won his next race that very day, by nine lengths!

Another intervention began during a subsequent visit. JJ had been sold and my friend was wondering how he was doing in his new surroundings. At the time, I had a terrible headache but decided to give it a try. JJ not only told me that he was very happy, but that he could help me with my headache! I gave him permission and soon experienced him galloping around in my head. The pounding of the hooves seemed to be breaking up the tension that was causing my pain. The pain got a little worse before it got better, but in a matter of a few minutes my headache completely disappeared. What an amazing experience this was for me, and he was excited and joyful that he got to return the kindness I had done for him the year before.

Another time I was doing a long distance reading over the phone for a new client. For some reason it seemed like the information I was receiving was coming in a foreign language, and I could not figure out what her guides were trying to tell me. I asked for an interpreter and suddenly received a very clear image of a cat on a desk. I asked my client if she had a cat. Not only did she affirm that she did, but also explained that her cat had just jumped up on her desk and was sitting on her computer keyboard. So, I asked the image of the cat if she was there to interpret for us. "Yes," she replied and proceeded to tell me all that was being said by my client's guides. It was an amazing reading, and I was sure to thank her for her help!

Dogs have been guardians to humans for thousands of years. I had a client come into my office who brought her two very large dogs. The reading was about another woman that had a tendency to be psychically very intrusive. My client was concerned about her psychic privacy. Looking at her two regal dogs, I tuned in and asked them if they could help. They responded eagerly explaining that protecting my client was their primary role in her life. Next, these dogs showed me four warriors who were now positioned at each corner of my room. These warriors were creating a psychic barrier that could not be breached by anyone. I explained to my client what was happening. While she knew the dogs were there to protect her, she was amazed to know that they could also protect her psychically. This brought her great comfort and we had a very fruitful and relaxed reading. I have since called on her dogs for psychic protection in other readings and they have been present with the warriors even many years later.

Another time, I was working with a young woman when I received a very clear picture of a black cat sitting on the roof of a garage. The cat told me that his name was Leo, and to tell my client that he would always be with her as one of her guides, as he had throughout many of her life times. When I related this to my client she confirmed that her beloved black cat, Leo, had died just the week before and that his favorite place to hang out had been the roof of her garage. She had been crying herself to sleep every night, missing Leo. She left the reading with a sense of peace knowing that Leo would always be with her.

The animals whom I have worked with communicate very clearly through both pictures and feelings. Animals are a part of our lives and very active with us on emotional levels. Their needs are basic, and they consider themselves family members. They will take on our emotions and even our physical health and emotional health issues, in order to help us. When you talk to your animals, be sure to also send them pictures from your mind and feelings that you are experiencing to help them understand. Learn to trust the pictures and feelings they probably are sending to you. With a little practice you can have a very deep, loving, and psychic relationship with your pets.

About Mary O'Maley, MSHN, CHtI

Mary O'Maley holds a MS in Holistic Nutritional Health Science and is a Certified Hypnotherapist and Hypnotherapy Instructor with International Hypnosis Federation.   She is recipient of the prestigious IHF Award of Excellence & Chapter Woman of the Year from American Business Woman's Association. Mary specializes in Past Life Regression, Intuitive Nutritional Counseling, Life Coaching, five energy healing modalities, psychic and medium readings, and hosts various programs and events.

Mary O'Maley, as Life Coach, created the Retreat-Reconnect-Recharge-ReEmerge Coaching.   This R4 Coaching provides indepth, personal-retreat experiences which help you access, trust, and follow your inner wisdom.

Certified in Reiki, Access Energy Clearing, Matrix Energetics and Reconnective Healing, Mary O'Maley also developed and provides Crystal Chakra Balancing. Crystal Chakra Balancing was discovered through Mary O'Maley's Akashic Records work.

Mary O'Maley teaches basic and intermediate hypnotherapy through IHF, nutritional approaches to health at various medical facilities, and metaphysical information at various international conferences and local venues.

Mary O'Maley's metaphysical studies allowed her to reignite her psychic and mediumship gifts which she uses for home, gallery and individual readings given since 1997. She is certified and tested as a member of Best American Psychics. Mary O'Maley hosts and produces The Merry Medium Show. On The Merry Medium Show, Mary interviews many wonderful spiritual explorers from the metaphysical and holistic communities. Podcasts of The Merry Medium Show are available at blogtalkradio.com/the-merry-medium. She also hosts live events in the Los Angeles area: The Merry Medium and Friends – Where Science and Spirit Meet Live Events.

To reach Mary O'Maley for her alternative health services, psychic and mediumship readings, radio programs, live events, materials, workbooks and books, contact her at http://www.maryomaley.com or call 424-234-9260.

CHAPTER 23

TAROT MEDITATION FOR SOULFUL CONNECTION
BY BRIGIT ESSELMONT

When I was preparing to give birth to my daughter, I saw first-hand the power of meditation and guided visualization. Meditation and visualization connect me with my inner wisdom and manifests positive change in my life. Using deep relaxation, focused breathing, positive affirmations, and guided imagery techniques for the weeks leading up to her birth, I was able to shift my mindset. In a relatively short time, I moved from feeling fearful about the upcoming birth to being excited. All of that inner work had an outward manifestation, too. By tapping into my subconscious mind and connecting with my inner wisdom, I gained confidence—and manifested the joyful birth I wanted!

As a professional Tarot reader and teacher, I wanted to be able to take that profound experience that I had while birthing my daughters and bring it to the world of Tarot. This deep meditation and guided visualization creates greater depth and spiritual insight into Tarot readings. So I started meditating with the Tarot cards and exploring the deeply symbolic imagery contained within. My mind opened up to the infinite possibilities contained within the cards, and I learned to trust my inner wisdom. I began to see things in the cards that I had never seen before. Some were unique to my personal experiences and inner knowing. From there, my Tarot readings flowed easily and effortlessly. This is where the magic happened!

Meditating with the Tarot

Have you felt you have not been living the life you would like to live? That you are not fulfilling your true potential? Do you want to manifest positive changes in your life? Or, are you on the path towards healing? Are you ready to learn from a difficult life experience or cycle—to integrate its spiritual lessons in a meaningful way? Perhaps you are struggling with your Tarot studies, wanting to get beyond simple memorization of card meanings and, instead, bring the cards' potent energy more fully into your life.

Meditating with the Tarot is an intensely deep and profound way to connect with the cards and more importantly to yourself. The rich, symbolic nature of the cards makes them ideal for exploring your subconscious. Deep insights come to the surface and you find yourself connecting with your inner wisdom and your soul in ways that you have never before experienced. Tarot meditations help you connect deeply with your fullest potential, heal emotional wounds, and dive beneath the surface. These Tarot meditations reveal solutions and meanings that are unique and significant to you. Meditations lift the lamp of the Tarot's wisdom and shine that light upon your personal spiritual path, awakening your innermost mind.

How to Meditate with the Tarot

So how do you go about creating these powerful meditations with the Tarot?

First, choose a Tarot card with which you want to work. Contemplate what you would like to learn, to change or to experience. Perhaps you want to connect with a healing energy. Perhaps you are ready for a change in your life, or you are ready to more deeply understand and explore something. Next, gaze at that Tarot card for a couple of minutes. Soak in the imagery. You do not need to consciously 'memorize' the imagery or interpret what it all means. Just let your subconscious absorb the picture.

Then, find a comfortably seated position. Gently close your eyes. Focus on your breathing and deeply relax. Now, bring up the imagery of the card and step inside. Take some time to explore the symbolism, energy, and attitude of the card. Experience the card. You can even interact with the characters in the card. Create a dialogue. Become those people in that situation in your imagination. You can take a journey in the card somewhere. Next, thank the card and then bring yourself back into your conscious surroundings.

After the meditation, bring your deep insights to conscious awareness by reflecting on your experience and writing it in your journal. Embody your lessons further by creating a ritual or practice which you can conduct regularly. For example, a meditation with the Sun Card inspired me to write a gratitude list each day for the three aspects of my life that are now in abundance.

Actively Engaging with the Tarot Cards Unlocks its Potential

When you actively engage in the Tarot Cards – through meditation, journaling, and other heart-centered activities, you unlock your potential and open yourself up to deeply personal and soulful connections with the Tarot messages. Tarot begins to 'live' through you, and your mind opens up to its infinite wisdom and its infinite potential by connecting in this way.

Here are two of many profound experiences people have shared on my website while meditating with the Tarot.

"I consider myself a person who is drawn to the light not the dark and here I was in the Devil's own place and it was familiar, exciting, and full of anticipation. It felt alive and like a happening

place. I have never thought I was this type of person. He knew me well. Was I this in a past life?" – Carol, meditating with the Devil card

"When I entered into the body of The Empress I looked out through my mother's eyes. I saw how content and happy she was to have created me. I saw what it meant to love, honor and respect both my ability to create and my creations themselves. I knew that, even though I never want to have children myself, I can understand and relate to this energy because of the pure, whole-hearted example my own mother set for me as a feminine creator." – Deirdre, meditating with the Empress

How will you connect with your inner wisdom, using the Tarot as your guide? I invite you to step into exploring who you are or wish to be with this powerful tool.

About Brigit Esselmont

Brigit Esselmont is a Tarotpreneur, intuitive reader, passionate teacher, author and dream manifester. She is the founder of Biddy Tarot at www.biddytarot.com and TarotFoundations.com. These sites and Brigit inspire over a million people each year to transform their lives with the Tarot.

Inspired by her own experiences of meditation and guided visualization, Brigit created ***Soul Meditations: A Journey through the Major Arcana*** which combines guided imagery with Tarot meditations and activities which are designed to embed your inner wisdom and intuition into your daily life. She has also created the popular ***Ultimate Guide to Tarot Card Meanings***, ***Tarot Foundations***, and her most recent program, ***Soul Meditations: A Journey Through the Major Arcana***.

She also teaches Tarot Master classes and online courses to help others read Tarot with confidence.

Brigit believes anyone can read Tarot. She does not own a crystal ball, nor a crushed velvet dress. She is simply a down-to-earth, practical Taurus who likes to use the Tarot cards to enhance everyday life. When she is not reading Tarot, Brigit loves spending time with her two daughters and husband in Melbourne, Australia.

SECTION IV

SPIRITUAL JOURNEYS

YOUR

SOARING PHOENIX

TAKES FLIGHT

Immortal my soul,
Your consciousness now escapes,
Rove past time and space.

Slipping in and out,
Dancing, flying, traveling,
Limits are melted,

Away.

Dr. Carol Franics

173

INTRODUCTION

SPIRITUAL JOURNEYS:
YOUR SOARING PHOENIX TAKES FLIGHT
BY DR. CAROL FRANCIS

I have traveled beyond time and space. Chances are, you have, too. Each author in this section makes these spiritual journeys as a matter of regular practice. The results of such spiritual journeys are phenomenal. So . . .

Prepare for take-off.

Who will help you in your next *Soaring Phoenix* adventures? Near Death Experiencers, Astral Travelers, Remote Viewers, Akashic Readers, Receivers of messages from the dead, Past-Life Regression Explorers, Walk-Ins, Prophetic Dreamers, and Parallel Universe Leapers continue to confound humans. For the spiritually awakened, these tools of traveling in and out of time and space become invaluable equipment for expanding spiritual consciousness.

The tools for traveling in and beyond 3-D, time-space, and bodily limits, presented in this Section, help you use your Phoenix wings fluidly. These authors help you explore beyond commonly perceived time-space and life-death limits. Clearly, the more you practice flying and landing, the more confidence and skills you will develop in your spiritual journeys. The farther you venture and experiment or test, the more you will learn that *we are not mere mortals.*

Unfasten your seatbelt.

Fly Safely.

Soar Beyond Mere Mortal Perceptions

Chapters in Section IV include the following guidance.

Communicate Beyond the Veil of Death by **Dr. Carol Francis** encourages journeying into the locations where loved-ones who have passed on now reside: a tricky journey?

Discover Through Past Life Explorations by **Dr. Heather Friedman Rivera** demonstrates the use of Past Life Regression work which is a spiritual journey into lives you have not yet remembered, and how those lives impact your present life.

Dr. Shelley's Time Travel © by **Shelley Stockwell-Nicholas, Ph.D.** demonstrates journeys of your consciousness used to heal and relieve current life situations and is a chapter from her bestselling book, *Time Travel.*

The Wild and Whacky World of Regression Therapy by **Mary O'Maley, MSHN, ChtI,** demonstrates other journeys associated to regression therapies which help you leap beyond your fear of time travel.

Shamanic Journeys by **Dr. Carol Francis** explains soul retrieval, journeys to different realms of reality, and how to use trance work for shamanic travels. One meditation is provided which helps you enter into the process of shamanic exploration.

Shamanic Soul Retrieval: The Glass Soul by **Debra Fentress** shows how shamanic techniques become a beautiful gentle journey on behalf of another aching soul who needs a lost part of her returned home safe and sound.

Dr. Steve G. Jones, a bestselling author and creator of thousands of hypnosis audio and video tools, wished to share his **Four Tools for Spiritual Journeys** associated to his progression as a seeker.

Disengaging from your physical form easily through astral projection techniques is next. Explore beyond your five senses so you can enjoy a free-floating journey throughout this planet, 3-D regions, and beyond time and space. Such is explored by **Dr. Carol Francis** in **Astral Projection, How and Why?**

Data collecting, life-reviews, autobiographical writings, explanations, perspectives, life-purpose, and personal discoveries await the traveler who journeys to the Akashic Records as discussed by author and lecturer **Barbara Schiffman, Cht., ARCT,** in **New Frontier of Conscious Evolution: The Akashic Records.**

Susan Mann journeyed the *Camino de Santiago de Compostela,* a physically strenuous 500 kilometer pilgrimage which can create a soulful ascension, communion with nature, connection with the Divine, and harmony with internationally diverse humans. Susan Mann describes lessons to be learned on the Camino in: **Spiritual Journeys on Physical Paths: Camino and Synchronicity.**

Donald Saunders' profound and enlightening information-download occurred on some seemingly random morning. That instantaneous knowing resulted in clarifications about how life's manifestations and spiritual power tools are gained. Donald Saunders explains 10 basic tenets of such wisdom in his chapter, **The Knowledge,** which is a partial synopsis of insights shared in his powerful book *The Knowledge.*

Kathi Kenedi describes the Walk-In experience in **The Dream and The Walk-In** wherein one spirit suddenly appears

within the body and life of another. This unique experience is
rarely shared openly.

CHAPTER 24

COMMUNICATE BEYOND THE VEIL

BY DR. CAROL FRANCIS

Mediums interface with dead loved-ones to convey messages someone cannot receive otherwise. They channel, hear, see or empathically sense those disembodied individuals. Wonder if you could too? Wonder if you knew you could speak directly, easily, naturally with your loved-ones? In my opinion, communicating with nonphysical loved-ones with no mediator is yet another aspect of spiritual awakening we all can enjoy.

Actually, many parents, lovers, siblings, and friends secretly do talk with their dead loved-ones. Sadly, they do not often realize that a two-way communique is available beyond the barrier of death. I realize that some spiritual teachers report that our loved-ones are stopped from their after-life evolution if we continue to interact with them too much. This belief discourages people from connecting easily with those gone. Perhaps, they are just a spiritual phone call away and eager to connect.

Consider for a moment that life after death is not based on our time-space perspective. Additionally, our identity is not limited to one sense of self. Therefore, reaching out to our loved-ones is touching one of their identities, the one we know. We are reaching into realms that are not limited by time, or by distance, or by effort.

For example, when Anita Moorjani was dead, she was also aware of her doctors, husband, mother and brother grieving and conversing in different locations. She was also aware of her new self, in her life after death, and she was aware of simultaneous lives. Here is her description:

"Although I was no longer using my five physical senses, I had unlimited perception, as if a new sense had become available, one that was more heightened than any of our usual faculties. I had a 360-degree peripheral vision with total awareness of my surroundings. And as amazing as it all sounds, it still felt almost normal. Being in a body now felt confining.

Time felt different in that realm, too, and I felt all moments at once. I was aware of everything that pertained to me—past, present, and future—simultaneously. I became conscious of what seemed to be simultaneous lives playing out." (1)

Interacting with those who dwell in the nonphysical arenas is an art of listening, watching, and attending to signals. Signals bleep at us constantly. But if our equipment to receive the bleeps is turned off, no signals are received. Yes, it is just like all our modern devices.

Seven Steps for Communicating With Passed-Over Loved-Ones

Step One: *Believing* you can receive messages is akin to turning the toggle switch "on." Belief is step one. Believe even for a moment. Believe with only a part of your heart or mind. Focus on that part of you which can believe. For a moment suspend your skeptical sides.

Step Two: Next, believing "they" can communicate with you, fuels your *efforts* involved in listening.

Step Three: *Ask your questions* clearly; initiate the conversations.

Step Four: *Initiate and ask* questions which can be answered directly and easily at first. Why easy questions? Because, you are learning a new language used between two familiar people. Ask questions which have easy answers at first if you have considerable doubts.

Step Five: *Put effort into listening* just as you would with your boss, employee, child, or spouse. Listen by watching too. Be attentive to details of all sorts. *Listen* on many frequencies. Authors Trish and Rob MacGregor who wrote *Synchronicity and the Other Side: Your Guide to Meaningful Connections with the Afterlife (2)* provides more details on such listening tools as well.

Step Six: *Writing the results*, step six, helps your personal internal-skeptic collect research materials and helps you pay attention and listen. We know that writing dreams every day increases the memory of dreams and sensitivity to messages of dreams. In like manner, writing perceived communications from the other realms, daily, increases your ability to hear their language. For me, this is a type of fact finding, as well.

Step Seven: Finally, *stay grounded* in your everyday life, chores, hobbies, and loves. Evolve your physical life too, because your loved-one, who has died, is definitely evolving their life-experiences as well. Life, and life-after-death, move on. Feeling connected, via your spiritual phone calls, will eventually provide clarity and comfort and even some humorous exchanges.

My MOM, Simple Examples

My mother's passing illustrates these tools aptly.

A few days after her restless death, I was driving a pensive, long haul home from her house. I so wanted to talk with mom. So many more conversations I desired even though we had 58 years as a mother-daughter team. Actually, three miles from home, I felt rather foolish about feeling so maudlin about her death. I knew she was here and there, a spiritual being. So why not talk now to her. Give her a spiritual call.

I turned my left blinker on so I could turn onto the next narrow road before arriving home and asked, "Okay mom. So now that you are fully there, what is the most important thing for me to know about? What information is the most important information you want to share with me?"

One second passed. I merged into the left hand turning lane and quickly a Silver Lexus SS 500 merged in front of me with my low beams focused on his license plate. She spoke.

God *Hearts* U

(The "Heart" symbol was used.)

Mom's message emerged instantaneously. I asked, she answered.

Digest that message for a moment before your internal skeptic begins to argue with this reality.

Remember, one license plate per car, and no license plates can be identical with another in the same state. Next, consider, I had travelled over 120 miles and only in that second, did this message appear as I was moving on to a rather narrow passage where few cars chose to turn. Thirdly, that is a very specific and pertinent answer, on the only car in California with that license plate. Clearly, that message is the most relevant and pithy message mom could ever convey. Yes, I took photographs for verification.

One week later, while washing my teeth for bed, I asked mom what she was learning. Within minutes, my cellphone in the adjacent empty room uncharacteristically turned on and loudly played an odd YouTube music video. This has never happened in the several years owning this iphone4s. Google's YouTube does not spontaneously begin playing on iphones even when you use that app. Mom's message was repeated over and over in this selfie-singing video from an unknown Asian teen with the repeated chorus line, "I now know I am loved. Yes, I now know I am loved..." Yep, that fit my mom's needs perfectly and of course touched me deeply.

Mom was a classical cellist with the Philadelphia Philharmonic Orchestra and a performing Pianist. During my childhood, she woke us up on easy Sunday mornings with Ravel, Chopin, Handel, and Beethoven. She would also sing in her grand alto-soprano voice, typically "Danny Boy," "Moon River,"and "16 Tons." This Sunday night, I told her that I missed her music. The next morning at 4:45 AM exactly 11 months after she died, our outdated, unused, stereo system began to hauntingly play Ravel's Bolero. I was sure I was dreaming and rolled over. 4:47 AM, my son swung his door open asking me why I was playing music downstairs so early and so loudly, as Bolero was swelling to a blare. Then I knew I was not dreaming. We crept downstairs looking for the source of the music. Weird. Yes. Even weirder is that this antiquated sound system, which we no longer used, requires one to push three buttons and then to twist one dial in order to play that track on that CD. Ravel's Bolero was among the last three tunes my mom and I shared before she passed. "Good morning to you too, mom. Thanks for the good-morning concert yet again."

Today, while researching materials pertinent to this chapter, I decided atypically to gather my materials onto the back patio for the first outdoor-day of spring. While reading about another near-death survivor, I asked what my mother felt while in that same state too. Within minutes, the first four lines of "Danny Boy" echoed up our canyon from some house, miles below with a female voice singing my mother's words to me:

Oh, Danny Boy, the pipes, the pipes are calling

From glen to glen, and down the mountain side,

The summer's gone, and all the roses falling,

It's you, it's you must go and I must bide. (3)

Christmas and special holidays become reminiscent times of woe and sadness when loved-ones are not there to create yet another memory captured in family time. Yet my mother again decided to visit me during that year's Christmas party when an unknown and unexpected person, who kept lingering to speak with me privately, finally stepped in and said, "I must tell you. Your mom is here and she wants you to know she is clear, finally. She is clear. Her mind is clear. And, she saw you celebrate her birthday in August." My mother's deathbed brain-fog was gone, and yes, she knew I celebrated her birthday too. Special days are still together. This message was delivered from a beautifully brave medium;—nice touch mom—bold and direct.

The final event to convey on this topic occurred when my mother was two weeks from dying. She truly wanted to get "death" over but was also so afraid to leave, having no particular comforting religious or spiritual beliefs. Her body was inflexible, frail, immovable, and her mind typically unalert these last days.

Early that day, she called and left a message: a very rare event. "Carol, I must tell you something really important. It's really very important. I will tell you when you get here!" I began to worry. As soon as I arrived at her home and relieved a caregiver, she sat up energetically in bed, crossed her legs like a teenager, glued her deep blue Irish eyes on me, and insisted that I sit and listen to her most important news. She began, "I was there. I went there. To that place where I'll be going." She had visited *her life after death*. "It was amazing," she continued. "The flowers densely covered the fields and were singing. They were yellow and pink. Music emanated from each flower with incredible harmony. The music

184

was beautiful. Their colors...I have never seen such colors, Carol. Carol, I was there. That's where I'm going." In 1950, my mother had a Near Death Experience while giving birth. Once, she explained how beautiful flowers surrounded her then in her out-of-body moment too. Ever since that day in 1950, my mother had been painting flowers trying to capture her life in that beyond. Frustrated with her flower water-colors, she explained that her paintings never matched radiant colors she had seen. Hmm, I wonder if she is painting musical flowers now?

My mother and I currently do not now occupy the same 3-D physical plane together. Nonetheless, since time, space, identity, and limits are not pertinent, we can still connect.

I encourage you to do the same.

Begin your loving conversations, then listen, watch. Thereafter, attend to the amazing messages they wish to share with you right now. You share too, often and peacefully confident, even during holidays or special occasions.

Many additional moments have been shared between myself and others whom I love. I confirm repeatedly that the illusion of death and distance is exactly that, the Hindu Maya of illusion. We might as well ignore death's veil and plow forward; ask, talk, listen, and watch each other through the thin lacy veil that barely separates us physically.

References

1.   Moorjani, Anita (2012). *Dying to Be Me: Journey From Cancer, To Near Death, To True Healing*. Carlsbad: Hay House, Inc. (2012), Page 66.

2.   Trish and Rob MacGregor who wrote *Synchronicity and the Other Side: Your Guide to Meaningful Connections with the Afterlife*

3. *Danny Boy* Lyrics by Frederick Weatherly (1913)

About Dr. Carol Francis

In addition to her spiritual counseling and intuitive work with metaphysically inclined seekers, Dr. Carol Francis has practiced for 37 years as a Clinical Psychologist, Life Coach, Clinical Hypnotherapist, and Marriage, Family & Child Counselor. She assists individuals, couples and children who seek to optimize their current situation and overcome complications of daily living. These individuals seek deep relief and growth for depression, anxiety, stress, career moves, family discord, child and parenting issues, relationship dissatisfaction, habit control, and the psychology of financial success. Practicing and licensed in Southern California for over 37 years, Dr. Carol Francis can be reached at drcarolfrancis.com or 310-543-1824.

Publications by Dr. Carol Francis

Study Skills for Successful High School and College Students

Helping Children with Divorce

Schizoid Anxiety

Helping Children with Natural and Manmade Disasters

"Horrific Parental Imaginings"

"Therapist's Countertransference with Abuse Couples"

KISS Method for Stop Smoking and KISS Cigarettes Goodbye

If You Can't Stop Eating, Maybe You're Hungry: Reset Your Cravings

Re-Uniting Soldiers with Families

Evolving Women's Consciousness: Dialogue with 21st Century Women.

Spiritual Paths, Spiritual Gurus: Your Choice

Spiritual Journeys: Astral Projection, Shamanism, Akashic Records

Your Akashic Records

DrCarolFrancisTalkRadio.com and DrCarolFrancis.com contain more information regarding programs, recordings, and helpful services.

FRANCIS & O'MALEY

CHAPTER 25

DISCOVER THROUGH
PAST LIFE EXPLORATIONS
BY DR. HEATHER FRIEDMAN RIVERA

Spirituality was not a large part of my life. As a young child, I was convinced that I would rot in the ground after death—nothing more. I was not raised with the hopeful stories of bouncing around on fluffy clouds in heaven. As a child I had wished I could. One of my classmates told me about heaven. She pointed to a large cloud in the blue sky and said, "We can play up there together someday."

I nodded in agreement, but secretly believed I would be lying under the dirt with worms crawling through my eye sockets.

As a teen, the closest brush with spirituality was reading passages from Henry David Thoreau's *Walden*. I sat alone with his words surrounded by nature and felt my heart expand and tears well-up in my eyes. This was my sacred time.

At age thirty-three, I was a content and driven agnostic woman whose life did not have room for spirituality—until I got sick. With a new diagnosis of Rheumatoid Arthritis I was devastated, and for the first time considered praying to G-d, whoever that was? I found a small stream away from people and sat down on the ground. "Um, I'm not really sure how to do this praying thing and I'm not sure if you know who I am but can you take away my arthritis?" I whispered to the gray air on an overcast morning. I waited and . . . nothing. No appearances, no voices, no answers—just a brief fluttering of a hummingbird nearby. He then whisked off leaving me alone and frustrated.

That moment, although not particularly exciting, was actually a turning point in my life. I stood and brushed off the dirt from my jeans and headed for a tea room to warm up. As I sipped my green tea, I made a list. What could I do to improve my health? On this list I put on the usual areas of concern: diet and exercise. Surprised, I also added meditation and spirituality. I made many changes over the next few years.

Buddhism was a comfortable fit for me since it did not challenge my non-spiritual upbringing. One Zen Center near my home became my refuge. I learned to meditate and find the stillness within. Not that it came easy to me, but after months of wrestling with my chaotic mind, I simply let go and let the quiet bubble up. I was left on my own to sit with myself and look within. I could handle that.

I ventured farther outside my comfort zone and read about unconventional, alternative and complementary therapies. I learned about acupuncture, biofeedback, channeling and even hypnosis. My younger self would have cringed to see me reading about anything "woo woo" but I was on a mission—to get better.

I found the subject of hypnosis interesting, but questioned what I was reading—especially past life regressions. I laughed inside and thought "Oh c'mon now." But another part of me was intrigued. Did we live before? And if so what did that mean?

I called a local hypnotherapist, Dr. Donna Kannard, who specializes in past life regression therapy and made an appointment. My interest was out of curiosity and an afternoon of entertainment. I told the hypnotherapist nothing of my search for better health. I also warned her that I was a skeptical, nervous and tense individual who probably could not be hypnotized. She listened to my concerns without judgment and in a soothing tone invited me to sit back in the chair.

With hesitation I leaned back into the reclining chair and closed my eyes. She guided me into hypnosis by having me imagine all my muscles from head to toe relaxing. Soon I was in a relaxed and peaceful state. Next, she had me descend an imaginary stairway in my mind—down, down into a garden. In the garden was a library. I entered this library where there was an entire section of books with my name on the binding. I pulled one out and sat at a table. As I turned the pages, Dr. Kannard told me that one page would call to me. I continued to flip through the pages. Then stopped on one: a drawing of a knight with a white horse kneeling before him. Before I could take another breath, I was pulled into the knight's body.

I was startled that not only was I able to be hypnotized but that somehow I was now experiencing this knight's life. It appeared that I was experiencing a past life. I felt the heaviness of armor, the hunger in my belly and the sense of duty. I was able to have two streams of thoughts in my head at the same time—those of the knight and those of Heather—myself as I currently knew me.

Then I found myself dying on a battle field of green, looking at the gray sky. As I choked and gagged on blood, I was also coughing and choking in the therapist's chair. Despite Dr. Kannard's instructions to detach and watch the scene as if observing a movie, I chose to stay with the knight and experience his death. He took his last breath and I left the body, rising higher and becoming huge. In this space out of the body, I had an overwhelming sense of love and peace, connectedness with all and with expansive Oneness. In this state I could have stayed forever.

I knew when I came back into my present-day body, that clearly this was a direct spiritual experience. Additionally, I immediately discovered that I had recovered from a major physical complication; this past life regression resulted in a profound physical healing while I was there. The experience was life-altering for me. I took a couple of days off work to process this restructuring of everything I thought I knew about life, death, purpose, and spirituality.

I also realize now I am not only Heather. I am also not only the knight, nor any of the other past lives I have remembered since that first experience.   Instead, I am an awareness currently inhabiting the body of Heather. During my out-of-body experience, I realized that I chose this current body for my greater good. My purpose now is to live fully in Heather's body, which includes being the nervous, tense, and skeptical person I was supposed to be. I do not have to pretend nor strive to be anyone else.

While I am in this body, I am to embrace who I am and discover how Heather would react to her life. That is this mission. So simple. This is, for me, spirituality.   Since that first experience as a knight, I have devoted my energies to research past life therapy and writing about it. My three books, *Healing the Present from the Past, Quiet Water,* and *Maiden Flight,* were born from my new understanding. Spirituality is not about being at peace at all times or sitting up on a mountain-top chanting "Om" but about embracing our humanness with all our flaws and the ups and downs of life. Life is about opening our eyes and responding with our wholeness to what is right in front of us.

Perhaps opening our eyes to who we have been in bodies of past lives and also who we are in-between each life-journey opens our consciousness about being connected and within expansive Oneness.

References

Rivera, Heather (2012). *Healing the Present from the Past.* Bloomington: Balboa Press.

Rivera, Heather (2014). *Quiet Water.* North Charleston: Createspace.

Rivera, Heather (2014) *Maiden Flight.*

About the Author:

Heather Rivera, RN, JD, PhD is an author and scientific past-life researcher. She co-founded PLR Institute for advancing past-life research. Dr. Heather speaks, writes and hosts retreats as well. To contact Dr. Rivera go to www.plrinstitute.org www.heatherrivera.com or drheatherrivera@gmail.com

FRANCIS & O'MALEY

CHAPTER 26

DR. SHELLEY'S TIME TRAVEL ©

BY SHELLEY STOCKWELL-NICOLAS, PH.D.

Who in the world is in here now?
For heaven's sake and holy cow.
Is it a sub-personality
Dressed like god inside of me?

Have you been to a place for the first time and felt that you have been there before? Have you caught a glimpse of reality in a dream? Or met someone new, yet, so familiar that you feel you've known them forever? Do certain cultures and peoples draw you to them while others leave you cold? What is déjà vu? What is déjà vu?

Time travel is the map to these deepest perceptions. Inside you live vivid scenarios of other places and times awaiting your access and exploration. Past life (regressions) and future life (progressions) benefit your life now. You access precious records within your body/mind, heal past pain, and revivify your dreams and goals. Each new awareness fills you with light. You become in-lightened. Some people experience psychic awareness during a journey. After accessing some 45 past lives I began trance channeling and that opens even more doors to my knowing!

Expect to feel relaxed and comfortable. Time travel brings inner peace.

The form your journey takes varies each time you depart and explore. Let it be. I have personally accessed lives of men, women, and animals. I even had a client who was a granite boulder who transformed as a result of volcanic activity. Avoid any expectations at all. Be open and see, hear, taste, and touch what you find.

In the center of every fear is a desire. If you are afraid that you will lose control and feel helpless, understand that you take control of your control when you make a choice to relinquish control. You are always in control. Anytime you want to, you can open your eyes and return to your present awareness.

AMAZING REGRESSION CASE STUDY

In the 1970s I was speaking to a Rotary club when an elder gentleman asked me if I did past life regressions. "I've dabbled in it", I replied.

Two months later, this gentleman was in my office. During my pre-interview I asked him about his health. "I've been plagued with asthma my entire life." he replied.

"How's your memory?"

"Very good" he said.

"Go back to a place in time, in this lifetime, when you are very young."

"How old are you?" I asked him and a tearful, little voice answered "I'm two." And he began to cry.

"What is going on? "Why are you crying Little boy" I asked.

"It's the day before Christmas and I want to open my presents. My daddy won't let me. He says I have to wait until Christmas comes."

And the man on my sofa began to cry and then launched into an asthma attack.

"Great" I thought and I carefully showed him how to "turn off" his asthma like turning down a gauge and when he did, his breathing returned to normal. "Very good; open your eyes and come back." And so he did.

"What do you know about past life regressions?" I asked.

"Nothing", he said "I'm simply curious."

"Have you ever read anything about regressions?" I asked.

"No, I've only heard it could be done."

"Fine," I thought "hypnotherapy is a fantastic tool to eliminate the symptoms of asthma so this session was already successful but now I had the challenge of regressing this gentle, retired aerospace engineer, in his gray suit to another lifetime.

He closed his eyes and embarked on a monumental past life journey that caused me to forever be smitten with past life regression. Since then I have done hundreds of time travel sessions, and continue being in awe of the vast imagining and power of our creative subconscious mind.

His session went something like this:

"Go back farther" I said. "To an earlier place in time."

The man on my sofa became still and silent, emerging into a state known as a catatonic trance. After several very long moments, I noticed that his hand twitched slightly.

"What do you have in your hand?" I asked.

"An auger."

"What do you do with it?" I asked.

"I run it across the stones."

"Where are the stones?"

"In the atrium of my house."

"Where do you live?"

"In Rome."

This elderly man now was an eight year old Greek boy who told me details of his life in Rome. He presented vivid accounts of his clothes, his toys, his food, his religion, his friends. His mother was a cold socialite, his father was an orator.

"I am learning to write. I write on the tablets and with sticks in the sand."

"Here's a stick" I said, handing him a pencil and paper. He began to write in Greek! (Later I learned that the man on the sofa did not know Greek). It seems that this boy grew up to be a good man, who never married; he never fully got over his mother's rejection. He went on to change the course of boating. Seafaring vessels had been wide and he created a narrow boat and took many people to islands off of Italy.

"How did he die?" I asked the entity.

"When he was forty he went to an island where there were elephants and he was crushed by an elephant."

At this, the engineer, on my sofa, launched into the most awful asthma attack I've ever witnessed. "Take a deep breath." I said. "Turn off your asthma" And he did.

Thus, a three-hour past-life regression session came to a close.

Several years later I called up this gentleman. "Do you remember me?" I asked.

"Do I remember you! You changed my life. That boy is me. I am that boy. I have carried him with me my whole life and I feel a great sense of peace having reunited with him once again."

"How is your asthma? I asked

"I've never had another attack since then. I had a couple of instances when I felt tightness, but I simply took a deep breath and turned down the dial."

I have been hooked with the work ever since.

HOW TO EASILY TRAVEL TIME

You can time travel using this simple exercise to send you on your way:

1. Take a deep cleansing breath and center yourself.

2. Bless yourself on all levels: mentally, physically, spiritually and emotionally asking that all the teachings of this journey are for your highest good.

3. Without censoring, editing or analyzing, imagine yourself walking down a long hallway into your past. As you walk, you pass many doors. Each door opens to a past life. You come to a door that will benefit your knowing. It beckons you "enter" and you do.

4. Notice everything in this place. How it smells, tastes, looks, sounds. Look at your feet. What are you wearing? Are you male or female? What is going on for you here? How did you die? Go to the Light. What happens when the light comes upon you. What did you learn from this lifetime? And how does that learning influence you in your present twenty-first century lifetime?

5. Come on back and stretch.

Oriental philosophy claims that we each have some 800 lifetime memories stored within. May you never feel lonely again!

Reference

This chapter is a reprint of an excerpt which was permitted by the publisher and author. Excerpts from "TIME TRAVEL: The Do-It-Yourself Past Life Journey Handbook"

About Dr. Shelley Stockwell

Dr. Shelley Stockwell-Nicholas is the author of many fantastic books including *Hypnosis - Smile on Your Face, Money in Your Pocket, Denial - It's not a River in Egypt, Stockwell's Hypnosis Dictionary Scriptbook* and over 20 more titles. You can find more information and get your instant audio downloads from Creativity Unlimited Press store located at hypnosisfederation.com.

Dr. Shelley is the founder and President of the International Hypnosis Federation and busy international keynote conference speaker.

Dr. Shelley hosted the nationally syndicated television show "BackTrack" ("Regressiones) and appears on radio and television shows such as Phil Donahue, Chanel 9 & 11 News, Mike and Maty, The Other Side, Strange Universe, Van Praague's Beyond, The Oxygen Network, and David Letterman. Dr. Shelley writes for Entrepreneur Magazine, Redbook, USA Today, The Los Angeles Times, Women First, Women's Day and of course The National Enquirer.

CHAPTER 27

THE WILD AND WHACKY WORLD
OF REGRESSION THERAPY
BY MARY O'MALEY, MSHN, CHTI

To me there is nothing more fascinating than to explore myself throughout time and space -- well, except for exploring with you!

We have the wisdom of the Universe inside of us. Answers to every question are available.   The possibility for every Spiritual or Metaphysical exploration begins with our inner awareness. From you, inside of you, there is a voice that is uniquely and beautifully yours and connected to All There Is. The information is transmitted through pictures and feelings and stories that seem to come from our imagination. The reality is that all communication is processed through our imagination.   I believe that what we commonly refer to as Regression Therapy should really be called Expansion Therapy since it expands our perception of truth and self-knowledge through imagination.

The word "regression" is defined as "The act of going back to a previous place or state; return or reversion."(1)   However, what I have discovered over these many years of being a hypnotherapist is that we do not always go backwards. Actually, we can go forward in time and even sideways. We can also use Regression Therapy to

201

go inwards, allowing us to have conversations with parts of our body or with sub-personalities.

We can move around in space and time in the state of regression and explore different time periods, cultures and countries. We can even go to Mars or the Moon or even another Universe if we choose. Dr. Brian Weiss noted in his ground breaking book, *Many Lives, Many Masters* (2), we can even hold conversations with other entities while we are on an Expansion Journey.

As a tool for advancing your boundaries in Spirituality, Expansion Therapy is an easy way to get started. If you are new to the mechanisms of the trance journey state, I recommend starting with a qualified, experienced and open minded hypnotherapist as your guide. To assist your trance soul-journey expansion, I created "The Seven P's of Regression Therapy" to equip hypnotherapists and you, as well.

"The Seven P's of Regression Therapy", is the template I created and use for teaching hypnotherapy in my Certified Hypnosis Courses. While these Seven P's are ones which I use and experience, do not let them limit you in your exploration to other possibilities.

In my practice of hypnotherapy, these sessions are also used as opportunities to heal. I am often asked, "Is this real or just my imagination?" Well, I have come to the conclusion that it just does not matter since it works! I have included some explanations and examples which I hope will help you understand the power of "The Seven P's of Regression Therapy".

The Seven P's of Regression/Expansion Therapy

Present – *Regression to any experience within your present life span.*

I once worked with a client who was terrified of being alone and did not know why. She actually came to me for a Past Life Regression to search for an explanation. During the regression she saw herself, in her present life, as a 3 year old child playing in a room where her uncle was seated, reading a newspaper. As she played, she had wandered under the long drapes at the window. When she came out from under the drapes, she was all alone in the room and became terrified. During the regression, she was able to see that her uncle had left the room not realizing she was still there. For some reason, her unconscious mind had held onto this moment as if it were a trauma, and it was now causing problems for her as an adult. Using Regression Therapy, she was able to comfort her 3 year-old-self and explain that she was never really alone and that her adult self would always be with her.

Past Life – *Regression to any experience that appears to be in the time before this present life span.*

Many years ago when I was a brand new hypnotist, my life was a mess. I was a single mom, on disability, struggling with some depression and was barely able to pay rent. I had many good excuses for not being able to start my hypnotherapy business.

I was asked to volunteer for a past life regression class given by my friend and beloved mentor, Shelly Stockwell Nicholas. During my regression, I was a young woman, 16 or 17 years old, in England around the year 450 AD. In my village I had been trained as a healer. Vikings (I think?) were destroying the villages around us but their men had become very ill and were dying. I was given to their camp as a healer in exchange for not destroying my village. When I got to their camp, I realized it was too late for most of them to be helped and many continued to die during the few days I was with them. They decided they had been duped. They tied me to a pole and set me on fire, and then killed everyone in my village anyway.

As I died, I made the decision that I could not be trusted as a healer since I had failed, and everyone in my village died because of my failure. As I moved into the after death state I was encouraged to find the truth of this experience. It suddenly became clear to me that my captives had planned on annihilating my village in any case, and happily used my perceived failure as an excuse. I was able to resolve this experience and acknowledge that I actually feared being in any healing-type industry because of this experience. From my post-life perspective I forgave myself, and we ended the session.

Strangely enough, even though my material circumstances had not changed, I was able to start my hypnotherapy business less than a week later. A friend studying graphic design helped me create business cards and professional brochures (I only had to pay for the paper). Another new acquaintance offered me use of her lovely office space and I only had to pay for the hours I used it. Wow! It was clearly only my own past life perceptions and decisions that had been holding me back!

Post Life– *Progression to a future time.*

I have used Post Life Progression in two different ways. First was to visit the end of my life. I did not like what I saw and asked my "Superconscious or Wise Mind" what I could do to change the outcome. Not only did I receive an answer but also a commitment from my subconscious mind to help me make the necessary changes that would lead to a more acceptable outcome.

Secondly, six of us, all previously strangers to each other, were *prog*ressed in class to the year 3000 AD on Earth. Not everything we experienced was the same as we were looking from different perspectives. Nonetheless, we brought back so much information that was the same or very similar that it was almost spooky. Two of us actually experienced having to travel back to the Earth from another planet!

Parallel Life – *Any experience related to the same point in time but from a different space or dimension.*

During another class, under a regression trance, we were asked to find out if we were having other experiences on Earth at the present time, in other bodies. Not understanding the expansiveness of my soul I was surprised to find out that I was also a 46 year old woman in New Zealand, living with and caring for elderly parents and their farm; a young African man being trained as a traditional healer; and, a 58 year old woman that had just died during a mud slide in Central America. This last parallel life I was able to verify as a possibility. I found in a news report that many had recently died in mud slides there, unbeknown to me. But, I suspect many of these experiences are also being lived in other dimensions at the same time, too.

Another odd thing that happened was I had several clients come in that swore they were experiencing two different lives at the same time. Under hypnosis they were able to receive important information and also to reset the dimensional boundaries that had been breached. (Please note that under normal circumstances I usually refer these type of issues with clients to a Psychologist who is well educated in the art of hypnosis.)

This can also be used to answer the question, "What if I had done that instead of this?" by progressing along the dimensional time line of that other possibility. For instance, what if I had married Jim instead of Fred? By following the alternate time line of marrying Jim you may find the outcome to be a negative experience, and release an unconscious form of stress.

Physical Point of Origin – *Using regression therapy to access a physical point on the body – useful in pain relief and physical healing.*

Talking directly to a body part that is in trouble is an amazing process. Quite often the body part will tell you what nutrients, types of exercise, or stress release it needs in order to heal. Sometimes we find that the body is carrying a memory from another life time that needs to be acknowledged. Spontaneous healing is not unheard of with this method.

I once regressed into my genetic structure through a process created by Kathi Kenedi, CHtI, called "Genetic Consciousness." I went to a past life and when she asked me what year it was, the answer that came was "the earth is still hot." I saw myself as a humanoid type being, a little like Gollum looked from Lord of the Rings.

Parts Therapy – *Accessing an aspect of one's personality to help change a behavior.*

Parts Therapy is classic hypnotherapy. Imagine you are a smoker and just cannot quit. The part of your personality that is in charge of that behavior pattern is incredibly strong. So, we ask that part of the personality to leave, or to switch to being in charge of a behavior that is healthier, like regular exercise. We can also ask that part when and under what circumstances it came into being and dissolve its power by acknowledging its purpose and then letting it know it is no longer needed for that purpose. We may also engage other sub-personalities to help with the process.

Pop-Ins – *Any communication that appears to be from an entity other than the subject.*

Pop-Ins experiences are better known as channeling, but can happen spontaneously, although it is rare in a hypnosis session. The first time it happened to me I came instantly out of hypnosis, was off the couch and halfway down the driveway before my teacher, Shelley Stockwell Nicholas, caught me and explained that if I do it, it means I could have clients who might too; and I needed to know how to handle it. What a shock! I am now comfortable with this phenomenon, completely in charge of what I allow, and look forward to receiving these incredible messages.

Source Regression (the 's part of the 7 P's <grin>) *Using senses such as a smell, sound, feeling, connection to a person, place or thing as the focus of a regression.*

I once worked with a man who was completely captivated by the sounds of buoy-type bells in the harbor. Under hypnosis I had him follow the sound of the bells to a time and place where they were significant in his life. He found himself as a warrior on a Japanese ship in the 1600's, going to war. He acquitted himself so well during the battle that, even though he died in that battle, his heroism brought great fortune to his family. He was very proud of his accomplishments.

Sometimes we meet people whom we are sure we must have known in another time. By tuning into the energy of that person, we can easily regress to a point when our souls were together in another time and space.

Source regression is one of the easiest to do on your own. Pick a time or place or person to which you are drawn and let that be your focus. Allow yourself to relax and begin to daydream and feel yourself drifting into the energy of time and space. Let your mind tell you a story about your time, place or person. Really pay attention to what you see, hear, feel, smell and taste. At the end of the story, ask your higher self if there is anything else you need to know about this story. Is there anyone you need to forgive, including yourself? Did you make a decision during this story that no longer serves you today? The following link will take you to a radio show in which I led a past life regression which you can use to help with your experience. http://maryomaley.com/?p=28

Regression/Expansion Therapy was the doorway into spirituality for me. It is also the key to the doorway into all of the advanced aspects of spirituality and exploration with which I work and enjoy today. I hope this information helps you on your Expansion Journey.

References:

This chapter is from Mary O'Maley's unpublished essay entitled fully:

The Wild and Whacky World of Regression Therapy:

Exploring Yourself Throughout Space and Time with

Expansion Therapy & Regression Therapy (2012).

1. www.Dictionary.com

2. Weiss, Brian (1998). *Many Lives, Many Masters.* New York: Simon and Schuster, Inc.

About Mary O'Maley, MSHN, CHtI

Mary O'Maley holds a MS in Holistic Nutritional Health Science and is a Certified Hypnotherapist and Hypnotherapy Instructor with International Hypnosis Federation. She is recipient of the prestigious IHF Award of Excellence & Chapter Woman of the Year from American Business Woman's Association. Mary specializes in Past Life Regression, Intuitive Nutritional Counseling, Life Coaching, five energy healing modalities, psychic and medium readings, and hosts various programs and events.

Mary O'Maley, as Life Coach, created the Retreat-Reconnect-Recharge-ReEmerge Coaching. This R4 Coaching provides in-depth, personal-retreat experiences which help you access, trust, and follow your inner wisdom.

Certified in Reiki, Access Energy Clearing, Matrix Energetics and Reconnective Healing, Mary O'Maley also developed and provides Crystal Chakra Balancing. Crystal Chakra Balancing was discovered through Mary O'Maley's Akashic Records work.

Mary O'Maley teaches basic and intermediate hypnotherapy through IHF, nutritional approaches to health at various medical facilities, and metaphysical information at various international conferences and local venues.

Mary O'Maley's metaphysical studies allowed her to reignite her psychic and mediumship gifts which she uses for home, gallery and individual readings given since 1997. She is certified and tested as a member of Best American Psychics. Mary O'Maley hosts and produces The Merry Medium Show. On The Merry Medium Show, Mary interviews many wonderful spiritual explorers from the metaphysical and holistic communities. Podcasts of The Merry Medium Show are available at blogtalkradio.com/the-merry-medium. She also hosts live events in the Los Angeles area: **The Merry Medium and Friends – Where Science and Spirit Meet Live Events.**

To reach Mary O'Maley for her alternative health services, psychic and mediumship readings, radio programs, live events, materials, workbooks and books, contact her at http://www.maryomaley.com or call 424-234-9260.

CHAPTER 28

SHAMANIC JOURNEYS
BY DR. CAROL FRANCIS

Shamans (the witch doctors or medicine men, as Hollywood characterized them in the mid 1900's) held the spiritual dimensions of his/her people's health and political power in his/her spiritual hands. Intricate ceremonies or spontaneous prayer-rituals would summons spirits to come, to help, or to flee from a tribal member's sick body. Hunting, battle preparations, peace negotiations, crop-planting, eating, marriage, dying, moving, control over weather, or even neighborly squabbles, were and are assisted by shamanic spiritual rituals.

Medicines were prepared shamanically too, from herbs, plants, or soil, with animal parts contributing to the concoctions. Bathing, vision quests in the wilderness, or hallucinogenically-induced spiritual quests were sometimes added to the rituals leading toward healing, guidance or resolutions. In some of these indigenous cultures, spirits were significantly a part of every dimension of life during each segment of the day. The shaman guided frequently. The shaman was consulted when life became troubled or vexed with extraordinary burdens.

Michael Harner and Sandra Ingerman have attempted to bring the daily use of shamanistic practices they experienced firsthand into the western society. They were not the first. Writings about Don Juan and his cultic-type practices in Central America were keenly studied by many in the mid 1900's, brought into the urban consciousness by a focused student, Carlos Castaneda. Peruvian anthropologist, Carlos Castaneda, captured the complex teachings of Don Juan, as a teacher of Mexican Yaqui brujo (sorcerer or shaman). Don Juan was dark, dynamic, powerful and mysterious in his shamanic teachings. Unfortunately, Don Juan made the Shamans' Path inaccessible to those who had earthly responsibilities or who did not wish to brave frightening spirits, agonizing nights, or drug-induced insightfulness.

Michael Harner and Sandra Ingerman have made the path of shamanism accessible and powerfully transforming for the urbanite. In their footsteps, many modern authors have modernized the process of these journeys as well. Such autobiographies are rich with narratives of women and men across the planet with unique spiritual abilities to communicate, conquer, and dominate the realm of spiritual entities for the welfare of humankind.

Let's travel the shamanic path in these next few pages. Perhaps this is the dynamic spiritual connection that appeals to the sensibilities of *Your Soaring Phoenix*. Please know that what follows are generalities and the specifics associated to any tribe or indigenous group is worthy of individualized study.

Mapping Spiritual Domains

Upper, lower and middle worlds exist within most shamanic traditions. The Upper Spirit-World consists of angel-like entities where divine, and perhaps not so divine, spirits reside. The Middle Spirit-World is where spirits are earthy and associated with plants, animals, humans, and planetary phenomena. The Lower Spirit-World may consist of mythical-like creatures that can assist or cause havoc in all worlds, as with the Upper Spirit-World. Soul Retrievals or Soul Extractions, as described by Debra Fentress in the next chapter typically occur within the Middle

Spirit-World. Astral Travel, discussed later, potentially occur in all realms. Remote Viewing is a Middle Worlds process typically. Spirit guides, medium communication, or connections with angels typically involve the Middle and Upper Spirit-Worlds. Healing practices can cross all domains.

Pantheism, the presence of God or gods, in everything, is common to these paths. In like manner, a Supreme God and associated spiritually divine entities exist as well. In addition, spirits of the dead or angels are present, too. In essence the spiritual dimensions are present in one form or another in everything, every event, every person and every realm and on multiple levels.

Shamanic Journeys

The adventurous part of the shamanic practitioner's life is to travel to all the realms of the spirits and become acquainted with all that dwell therein. Shamanic Journeys might go to the spirit of a plant that might be used to heal someone. Shamanic Journeys might be aimed to solicit assistance from a series of gods, angels or entities in order to win an abusive battle or coerce the weather to be gentle.

Shamans travel with the aid of meditations (as we might call them today) or ecstatic mind-altering practices. These ecstatic practices might include repetitive movements, extreme starvation fasts, hallucinogenic plants, chants and songs, dances, or any other hypnogogic-inducing rituals.

Shamans also carry their medicine bags filled with herbs, plants, precious gems, earthly stones, talismans or artifacts. Shamans are accompanied on these spiritual journeys by spirits of animals and plants who would guide, protect and accompany the Shaman through the spiritual realms.

The Shamans' power includes summoning the spirits to the earthly plane or traveling to the spirits' domains. Shamans are mediators between ordinary people and the spiritual realm. The Shaman might be the liaison, negotiator, pleader, messenger, solicitor, warrior, or kingly proclamator between the spirits and the humans involved.

Michael Harner (1) devised a method whereby each person could travel to these realms and visit the spirits dwelling therein. Through ecstatic chanting, singing, dancing and especially drumming, you, in meditation, would loosen your hold on this earthly realm and spiritually travel to those other realms.

Your first spiritual journey would be to acquaint yourself with friendly animal spirits and find one in particular who would acknowledge you, three times, and then agree to become your accompaniment during each moment of your life whether during a Shamanic Journey in the spiritual realms or in ordinary life.

During subsequent journeys, you would ask your core question, three times, and then descend or ascend to one of the spiritual realms with the aid of your ecstatic drumming meditation and animal spirit guide. You would reunite with your animal spirit and journey to find the answers to your core question. What you might see, sense, dialogue, or receive as an iconic gift, would provide you with the answer or solution to your core question. Your task is to apply such answers to your ordinary life.

Michael Harner at one time wanted all Shamanic Journey persons to describe and map-out their journeys in an attempt to see if there are universal locations within the spiritual realms. He discovered through his anthropological research, that each culture seemed to have a specific proclivity toward certain types of evil and good spirits, as well as similar descriptions about their locations within these realms. He was more intrigued by how different cultures also seemed to have similarities that seemed trans-culturally described. Similar spirits performed similar tasks in similar nonphysical locations across many physical cultures, Harner discovered.

Sandra Ingerman, (2) keenly promoted the use of these urban shamanic journeys to provide help within the healing professions as well. She used these Shamanic Journeys, as did the indigenous shamans, to extract unfavorable spirits or souls from a person's body, personality or past existence. She would also put to rest unsettled spirits aggravated by past events or disturbing complications. She would retrieve lost portions of a soul or create a spiritual healing ceremony in the spiritual realm and then the material realm.

If a spirit of a plant, mineral, concoction, or animal would be helpful as a presence or medicine, Sandra Ingerman would bring that back for her patient to keep as a spiritual companion until the healing occurred. If an individual lost a portion of their being, their personality or their personal essence, Shamans would retrieve those disowned parts of the patient, and return that part to the patient. Spirit retrieval, spirit extraction, spirit negotiation, spirit solicitation, or medicinal formulas become ways Shamans heal their tribal fellow men and women.

I have studied Shamanism for over two decades with Native American Indian initiates in the Southwestern United States, Peruvian Shamans from Inca descendants, Quechuan Shamans in the Andes, and Amori Shamans in Southern Peru, and the tip of Bolivia, Plant Shamans, Music Shamans, and professors of urban Shamanic practices. Since 1995, I have enjoyed holding many drumming and healing circles of my own. I have grown fond of the power of these Journeys for individual clients, too. I also greatly appreciate how accessible and doable these Journeys become after merely a few such ceremonies are taught and conducted. You can interface with your Gurus in the Spiritual Realms. You can travel and interface with fellow travelers in discussion, meditation and wonderment as well.

Mediation, for many, is a vexingly boring or perplexingly undoable as an empty mental, spiritual state. Repeatedly, many who try to meditate in a state of mindlessness as with certain

Eastern traditions (Yogic, Hinduism, Buddhism) or with certain mystical Christian or Kabbalistic traditions, find that nothingness produces yawning nothingness. Typically, I hear this reaction from folks who believe that they must attain an empty, mindless state in order to be meditating at all. Clearly, empty mindless states during meditation provide powerful results when such is doable and indicated.

In contrast, meditation for the shamanically trained individual is an adventure. This adventure includes sights, sounds, smells, alternate realities, alternate beings, symbolism and literalism, dangers, battles, struggles, communiques, time travel, astral projection, akashic examination, emotional swings, and the accomplishment of a task (if done for healing or answering of questions). Meditation, shamanically, requires an open mind that is not going to remain empty since so many experiences and spirits will be encountered quite proactively.

For many, this Path is too fanciful or riddled with imaginary unrealities. Perhaps that is your reaction as well. But once an individual has experienced the power of such Journeys, the fancifulness is taken more seriously. Perhaps this Path reveals the multi-dimensional nature of many realities and catapults us out of the restrictions of logic, reason and the illusions of "facts!"

Dogmatism is definitely not likely to arise from you after embarking on these Journeys. The test of truth is tricky because of the imaginative nature of this Path. Often the test is in the form of physical healings, psychological well-being, karmic healings, odd and significant circumstantial changes, or psychically gained factual information. The pleasure of these Journeys is how they expand one's perspectives, sense of power, ecstatic states of meditation, and communion with spirits.

The Shamanic Journeys have been a part of the human race for thousands of years. They seem to pre-date all systems of religious or spiritual understandings in recorded history. Longevity alone does not validate this path, but it suggests that exploring this path is worth some time and open-minded exploration.

Components of Shamanic Journeys are written into *every* religious sacred document which records communication between the human and spirit realms as well. This factor alone suggests that the serious student of spiritual paths needs to consider how they might actually have such Journeys of their own instead of merely reading about others who have moved within these realms with vivid experiences.

If for no other reason, improve your meditation skills, enhance your flexibility of thinking or sensing truths, and expand your perspectives about potential spiritual realms, yet unknown to us materialists. Shamanic Journeys can be easily practiced with Michael Harner's book *The Way of the Shaman (1)*. Below however, you will be guided to have a Shamanic Journey. Record your voice reading these words below with soft and rhythmic music for 20 minutes in length playing in the background. Additionally, stereophonic drumming and rhythmic music is on mpg3s by Dr. Carol Francis for several meditations, available through DrCarolFrancis.com, Amazon.com, YouTube.com/spiritualjourneytools.com or DrCarolFrancisTalkRadio.com. The meditation below is one of the meditations on that CD.

Meditation for Shamanic Journey and Spiritual Animal Guides

You are sitting or lying comfortably with no distractions likely to occur for the next 20 minutes. Your eyes are closed but your mind, soul, and emotions are awake and open for any experience worthy of your time and effort. Suspend for these 20 minutes your skills at scrutinizing reality and evaluating validity. These skills are supportive of you during much of your day. For now, you will enable yourself to experience the realms of alternate realities much more satisfyingly if you open yourself to the unknown and the unusual. So temporarily calm your skeptic.

Next, establish your intention, your purpose statement, and your goals for the next 20 minutes to do the following. First, establish the intent to visit Spirit and the various spiritual domains without expectations or censorship.   Three times, repeat to your heart, soul, and mind the following:

"I now give myself this opportunity to visit spiritual domains and spirits who may be unknown or known to me at this time. I intend that each such visit will be to my benefit, with benign, respectful, and earnest spirits.   In like manner, I will travel in these domains with respect as well."

Repeat the above statement two more times.

Second, repeat three times the following, or your version of the following:

"As I approach the spiritual domain and spirits therein, I request that the following information, solution, or task be accomplished. (State clearly and succinctly the outcome you are looking for in your journey.) Repeat your request three times.

Make your request or statement in the affirmative, that is to say, what you DO want not what you DON'T want to discover or resolve. For example, "My dear wife is ill with pneumonia, and I request that the spirit domain provide healing and the healing materials which will assist her." Another example, "My bills are voluminous and I need assistance with budgeting and creating financial means for payments of such. Please provide the tools, healing, directions which will assist with such."

Refrain from, "I hate my boss, I don't want to work there anymore," or "I don't want to be overweight." Instead, cast such concerns in the affirmative, "I need clear direction on my employment situation and which way to go to remedy my troubled relationship with my boss," or "I now ask for the assistance I need to move my weight to my next healthiest level."

Three times, repeat your request, affirmatively written, clearly, briefly and with deep emotional passion and enthusiasm. Do so now.

You will now use imagination, your senses, your desires, and your question or request as the tools you need for this adventure.

Please imagine yourself looking down a beautiful stairway and note the materials, lighting, flooring, colors, sounds, smells, textures of your surroundings. You note that below, you hear inviting music and sense a magical space being prepared for you to enter. Begin, step by step, moving down and with each step you take, one, two, three, four, five. . . you feel your body relaxing and growing pleasantly in-line with itself. Your mind feels focused but open. Your sense of having to put effort and hard work into your moment begins to melt away. Your stride down the stairs becomes slower and slower with each muscle and movement of your legs, torso and arms becoming comfortably rhythmic and easy. Six, seven, down at eight, nine, ten, slowly comfortably down deeper at eleven, twelve, . . . Note the smells, sounds, textures, ambiance, sights, colors, objects, shapes, and the easiness of your body's stride. . . thirteen, fourteen, fifteen, down again at sixteen, seventeen, eighteen, nineteen and arriving at the bottom at twenty.

Now you are on the bottom platform and feel at peace, alert, and gentle with yourself. The door ahead is beautifully carved from either marble, wood, or glass and you notice the design. Prepare to enter into another realm where there may be familiar and unfamiliar sights, sounds, objects, lighting, life-forms. It may surprise you with its beauty or intrigue.

Open the door, step inside and experience your new surroundings. Take in from your visual, auditory, olfactory, tactile, taste, mental senses, muscle-skeleton sensations, emotional and spiritual senses.

Enjoy, walk forward, float forward, fly forward. Move gently and aware, peacefully and alert.

Once you have absorbed your surroundings, acknowledge with respectful greetings the life-forms. Then, repeat your intention, goal, or request, again three times.

When one of these life-forms looks you in the eyes and comes forth, introduce yourself to this new guide. All the normal greetings will suffice. Enjoy, settle-in to meeting this life-form. Ask out of curiosity what you will. Listen. Listen some more.

After greetings and comfortableness are reasonably established, ask your request, again three times. Listen, follow, watch, receive, and ask for clarifications. When your visit is up, summoned home by the shifting drumming (on the CD/MP3, drums halt, then there are two beats and another halt; and after three times of this halt and two beats, rapid drumming begins and returns you back to ordinary reality). Say your salutations and many thanks. Be ever so grateful in your spirit. You can visit again for greater clarification and further exploration.

Return through the carved door, move up the stairs, open your eyes, readjust to this realm, and now write your answers and insights. Then, if you were told to get, take, receive or do anything in this realm, follow-through immediately if possible. Timing may be essential. What is a remedy in one moment may not be a match in the next. In addition, this shows the power of your intentionality and your respect for your guide. If you do not like or feel at ease with the advice, you are in control and can choose to wait to act until you have further wisdom, clarity, and guidance. Never relinquish your wisdom. Never feel wrong to remain as wise as you know to be. You can say no or wait if that is your wisdom. Yet, also leave conscious room for your wisdom to evolve progressively, respectfully. Perhaps the advice or gifts you were given in this Journey makes little sense to you today, but tomorrow relevant insights might flood your thoughts.

Michael Harner warned that not all spirit guides are equal in helpfulness or in kindness. His visit to many indigenous communities and travels with Shamans throughout the world, revealed the beneficent and ugly side of the spirit realms. Do not therefore, if this is also your experience, hang-out with any spirits who are less virtuous than what you would demand of a trustworthy guide. In addition, scrutinize their solutions with your own knowledge, your academic research, and your own virtuous values. As with any guides, gurus or paths, you ultimately must decide their veracity and helpfulness. Be open and be alert and be as wise as you are able.

Enjoy this Journey at any time during your day or night. After three to five such Journeys, you may begin to map out the realms you are visiting and notice the messages you regularly seem to collect. Reflection on these Shamanic Journeys is often quite fruitful. If you cannot access my sound tracks or other such background sounds or actual drumming circles or activities, you can find suitable music on YouTube, Pandora.com, LastFM.com or music software programs (Garage Band, for example) which have drumming options. Slower rhythms which match your slow heart beat are optimal.

References:

This chapter is a reprint from *Spiritual Gurus, Spiritual Paths: Your Choice* By Dr. Carol Francis (2010). Rancho Palos Verdes: Make Life Happen Publishing.

Harner, Michael (1980). *The Way of the Shaman.* San Francisco: Harper and Row.

Ingerman, Sandra. *Soul Retrieval: Mending the Fragmented Self.* HarperCollins Publishers.

About Dr. Carol Francis

In addition to her spiritual counseling and intuitive work with metaphysically inclined seekers, Dr. Carol Francis has practiced for 37 years as a Clinical Psychologist, Life Coach, Clinical Hypnotherapist, and Marriage, Family & Child Counselor. She assists individuals, couples and children who seek to optimize their current situation and overcome complications of daily living. These individuals seek deep relief and growth for depression, anxiety, stress, career moves, family discord, child and parenting issues, relationship dissatisfaction, habit control, and the psychology of financial success. Practicing and licensed in Southern California for over 37 years, Dr. Carol Francis can be reached at drcarolfrancis.com or 310-543-1824, drcarolfrancis.com or visit DrCarolFrancisTalkRadio.com.

Publications by Dr. Carol Francis

Study Skills for Successful High School and College Students

Helping Children with Divorce

Schizoid Anxiety

Helping Children with Natural and Manmade Disasters

"Horrific Parental Imaginings"

"Therapist's Countertransference with Abuse Couples"

KISS Method for Stop Smoking and KISS Cigarettes Goodbye

If You Can't Stop Eating, Maybe You're Hungry: Reset Your Cravings

Re-Uniting Soldiers with Families

Evolving Women's Consciousness: Dialogue with 21st Century Women.

Spiritual Paths, Spiritual Gurus: Your Choice

Astral Projection and Spiritual Journeys

Your Akashic Records

Media Productions of Dr. Carol Francis

Dr. Carol Francis Talk Radio has been active since 2008 with hundreds of thousands of listeners across the internet planet. Archived programs are available at DrCarolFrancisTalkRadio.com and BlogTalkRadio.com/dr-carol-francis.

Dr. Carol Francis has interviewed internationally on KABC, KLOS, KROQ, and Associated Radio Programs as well.

Her *Spiritual Readings Radio Show* is live and archived at BlogTalkRadio.com/spiritual-readings.

For even more helpful information, Dr. Carol Francis Videos, Lectures, Dr. Carol Francis Television Shows and Presentations are archived at YouTube.com/Dr. Carol Francis or Vimeo.com/Dr. Carol Francis

FRANCIS & O'MALEY

CHAPTER 29

SHAMANIC SOUL RETRIEVAL: THE GLASS SOUL

BY DEBRA FENTRESS

As I entered the world of jagged broken glass and mirrors, I realized that everywhere I looked were disjointed reflections of myself. Shards of glass and mirrors were all over, even under my feet. Even the trees were made of sharp fragments of glass and mirrors. Every movement could mean blood and pain. What was going on?

The view of our world defines how we see ourselves and our relationship to everything else. Rarely do we change this world view. However, when our "higher purpose," or our soul's paths, become our focus, we must shift the context in which we view our world. Without doing this, we can only see one facet of others and ourselves. Finding our higher purpose or our soul's essence requires us to be open to other ways of accessing any deep unconscious blocks and limitations.

I am often asked, in my coaching practice, to help clients move past barriers and stuck states, especially regarding their spiritual path. Many of these clients feel as if there is something missing, even those who have progressed on their soul-journey paths. So, I tell them the story of the Glass Soul to illustrate how all of us, regardless of how long we have worked on ourselves and practiced spiritual techniques, can be blind to the workings of the inner soul.

Once, a professional woman sought my help who had lost her will to live. She was drinking heavily and having continuous accidents. During our initial meeting, she talked about "not being herself," and "feeling lost and alone." All her rationalizing and spiritual work was not helping, so she began to numb her feelings with alcohol. Listening to her, I sensed she was dealing with deep old soul loss.

In ancient healing systems, soul loss or soul sickness was considered a cause of imbalance leading to physical, mental and emotional illness. Part of the soul wants to escape. We often experience it as an "out of body" feeling or disassociation. The part of the soul that is "lost" is stuck in the issue at the age during which it occurred. Unfortunately, we may or may not be aware of the moments when the part of our soul left.

It is useless to tell someone experiencing soul loss or sickness to "snap out of it." Many do not even realize when or where they experienced the loss (sickness) and most do not know what to do. Healing cannot take place on the rational level. Healing, in these situations, must come from the sacred realm of the soul. This sacred work is called Soul Retrieval.

Working with others to reclaim soul loss is a powerful process experienced through the practitioner's own soul. Not only do we help them, we become our true self by accessing the connection with ourselves, with others and our world. In this case, I explained soul loss to her in modern language. I told her I thought we needed to do a self-empowering visualization in order to heal the missing pieces. I cautioned her that the world of her lost soul parts would be metaphorical and allegorical.

As I moved carefully along that jagged road, I scanned her universe for "lost" pieces of her soul. Everywhere were broken bits of glass and pieces of mirrors. Everything was made of these pieces, mirroring themselves. Eventually I found three aspects of her soul.

The one that made the biggest impact on both my client and me was a small child. I found her hiding in a glass closet. She was crying and holding onto a mason jar filled with liquid. I picked her up and tried to comfort her, telling her I was there to take her home. Because we are traveling in the underworld, everything (mineral, matter, and even a baby) can dialogue with me. She said she did want to go home, but, not under the same circumstances which caused her to leave. I assured her, things were different. Her "being" was an adult now and could protect her.

After completing the reintegration of her lost soul parts, I brought my client back to this reality. As I relayed the story of the baby, she began to cry. She told me that as a very young child, her mother would lock her in the closet with a jar of gin and water to get her to be quiet! Since I had not talked to her about her childhood prior to the Soul Retrieval, the fact that I found the baby with the Mason jar was hugely convincing to her that something profound had taken place in our work. Later she told me she felt like she had rediscovered herself and was beginning to be happy again.

Although there was more work to be done, this Soul Retrieval allowed her to connect with the powerful source of life energy within her, which were the pieces of her soul which had been lost along the way. This brought her wholeness back into being. In the following months, she stopped drinking, got back to work, and began to rebuild her life.

Our worldview gives us the parameters of our physical world, our identity and even our spiritual advancement. We are attached to it; or, in the shamanic vernacular, we are dreaming our existence into being.

When we allow the gaze to soften, we can experience a whole new realm of spiritual possibilities. When we connect to the voice of our soul, even those parts of our soul which are "lost," we can uncover the hidden fears and ego-based boundaries we have built into our lives. From our hearts we can discover the origins, break the boundaries, and begin the ascent again.

About Debra Fentress

Debra has a background in Psychology, is a published author, Master Trainer of NLP, Certified Hypnotherapist and a Shamanic facilitator. Debra Fentress is the founder and lead trainer for Spirit's Muse. Debra's focus is on assisting individuals to actualize their true self through the expression of their soul.

From an early age, Debra was introduced to nature based, shamanic practices and disciplines as well as Christian teachings. Her ability to "see" disease within the energy patterns of individuals caused many misunderstandings with others as she grew up. For years, she went silent about her gifts, studying secretly on her own and mastering the tools and techniques of esoteric teachings.

As a lifelong student of personal growth, she studied with Hank Wesselman (author of Spiritwalker), with Helen Bangs as early as 1972 and was a lead trainer for Advanced Neuro Dynamics, an international training company. She has been authorized as a facilitator of "Shamanic Journeys," as a Spiritual Counselor and Minister.

Debra is considered an expert in the field of universal and personal energy. Known for her ability to "hook you up," she is sought after by those who understand the utilization of the universal field.   To contact Debra Fentress e-mail her at www.SpiritsMuse.com.

CHAPTER 30

FOUR TOOLS FOR SPIRITUAL JOURNEYS
BY DR. STEVE G. JONES

Activities and actions performed on a regular basis in order to cultivate spiritual development are called spiritual practices or spiritual disciplines. The foremost purpose of these practices is to train your mind and body so they become aligned with your spiritual potential. Such tools help you start discovering gifts and blessings within you, breeding satisfaction and contentment. Spiritual practices nourish our bodies and prepare us fully to do what we have been sent on this planet to do, too. Your life becomes enjoyable for you and a message for others, when you enhance your spirituality.

Spiritual practices move a person along a determined path, which leads them toward their goals in life. Such goals related to walking on this path may be different for each individual: salvation, liberation, or union with God. Some people have spiritual practices to rediscover themselves while others seek freedom from worldly things or wish to reach inner peace. There are those people too who use spiritual practices in order to become close to their Supernatural Being. Whatever the reason is, the end result is always the same: the person strengthens their relationship with themselves and the Universe.

Anything in your life can be a spiritual practice. The spiritual practices you select become wonderful parts of your daily routine.

Going for a walk, yoga, massage, or any other activity which relaxes you and leads you towards a better life, is marked as your spiritual practice. However, there are a few advanced processes which I will discuss in this chapter. They are practiced by people who are profoundly involved in diverse explorations of the spiritual realm.

Hypnosis

Hypnosis is a way to get to the bottom of what it means to exist. The hypnotized person experiences the state of consciousness and has the power to perform voluntary actions, but is also highly responsive to suggestions and directions. This practice takes the person to a deep state of consciousness where one looks for answers to some perennial questions. Who am I? Why have I been sent to this planet? What is the purpose behind it? Many people make an effort to look for the answers, and, when they do, they start living a meaningful life.

The specific details are unique to each person but the purposes of hypnosis are to attain spiritual enlightenment, emotional healing, and personal growth. Without any knowledge of our soul's purpose, we get caught in states of anxiety and stress. Reaching to the level where you actually start knowing yourself is the key to a successful and happy living. You not only understand your life's purpose, but you also begin to recognize the deeper meaning and value of being on this planet. Working on a deeper level produces life-transforming results.

Meditation

Meditation is a self-exploratory journey. Here your soul finds a welcome break from all types of stressors which you are currently going through or have experienced in the past. Through meditation, you make peace with your history which is affecting your present, which will result in a more tranquil future. In a relaxed state, you access both your conscious and unconscious mind, thus building a bridge in between. You manage stress, eliminate all the negative thoughts, and attain a balanced mind and body, which is filled with compassion, love, and an understanding of the true meaning of life.

Meditate your mind and soul to purity and it will reflect outward. Start accepting the reality that justice does not always prevail. You will come across a lot of negativity in your journey to attain success, but through meditation you can very easily become immune to it. Also, your aim in life should not be to accomplish everything; it should rather be to learn through various experiences. This will relieve your mind of many stressors too. Then, achievement of goals will become easy. Meditation is like an ultimate rest. It sharpens everything, clears one's mind, and keeps life fresh.

Law of Attraction

There is a continuous desire for "improving our life" in each one of us. We practice various spiritual processes to attain this. One of these processes is the Law of Attraction. This law states that whatever happens in our life is attracted by us whether it is good or bad. To attract something into our world, we have to focus on it, expect it, and accept it.

The Law of Attraction can be put to good use by drawing positive thoughts and physical items toward us. We can free our mind of all negative thoughts and then give space to righteous thinking. The way we think will be portrayed in our actions. When we think in positive ways, we act in positive ways. This practice will help us enhance our good habits because we will be focusing on them.

This Law Attraction is not related to our needs or desires. Instead, it is related to our way of thinking. It is about what we are attracting towards us, consciously or subconsciously. Consider that whatever you desire or wish for yourself, you can do such for others. If you want more friends, be friends with others. If you want more and more food, feed others. What goes around comes around.

Astral Projection

Astral projection is the act of separating your spirit from your physical body. It is an out-of-body experience which is driven by nothing else but our thoughts. People who practice this strongly believe that in order to move into new dimensions, we can first separate our astral body from our physical body. It takes some practice, but many people report joy, peace and satisfaction while traveling in the astral plane. Anyone can practice it and can change their way of thinking and living. To assist, consider TheArtOfAstralProjection.com.

About Dr. Steve G. Jones

"If you want to make a positive change in your life, Steve G. Jones can make the difference. He did with me." Tom Mankiewicz, Writer of **"Superman the Movie"**

Dr. Steve G. Jones is a member of the National Guild of Hypnotists, American Board of Hypnotherapy and president of the American Alliance of Hypnotists. Steve is a former member of the board of directors of the Los Angeles Chapter of the American Lung Association. Dr. Steve G. Jones, Ed.D., is a board certified Clinical Hypnotherapist who has been practicing hypnotherapy since the 1980's. He is the author of 25 books on such topics as hypnosis, the law of attraction and weight loss. Steve has also created over 9,000 hypnosis audio recordings and 22 different online certification programs, which are sold in over 140 countries. From 1990 to 1995, he was fortunate to counsel families and individuals. During this time he finished his degree in Psychology at the University of Florida and went on to graduate studies in Counseling. Steve has a Bachelor's Degree in Psychology from the University of Florida (1994), a Master's Degree in Education (M.Ed.) from Armstrong Atlantic State University (2007), a Specialist Degree (Ed.S) in Education (2009), a Doctorate in Education (Ed.D.) from Georgia Southern University (2013), and has studied Psychology at Harvard University. Dr. Steve G. Jones sees clients for a variety of conditions. Among them are weight loss, anxiety, smoking cessation, test taking, phobias (such as fear of flying), nail biting, road rage, anger management, IBS, general wellness, pre-surgical and pre-dental pain control, natural childbirth, and many others.

CHAPTER 31

ASTRAL PROJECTION
WHERE TO BEGIN YOUR SPIRITUAL ASTRAL JOURNEYS
BY DR. CAROL FRANCIS

Intriguingly, most of you likely have astral projected during your sleep. Your soul or spirit visited physical Earthly domains or Astral Plane locations. Then, you popped back into your body with a jolt! You felt as if you came from somewhere else, a bit disoriented to this time and space. You asked yourself, "Was that a dream?" Not necessarily.

Benefits of Astral Projection Journeys

Mastering the art of Astral Projection magnifies your knowledge that time, space, and death have little hold on your personal being. Additionally, verifying that such conscious travel did in fact take place builds the uncanny certainty that you can be in charge of leaving and returning to physical form at will. You can explore physical and nonphysical locations with amazing conscious dexterity and prove such as well.

Willfully moving out of your body then traveling with your consciousness, perceptual senses, and current personality intact is a form of Spiritual Soul Journeying. Many other types of Spiritual Soul Journeys are explored in my books *Spiritual Gurus, Spiritual*

Paths: Your Choice (1) and *Astral Projections and Astral Journeys* (2) and *Your Personal Akashic Records* (3).

Exiting Your Physical Body

Some astral journeyers exit their bodies fairly easily and others slip slowly out, a toe or finger at a time. Some are at ease with being associated with and dissociated from their bodies at will. Others are terrified to leave for fear of never returning. Some people even state that astral projection reminds them of scary, traumatic events of their personal past. For these individuals, out-of-body dissociation during trauma is often the only relief they secured during abusive or terrifying circumstances. If you associate fear with astral projection, your first challenge is to study the safety aspects of astral projection.

Ultimately, astral projection can produce high-level spiritual awareness, uncanny expansions of knowledge, and amazing psychic flexibility. Astral Projection is a tool associated with bi-location of the Swamis or Yogis, psychic fluidity, ESP, and time travel, too.

Teaching individuals astral projection has revealed three core truths to me. First, everyone leaves their physical body using different approaches, some of which I will reveal below. Second, everyone has a different awareness of their physical body while in their astral body. Third, the astral projection experiences you have which are verifiable, or produce resolutions, lead to more profound spiritual consciousness.

Truly, astral projection is a tool of *Your Soaring Phoenix* not to be missed. Breaking through the here and now perceptions of physical form and time-space experiences, expands your recognition of your power tools of perception, your connection to others you respectfully visit, and awareness of locations which you flexibly journey through without regard to time-space relativity.

Your concept of yourself and others expands. You recognize yourself as both physical and astral, both embedded in your current body and present in ethereal domains. You develop also beyond your temporal fears, limits, and powerlessness. Sensing fields of energy, wavelengths of sound, qubit of thoughts, emotions, sensations, and thought forms   all help you perceive what is invisible to your physical form. Detecting the presence of life-forms which have diverse qualities, or perceiving other humans in astral forms, clearly evolves your appreciation about what realities we barely understand beyond our immediate human moments.

In essence, through astral projection, you soar connected to your infinite and immortal self to explore the ethereal and unlimited vistas, using your astral body's tools of perception. You fly, walk, float, teleport, shape shift, superposition, bi-locate, assist, discover, interface, and become connected to the one, the elementals, the All and the Everything with increasing awareness. Universal love and soul-connections can also become clearer in the astral domains when you utilize the processes of astral projection as your vehicle of consciousness traveling.

Detailing the progressive steps which helped many learn to travel out-of-body, became Robert Monroe's mission after his spontaneous experiences (4).   I too, want many to experience astral projection and offer tools freely at YouTube.com/spiritualjourneytools.com. Also, Dr. Steve G. Jones' comprehensive practice sessions can be found on one of his main websites: TheArtOfAstralProjection.com (5).   Use these three journey person's diverse techniques to discover which methods most suit your style of voluntarily moving "out-of-body" and exploring. Read on as well for more suggestions helping you learn to easily astral project.

Methods of Practicing Astral Projection Departures

Enthusiastic and safe mindsets help all spiritual journeys to progress quicker and deeper. First, hone your sense of safety and eagerness associated to astral projection. White light meditations, angelic or trusted spirit guides, and baby-steps exiting your physical body can increase both safe and eager feelings.   Then, practice the progressive body-part exit method. Dr. Steve G. Jones provides such through hypnosis. With his deep relaxation, the listener slowly lifts body parts out until the whole astral body is separated from the physical body.   First, focus on lower extremities. Moving in and out from your feet, then your legs, torso, left and right arms, then head. Bit by bit, build confidence and a dualistic awareness of your physical body and your astral body. Ultimately, you can float your entire body up to the ceiling and back down. Take a look around while you are floating, too.

After these types of progressive exercises, you can practice moving up, down, left, right, under, then back into your body. Move your consciousness through walls, into adjacent rooms, floating above streets, visiting a friendly person, or travel to a place. You can verify what you perceive in your astral form later on in your physical body. Consider using the materials Dr. Steve G. Jones has developed if this gradual and relaxed hypnotic method matches your initial style. Again, Dr. Steve G. Jones's website is TheArtOfAstralProjection.com.

Here is another technique to begin astral projection work. First, close your eyes, meditate, and protect your body. Next, imagine "seeing" outside the back of your head and look around. Return to your physical body and open your eyes. Close your eyes and repeat. Then, after "seeing," try to shift to sensing your back's surroundings by extending your imagination. Pay attention to different physical senses such as sight, touching, hearing, tasting, and kinesthetics. You essentially are projecting your physical sensory awareness behind you. You are using mentalization or imagination associated to your basic five senses.

After playing with your five senses, practice using this same technique by moving around and sensing what you can above your head and below your feet. Keep doing these movements with your basic five senses with your eyes closed while oriented to your physical body's locations. Always, afterward, return to your body and gently open your eyes and stretch. Then check out your discoveries. Increase the distance you "move" with your five senses while doing these exercises. Eventually, your mentalization or imagination associated to using these five senses will become quite alert. As a result, you will notice a shift in your connection to your body when you move out of your physical body's primary location and return back into your body's primary location.

Next, realize that your astral body has many other tools for perceiving that are akin to intuition, psychic awareness, clairvoyance, and multi-dimensional "knowingness." You can observe, or rather, perceive auras, energetic fields, radio waves, or photon wave-lengths or particles, to name a few. So during your next journeys, try to expand your tools of perception beyond your five senses to include these other tools of perception that are cognitive, precognitive, empathic, intuitive and clairvoyant in style.

For example, you might link up your visual astral sensory tool with your emotional or empathic sensory tool. This will help you experience the presence of nostalgic objects in a room as well as the emotions and history of those objects. This is associated to clairsentience or clairvoyance. You might combine your auditory astral sensory tool with your kinesthetic astral senses to detect vibrations, movements, changes in temperatures, or subatomic particles of objects in motion or orderliness.

As you accumulate and master these perceptive tools, you can journey to familiar or unfamiliar locations on Earth, in the 3-D, micro and macro worlds, other dimensions, and parallel universes. Clearly, verifying such "out of the world locations" is not nearly as doable so if you are still needing evidence that Astral Projection has merit, then visit planes of existence that give you those opportunities frequently.

Those familiar with Chakra or energy fields of their own physical-spiritual form can exit and travel extending from these Chakra or energy fields as well. For example, your emotional-heart and your physical-heart can be perceived emanating from your chest. Hold your consciousness of these two arenas of your heart energy simultaneously. Flow in your mind outward from your physical-heart using the emotional experience of your emotional-heart as a trajectory. Aim your emotional-heart trajectory as a beam which your mind, or consciousness, follows. Aim this trajectory toward a person, pet, location or object that contains an emotional connection for you in this current life. Walk with your astral body upon or through this beam until you arrive as fully and completely as you can to that new location. Next, summons all your other sensory tools to that new location and become more and more present in that domain until you can collect details which you can verify later.

Interestingly, many spontaneous out-of-body experiences documented are associated to death or traumatic events. It seems likely that these astral projections which occur at times of death or trauma actually use the beam of this heart chakra to guide the astral traveler's emotionally laden steps. Other times, individuals describe exiting through their head, Crown Chakra, flowing out upon white beams of light to heaven-like domains.

Those who are kinesthetically attuned to their muscles and skeleton movements can use a method I expanded from The Wild Divine (6) meditation programs. First stand and move your physical right arm up and down several times, slowly, deliberately. Be sure to move with a clear and thoughtful notation of all the sensations created by such movement. Next, close your eyes, and move that same arm in your mind alone and re-experience all those same sensations yet without moving your physical arm. Do this same exercise repeatedly with arms, legs, head, feet, and fingers. Ultimately jump with your whole body physically, and then jump out and into your body using your astral consciousness. Repeat playfully many times, increasing your conscious dexterity.

You can also do a similar practice using only your sense organs. You may move your awareness of sensory input such as seeing or touching, and then close your eyes and then feel those senses working without your anatomical senses being involved during the mental act of sensing. For example, look at the red apple on the table near you. Touch that apple. Bite into that apple. Next, close your eyes, protect yourself meditatively, and then see the apple in detail with your imagination. Then touch that apple with your imagination. Now bite that apple with your imagination. Pop back into being physically aware. Then, close your eyes, and in your imagination walk around that apple, pick it up from behind to examine the other side and look at the spot where the apple was sitting and see what is under the physical apple. Then open your eyes and do the same. This is just one of many simple exercises you can create to practice astral perception or using senses in the astral domain.

These processes create flexibility in your mind, consciousness, and brain so you can begin to step out, move, and then step back into your body. Moving out repeatedly, moving farther out, up, down, floating, walking, passing through or over or under or inside other locations can be followed by moving back in your physical form using increasingly larger and bolder steps.

Notice that any of these activities can be used to further expand your consciousness. Then, using these activities to move your consciousness fluidly around to explore other-worldly domains becomes even more exciting. Creating opportunities to learn, to help others, and to comfort others through these tools is yet another level of letting your Phoenix soar using astral projection.

You Are Not Alone

Shamans of South America, North America, and Africa document these types of journeys regularly and historically (7, 8). Swamis and Yogis from India have done so as well (9). In the Western Hemisphere, it is solidifying to know that the functions of Out-of-Body experiences are being documented by fields of science. The following list merely scratches the surface of such research.

Resuscitation Medicine, currently clarified by Sam Parnia, M.D. (10), is the new field of medicine which explores death experiences documented by multiple technological devices that are correlated with near death or after death experiences. The very consistent and statistically researched reports of dead patients observing what occurs during the time of their death is corroborated by witnesses alive during the same time.

Stuart R. Hameroff, M.D., studies of Quantum Consciousness address the biologically quantum components of consciousness (11).

Astronaut Edgar Mitchell's Noetic Society provides multiple research articles accessible through, IONS, or Noetic.org which utilize standard scientific methods of observation, data collecting, statistical analysis, control studies and repeated test results associated to out-of-body processes (12).

Researcher Dr. Dave Radin and his associated researchers examine statistical and observable components of consciousness utilizing all the scientific methodologies described before (13).

B. J. Williams also provides constant streams of scientific articles examining past and current research related to phenomena such as PSI and ESP as associated to Quantum Physics, nonlocal influences, quantum entanglement, and quantum superposition which are all associated to Astral Projection as well. Actually, Dr. Williams is organizing more research studying Out-of-Body-Experiences experienced on demand, like Astral Projection (14, 15).

Embrace the journeys which await your heart.
Enjoy the travels calling your soul.
Wave the wings of Your Spirited Eagle.
Fly high with Your Soaring Phoenix.

References

1. Francis, Carol A. (2011). *Spiritual Gurus, Spiritual Paths: Your Choice.* Rancho Palos Verdes: Make Life Happen Publishing.

2. Francis, Carol A. (2014). Astral Projections and Soul Journeys. Rancho Palos Verdes: Make Life Happen Publishing.

3. Francis, Carol A. (2014). *Your Personal Akashic Records.* Rancho Palos Verdes: Make Life Happen Publishing.

4. Monroe, Robert (1971). *Journeys Out of the Body.* New York: Braodway Books.

5. Jones, Steve G. (2012). *The Art of Astral Projection* is a comprehensive astral projection how-to kit which encompasses many different perspectives and techniques.

6. *The Wild Divine* is a meditation computer program as well as mind over matter Software and hardware program that is based on brain entrainment research. More can be found at http://www.wilddivine.com/.

7. Harner, Michael (1980). *The Way of the Shaman.* San Francisco: Harper and Row.

8. Eliade, Mircea. Trask, Willard R. Doniger, Wendy. (1964). Shamanism: Archaic Techniques of Ecstasy (Bollingen Series LXXVI). Princeton University Press.

9. Yogananda, Paramahansa (1946). *Authobiography of a Yogi.* Authorized by the International Publications Council of Self-Realization Fellowship.

10. Parnia, Sam (2013). *Erasing Death: The Science that is Rewriting the Boundaries Between Life and Death.* HarperCollins Paperback.

11. Hameroff, Stuart R. Thorough list and access to Hameroff's research and papers can be found at quantumconsciousness.org.

12. Mitchell, Edgar and his Institute of Noetic Sciences can be found at http://noetic.org/.

13. Radin, Dave (2103). *Supernormal: Science, Yoga, and the Evidence for Extraordinary Psychic Abilities.* Publishers Weekly.

14. Williams, B. J., & Roll, W. G. (2006). *Psi, place memory, & laboratory space.* Proceedings of Presented Papers: The Parapsychological Association 49th Annual Convention (pp. 248-258). Petaluma, CA: Parapsychological Association, Inc.

15. Williams, B. J., & Roll, W. G. (2008). *Neuropsychological correlates of psi phenomena.* Proceedings of Presented Papers: The Parapsychological Association 51st Annual Convention (pp.264–287). Petaluma, CA: Parapsychological Association, Inc.

About Dr. Carol Francis

In addition to her spiritual counseling and intuitive work with metaphysically inclined seekers, Dr. Carol Francis has practiced for 37 years as a Clinical Psychologist, Life Coach, Clinical Hypnotherapist, and Marriage, Family & Child Counselor. She assists individuals, couples and children who seek to optimize their current situation and overcome complications of daily living. These individuals seek deep relief and growth for depression, anxiety, stress, career moves, family discord, child and parenting issues, relationship dissatisfaction, habit control, and the psychology of financial success. Practicing and licensed in Southern California for over 37 years, Dr. Carol Francis can be reached at drcarolfrancis.com or 310-543-1824.

Publications by Dr. Carol Francis

Study Skills for Successful High School and College Students

Helping Children with Divorce

Schizoid Anxiety

Helping Children with Natural and Manmade Disasters

"Horrific Parental Imaginings"

"Therapist's Countertransference with Abuse Couples"

KISS Method for Stop Smoking and KISS Cigarettes Goodbye

If You Can't Stop Eating, Maybe You're Hungry: Reset Your Cravings

Re-Uniting Soldiers with Families

Evolving Women's Consciousness: Dialogue with 21st Century Women.

Spiritual Paths, Spiritual Gurus: Your Choice

Spiritual Journeys: Astral Projection, Shamanism, Akashic Records

Your Akashic Records

Dr. Francis has contributed since 1977 to numerous newspapers and magazines, chapters in professional psychology anthologies, and blogs on family issues, personal development, and problem-solving concerns.

Media Productions of Dr. Carol Francis

Dr. Carol Francis Talk Radio has been active since 2008 with hundreds of thousands of listeners across the internet planet. Archived programs are available at DrCarolFrancisTalkRadio.com and BlogTalkRadio.com/dr-carol-francis.

Dr. Carol Francis has interviewed internationally on KABC, KLOS, KROQ, and Associated Radio Programs as well.

Her *Spiritual Readings Radio Show* is live and archived at BlogTalkRadio.com/spiritual-readings.

For even more helpful information, Dr. Carol Francis Videos, Lectures, Dr. Carol Francis Television Shows and Presentations are archived at YouTube.com/Dr. Carol Francis or Vimeo.com/Dr. Carol Francis

CHAPTER 32

NEW FRONTIER OF CONSCIOUS EVOLUTION: THE AKASHIC RECORDS

BY BARBARA SCHIFFMAN, CHT, ARCT

On Oprah Winfrey's "Super Soul Sunday," Deepak Chopra shared: "We are the consciousness that makes the Universe manifest." This Universal manifestation clearly begins at the spiritual level, with a Divine Spark. (1) It expands throughout Humanity's Soul Body where everything each human sees, hears, thinks, feels, does and says is recorded vibrationally in the intangible archive of our collective Souls.

This "Superconscious Soul Archive" has been called The Akashic Records by mystics and psychics including Edgar Cayce. About a hundred years ago, Cayce said he accessed the Akashic Records under deep trance hypnosis to receive Universal guidance for his clients on health and relationship issues. (2)

"Akashic" comes from "Akasha," the Sanskrit word for "the basis and essence of all things in the tangible world."(2) Akasha is similar to Ether, or "pure consciousness," which is one of Ayurvedic Medicine's Five Elements. This Akashic Soul-dimension is also mentioned by all major religions as "The Book of Life." It has been called the Collective Consciousness by psychotherapist Carl Jung (3) and, more recently, the Quantum Field or The Field by quantum physicists. (4)

Mythologist Joseph Campbell considers consciousness as a highly creative dimension. In his book, *Hero With a Thousand Faces (5)*, he wrote: "The constriction of consciousness, to which we owe the fact that we see not the source of the universal power but only the phenomenal forms reflected from that power, turns superconsciousness... into unconsciousness... and, at the same instant and by the same token, creates the world." Campbell is also quoted in *The Joseph Campbell Companion* (6) as saying: "I am more and more conscious that there is a plane of consciousness that we are all sharing, and that the brain is a limiting machine that pulls it in."

For many 21st century Soul Questers, this high frequency of consciousness is the new frontier where our individual daily lives and spiritual quests converge as a collective wavelength. More people than ever before are tuning directly into their souls for guidance or solace. Additionally, spiritual teachers often echo Jesuit philosopher-scientist Teilhard de Chardin: "We are not human beings having a spiritual experience; we are spiritual beings having a human experience." (7)

Hypnotherapist Michael Newton relates case studies of numerous hypnosis sessions in, *Journey of Souls (8)*, when his clients recall past lives plus "life between lives" which explain why we choose to visit Earth again and again. In addition, more authors are writing about "life between lives" such as four-year-old Colton Burpo's, *Heaven is For Real* (9), and Neurosurgeon Dr. Eben Alexander 's, *Proof of Heaven* (10). Alexander recounts his near-death coma when he experienced "the unity of all Souls." This sensation has also been reported by Near Death Experience (NDE) "survivors," especially Dannion Brinkley who was struck by lightning in 1975 and literally states he was "saved by the light" (11).

As a life-long Soul Quester, I am increasingly aware of my personal Soul as it expresses through my everyday life. The sense

248

of living from my Soul's point-of-view has increased because of accessing my own Akashic Records and reading others' Akashic Records since 2009. At the Soul-level, everything is "whole, complete and good" according to my personal mentor, Akashic expert and author, Linda Howe (12). There is nothing to fix, retrieve, rewrite, erase or feel guilty about. If we could have done things differently at any point in our lives up to now, we would have.

I tune into the Records via Linda Howe's Pathway Prayer Process (13). This Pathway Prayer Process is a specific vibrational "ritual" which "opens the Records." Using this process, I can receive the unconditional love, experience of unity, and universal wisdom guidance available there.

According to my Records, my current life (which is only one "chapter" in my individual Souls' "true-story-in-progress") is the evolution of numerous past lives through which my individual and humanity's collective Soul-patterns are evolving. This evolution occurs regardless of whether or not we "believe" in past lives or in our future lifetimes. Our future lifetimes are "yet to be written" and are not pre-destined. Past, present and future lifetimes are shaped by our daily choices and actions. Becoming conscious that we are "spiritual beings having human experiences" is the first step to making better, or at least different, choices than we did in previous lives and/or in this life. True evolution is generating a new result by doing something differently than before.

Other Akashic-access methods used by Soul-seekers include meditation, hypnosis, shamanic rituals and remote viewing. Many meditators envision the Records as "an infinite library." I love how in the movie "The Adjustment Bureau," Hollywood's best depiction of Akashic Records thus far, the Adjustors work in a library (14)

Some scientific thinkers, however, believe our sense of the Divine is generated merely by brain functions. In the 2005 book, *The God Gene: How Faith is Hardwired into Our Genes* (15),

Dean Hamer explores how brain synapses are stimulated by neurotransmitters associated with "mystic" experiences which seem to generate a sense of self-transcendence and an openness to "believe things that are not literally provable." Hamer does not seem to consider the existence of the Soul. Although we cannot see or feel them, Souls have been measured. In 1901, Dr. Duncan MacDougall (16) weighed five terminally ill patients just before and after their moments of death. After they ceased breathing, they were each 21 grams lighter. Since the air in their lungs did not account for this weight change, this indicates something else; their Souls perhaps, left their bodies.

It is my sincere hope that more people will consciously tune into their Souls and begin living from an Akashic perspective. This can help us generate enough "critical mass" to naturally shift humanity to a new octave with a focus on healing our planet and caring for each other, at the very least. That, to me, is what our Spiritual Quests are meant to do.

As Linda Howe shares: "The energy present in the Records is a very quick vibration with a great velocity... Being in the Records potentially takes participants into a state of unconditional love, acceptance, peace, power and light. The combination of knowledge and power found in the Records activates the highest good of all" (17).

References and Annotations by Author

1. Deepak Chopra/"Super Soul Sunday" quote from • October 14, 2012 - quote from Chopra on "Super Soul Sunday," per Joanne Guidoccio blog: http://joanneguidoccio.com/2012/11/05/oprah-and-deepak-chopra-2/• First-Look-Super-Soul-Sunday-with-Deepak-Chopra-Video: http://www.oprah.com/own-super-soul-sunday/First-Look-Super-Soul-Sunday-with-Deepak-Chopra-Video• Quote also given by Chopra in 5/18/12 Keynote address at

TiEcon 2012 - Breakthrough Thinkers Conference (non-profit int'l network of entrepreneurs and professionals): "It is our consciousness that makes the Universe manifest"on youtube video of Keynote @ minute 11:10 (out of 51.19): http://www.youtube.com/watch? v=e9ut88HJWvg&feature=share&list=PL685624D19B5310A8&index=5

2. Edgar Cayce reference -- from documentary "Legacy of Edgar Cayce" (produced by A.R.E.Foundation) -- in Part 2, available on YouTube (@ minute 3:50-4:24)http://www.youtube.com/watch? v=dM9ceQdzYdg&feature=share&list=PLF0F88CE6C9B6D874&index=1Quote = 3:50 -4:17"Cayce immersed himself in giving readings each day. He would lie down on the couch, become comfortable put his hands up to his forehead, and begin to pray. When he saw a brilliant flash he would lower his hands to his stomach and when his eyes began to flutter, his wife would give him the appropriate suggestion. In this state it seemed that he could answer any question or provide any type of information requested."Quote = 4:17-4:24 "According to the Readings each of us writes the story of our lives through our thoughts, our deeds and our activities with one another. These accounts are stored in what the Readings called the Akashic Records. And it was from this place, as well as from the minds of the individuals for whom he was giving the readings, that Edgar Cayce gathered his information..."

3. Carl Jung's Collective Unconsciousness can be further explored Jung.org

4. McTaggarat, Lynne (2008). *The Field: The Quest for the Secret Force of the Universe.* Harper Perennial, updated edition.

5. Campbell, Joseph (2008). *Hero With a Thousand Faces.* Page 222. New World Library.

6.   Campbell, Joseph (1995).   *The Joseph Campbell Companion: Refelctions on the Art of Living*. Page 131. Harper Perennial.

7. Teilhard de Chardin (1975). *Le Phenomene Humain*. Bernard Wall translation. First HARPER COLOPHON edition published 1975

8. Newton, Michael (1994). *Journey of Souls*. Llewellyn Publications.

9. Burpo, Todd. Vincent, Lynn. Burpo, Collins. (2010). *Heaven is For Real*. Thomas Nelson Publishers.

10. Alexander,Eben (2012).   *Proof of Heaven: A Neurosurgeon's Journey Into the After Life*. Simon & Schuster.

11. Brinkley, Dannion (2008). *Saved By the Light*. Harper One.

12, 13.   Howe, Linda (2011). *Healing Through the Akashic Records*.   Sounds True.   Also Linda Howe's writings can be accessed at www.AkashicStudies.com or akashicstudies.com.

14. The Adjustment Bureau (film).   YouTube Trailer: http://youtu.be/wZJoTP4nTaE. http://en.wikipedia.org/wiki/The_Adjustment_Bureau HuffPost film review - Cathleen Falsani - March 8, 2011 and look at .

15. Hamer, Dean (2005). *The God Gene: How Faith is Hardwired into our Genes*. Anchor Books.

16. MacDougall, Duncan, MD (1907) article appearing in American Medicine Journal, April 1907 and discoverable at - http://www.ghostweb.com/soul.html and also in NY Times article on March 11, 1907: http://query.nytimes.com/mem/archive-free/pdf? Res=9D07E5DC123EE033A25752C1A9659C946697D6CF.

17. Howe, Linda. Quote located at The Akashic Record on AkashicStudies.com website (Linda Howe's website): http://www.akashicstudies.com/akashic.html

About Barbara Schiffman

Barbara Schiffman is an Akashic Records Advanced Certified Teacher/Practitioner, a Certified Hypnotherapist and Soul Keys Hypnosis Therapist, and a Life&Soul Balance Coach. She helps people expand their lives and evolve their souls with more ease and grace.

Barbara wrote *The Akashic Muse*, about working in the Akashic Records "for writing and other creative endeavors." Barbara Schiffman is a popular speaker on topics about the Akashic Records and Life&Soul Balance.

Learn about her DailyOM.com e-courses plus her empowering books and coaching programs developed for people who are seeking joyful, resilient, and exhilarating lives at www.YourLifeandSoul.com.

CHAPTER 33

SPIRITUAL JOURNEYS ON PHYSICAL PATHS: CAMINO AND SYNCHRONICITY

BY SUSAN R. MANN

Incredible insights of intuition:
A Spontaneous Synchronistic Adventure of the Spirit

For more than a thousand years, the Camino de Santiago de Compostela has captured the hearts and minds of millions from around the world calling each pilgrim in a unique way to walk her path. The Camino walk is a tradition first established mainly for religious reasons. Now the Camino encompasses experiences also involving human interests and emotions. The "what," "why," and "how" of each pilgrim's story is truly personal, equally significant and life transforming. In some way we who walk this trail all share in the collective spirit that is the true heart of the Camino.

So how does a girl like me growing up at the beaches of La Jolla in Southern California find herself as a woman living in Spain - passionate for Galicia and all things Camino? For me, walking the Camino was a culmination of incredible coincidences or "synchronicities" occurring over years. No matter where I was in the world, the Camino called me. Part of the journey was truly being called to the Camino experience in the first place.

The Camino de Santiago de Compostela is an incredible adventure of discovery, a discovery of new cultures, traditions, people and passions. Also, the Camino has the power to transform someone's perspectives about life or change one's personality in Toto, in ways that are hard to describe. Each person has their own unique and personal experience. Often times, the biggest transformations happen in such subtle ways which are profoundly felt at one's core. Deep emotions and inspiring insights urge travelers to continue to open up. The Camino experience pushes the boundaries of our comfort zones forcing us to explore new territories of our feelings because of the atypical challenges of the Camino pilgrimage.

The Camino has been one of the greatest gifts of my life, and I am grateful to the loving support and encouragement from my family, friends and fellow pilgrims. For me, the Camino has been my best teacher about how to embrace and how to live by synchronistically. Living by synchronicity forces me to follow my intuition, look for connections, or notice opportunities that the universe has created just for me. Living by the guidance of synchronicity is a way of being and learning to live which I could never have imagined in my La Jolla life style. They say the Camino provides just what you need to truly learn and grow even though not everyone receives what they thought they were looking for or expecting.

The experience of hiking the Camino itself contains profound life lessons, and the process in many ways provides an opportunity for us to return to a flow similar to when we were children. This child-like flow is one of excitement, interest, a positive anticipation filled with emotions which move us to discover, feel, release and live more fully. Hours spent in nature, surrounded by beautiful sites, and sounds that inspire, clearly fill each day on the Camino. In addition, each moment requires a completely different set of actions, items, or decisions than what we would experience in our normal daily routines back home. We change on the

Camino in part because we must. Totally mixing-up what we are accustomed to provides a space in which to reflect and truly listen to oneself. Even more, we interact with others in a setting that provokes new exchanges. We have all set aside the world as we know it to step into one where we are not quite sure what to expect or what to do. We jump into a place where we explore while leaving our usual "masks" behind.

On the Camino, we changed our regular clothing and possessions. Each pilgrim must decide for themselves what to take and what they will carry as all must fit into a backpack that will be our body's burdensome companion. Interestingly, during my three different Camino experiences, one big area of change is what I released; I let go of what feels necessary. It can be so liberating to shed more and more of what you are carrying physically, mentally and spiritually. The lighter the load, the more you can find yourself completely swept away into the experience. One becomes present in each moment to the beauty of nature surrounding you. The enjoyment of time alone, as well as time spent with fellow pilgrims and the people living on the Camino, weigh nothing and mean so much.

Of course, the Camino pilgrim faces challenges just as when you were a child growing up. This newness fills you up with renewed energy which helps you meet those challenges in new ways. Opportunities always arise which help you discover how much support the universe wants to provide to help you to continue this journey for your spirit.

When one embraces their own journey following their passions and synchronicities, new life truly begins, a life of spiritual exploration and discovering. It is as if we have found a new compass and support which provides the energy and strength to go after our dreams, find and live our life's purpose, and participate in life from a new way of being.

Alan Watts, a famous philosopher, encouraged us to allow ourselves to be teased out of thoughts, old thoughts which are habitual and routine. Allowing ourselves to be teased out of our patterns and routines that no longer serve us is another Camino lesson. The Camino teases us out of old rigid perceptions and replaces those with new treasures which help your spirit soar.

The gifts which await each pilgrim are always a wonderful surprise. No two stories are the same, but all are inspiring. The Camino allows for an experience of being in the world and in nature. Walking the Camino is combination of processes and tasks which subtly blend together, helping us to release old fears, open blocked-energy and to build and strengthen us. Acceptance of ourselves and others increases, and we see how the world naturally aligns itself perfectly with the universe, bringing to us and through us experiences and opportunities to express and grow. We feel more deeply. Love expresses through us easily; like when we were children. Camino experiences of all types hold a mystery and a reward that are forever unfolding.

I wish for all a never ending loving life of exploration and discovery of your soaring spirits! Bo Camiño!!!

Learning to pay attention and follow our synchronicity provides an opportunity to live each day like a "treasure hunt." Daily, one is looking for the signs from God, who desires to bless our lives with support from the universe so that we can live sharing our passions. While using our gifts and talents working collaboratively with others, we collectively make a difference in the world.

Synchronicity supports receiving love from God and the universe so that we can be the love that we are while sharing that love and peace with others in joy and happiness.

Have fun looking for your signs: listening and paying attention to your true heart's desire, through the people you meet, the invitations from others that you receive, any words and symbols all around you. Enjoy living abundantly, relying on God who desires learning and expression.

Susan Mann, 2011 in *Spiritual Gurus, Spiritual Paths: Your Choice.*

Reference

Francis, Carol A. (2011). *Spiritual Gurus, Spiritual Paths: Your Choice.* Rancho Palos Verdes: Make Life Happen Publishing.

About Susan Mann

Susan Mann determined, through these many synergistic moments, that the Pilgrimage on the Santiago de Compostela, the Camino, through northern Spain was an ideal way to practice and to test this method of listening to the messages from Spirit. Susan Mann is producing a documentary about her experience which will likely be finished in 2012. JourneyToSantiago.com is her website. Her interview can be watched through DrCarolFrancisShow.com or heard on BlogTalkRadio.com/DrCarolFrancis.

Susan Mann has over twenty years of diverse business experience in sales, marketing advertising, public relations, product branding campaign promotion, product placement, sponsorship, business development, management, operations, distribution, magazine publication and raising venture capital. As an independent entertainment and media marketing consultant, she has produced commercials, corporate motion pictures, network promotional DVD's, developed program concepts for television, participated in single picture, multi-picture slate financing for films, film distribution company financing, and supported the formation of a production company and procurement of venture capital.

Susan participates in a variety of philanthropic endeavors supporting local charity events in her hometown of La Jolla, CA. While living on Hilton Head Island, SC, she supported the expansion of motion picture production through her participation on the South Carolina Film Commission Governor's Tax Incentive Subcommittee. Susan is a member of Women In Film. Susan is passionate about MFS mission to empower others through creative media arts learning and expression.

Susan Mann is a contributing author in *Evolving Women's Consciousness: Dialogues with 21st Century Women* and *Spiritual Gurus, Spiritual Paths: Your Choice.* You can contact Susan Mann on Facebook or at JourneyToSantiago.com.

CHAPTER 34

SPIRITUAL MESSAGES DOWNLOAD THE POWER OF KNOWING HOW LIFE WORKS
FROM *THE KNOWLEDGE*

BY DONALD SAUNDERS

INTRODUCTION BY DR. CAROL FRANCIS

Donald Saunders, the author of the next chapter, awoke one morning paralyzed for 26 minutes. Profound and strange ideas, concepts, messages, and explanations poured coherently into his mind and soul intensely.

The Knowledge: The Power of Knowing How Life Works is the profound series of books born during these 26 minutes.

Donald Saunders' experienced a spiritual awakening event that ascending souls tend to describe with singular transcending awe. Michael Talbot in *The Holographic Universe* names these all-knowing moments "instantaneous knowledge." Clair Cognizance is yet another term for such experiences.

Such information downloading, throughout recorded spiritual history, results in texts which have transformed continents for millennium. Most faith based holy cannons notably are recordings of these transcendent experiences into the spiritual omniscient domains. Many of you reading this book recognize this experience as moments of your enlightenment.

Donald Saunders recognized these 26 minutes as his moment of enlightenment and wished to share some of the basic principles revealed to him which clearly reveal to us the axiomatic introductory truths of *The Knowledge*.

THE KNOWLEDGE
BY DONALD SAUNDERS

Below you will find ten insights that arrived through me, on November 17, 2009 at 6:24 AM, for all of humanity to ponder. Only you can accept or reject them as part of your physical existence.

1. "YOU and only YOU," get to create the dream, that we have mistakenly labeled our "reality." You can combine all of your thoughts that you have about life and come up with the same daunting conclusion.

"YOU and only YOU" is one of the most critical insights to have arrived with "The Knowledge." It is the "thought thread" that ties life together. No matter how you approach your life, no matter how many outside influences you believe you have encountered, no matter how important you think you have become, or how insignificant you think yourself to be, it is up to "YOU and only YOU" to create the reality that surrounds you. "The Knowledge" will explain that we have actually created a non-reality.

2. "The Particle Soup of Life," is the fuel that drives our thoughts. Scientists at CERN have announced that they have

discovered the GOD particle. Little do they know that they will discover zillions of these sub-atomic particles that attract each other and contain our thoughts, feelings, beliefs, emotions, knowledge and information, all suspended in water molecules which act as the memory to be utilized in generation after generation. You create your own reality using this particle soup or database. Then as part of humanity, you contribute your reality into the overall consciousness that surrounds us all.

3."The Brain is Simply a Processor." The Brain does not create anything.

4. "The Dominant Thought Always Wins" no matter what the situation is. Political leaders, corporate executives, educational institutions and religious organizations will always control your thoughts if no one challenges their authority. Apply this thought to everything in your life, your relationships, your work environment and your life in general. Why is it significant? Because, if we all understand how powerful thoughts are and where they come from, we can create heaven on earth when we learn to eliminate greed and fear from our thoughts. If the masses were to unite in good, compassionate, and loving thoughts, there would be no need for dominant leaders in any realm, controlling our lives.

5. "Water has memory." "The Knowledge" carries with it the missing pieces of the humanity puzzle. Water is the "link" that ties our dream to our physical projection. Our physical existence and the sustainability of all living things revolve around water. Thoughts are frequencies and vibrations stored in sub-atomic particles (soon to be discovered) that contain water. These particles hold memory. "The Knowledge" mentions structured water, but not the water polluted by man and sold for profit. It is

referencing the water that is from the Earth, the water that God gave us before the pollution altered its capabilities.

6. "Realities are like brains, we all have one." Seven billion people, seven billion realities, all walk through the particle soup of life. Seven billion brains are all composed of three pounds of gray matter, packed with cells which are filled with "water." Yet, no one can tell you where thoughts come from...at least until now. Science can map the brain functions, but where does the information come from that the processor puts out. How does it all work? Example, seven billion people exist in the dream and you find one person to call a significant other. Seven billion people all go to different jobs and they each create different ideas about life as they draw from the particle soup.

7. "Wake up! It's only a DREAM." There is only one reality and one non-reality, which by the way, we confuse as reality; in fact, we call it life (Living In Fear of Eternity). The non-reality (life) that we have created during the separation is simply a dream that we project as our Ego. Our Ego has made us believe that we can create something better than the original IDEA. Dreams are simply our projections, created by the separation from the original IDEA. "You think you have a better idea, go ahead; I will be here when you are ready to come home. Before you go, take some water with you, it will help you remember from whence you came"...GOD.

8. "The collective God Consciousness is ONENESS." "The Knowledge" was clear, oneness came before separation. Let us roll up our sleeves and get to work, uniting science and religion back to one thought by "linking" oneness and separation in an understandable process, without a hidden agenda. In fact, think big, unite humanity. For fun, pick an earthly word to create separation: for now let us use the word "GOD." Bingo, automatic

separation of thought occurs. That was easy. 241 recognized religions separate us. Now, take the original IDEA of love and compassion and caring for each other and inject some war, politics, prejudice and confusion and the separation not only continues but it expands. How is it all working out so far? Hey, it is your Dream, that means that "You and only You," get to fix it, or not! That extends to me as well; the Dream in fact extends to all of us and so does the repairing Dream.

9. "The Collective Universal Consciousness is currently SEPARATION." Make it easy to remember, call it our *projected* LIFE. All of your thoughts, feelings, beliefs, emotions, knowledge, and information come from the collective accumulation of all of the "separated thoughts." For fun, I call it the particle soup. Not much more explanation is required, we are either "oneness," or we are "separated." I am not referring to string theory or the commercial buzzwords that "we are all one." Instead, consider this as the pure thought of "oneness" or the original Idea.

10. "Oneness to Separation -- how The Knowledge will sustain us." When "The Knowledge" arrived I could have asked why did it show up, or why did it arrive through me, but after about 30 seconds of insights into "The Knowledge," those questions disappeared. This thing we call "life" is not working for all of us. Sure, we have wealth, abundance, and people laugh and smile, take nice vacations and have great jobs, because they have created and are living an inspired "Dream." Peel back the onion and take a hard look at what those people are ignoring. We have war, poverty, fear, confusion, hunger, distrust, crime, separation of thought, greed, anger and the list goes on. We are NOT ONE; we are totally separated, oblivious to the original IDEA. "The Knowledge" was delivered to unite us and explain, "How this thing we call LIFE actually works." It was delivered for people to ponder

not to create separation caused by creating religion or a cult of any kind.

Ponder the possibilities of producing
Heaven on Earth through thoughts.

References

Saunders, Donald (2012). *The Knowledge: The Power of Knowing How Life Works*. Balboa Press.

About Donald Saunders

Donald Saunders is a business man helping companies grow and products flow for decades. Retiring from this field opened other avenues as keynote speaker and seminar leader at various resorts and conferences halls across the United States. After this intense claircognizant experience, Donald Saunders main goal is to share the wisdom in order to enhance each person's life.

Donald Saunders founded The BEAM Institute a Learning Oasis@Lake Las Vegas, www.thebeaminstitute.com also www.thepowerofknowinghowlifeworks.com 949-922-1703, The Dabney Consulting Group, LLC, Saunders Enterprises, LLC, and The Turquoise Door, LLC. He can be reached also at Email: donald.saunders@ llvresort.com

CHAPTER 35

THE DREAM AND THE WALK-IN
BY KATHI KENEDI

I heard the story over and over during my life. My mother was left in poor condition after the birth of my brother, her second child. For two years she experienced headaches, fatigue, depression and over all poor health. Her doctor recommended another pregnancy to correct the imbalance in her body. Since my parents wanted more children, this was a welcome prescription. Their first two children were unplanned gifts from God, so this was a new and exciting experience for them.

The doctor was right. The pregnancy corrected her discomfort and she felt wonderful. Her energy returned, her headaches were gone and she had a new lease on life. The first two months were bliss and then the dreams started. A recurring dream of giving birth to a little girl, watching her grow to three years old, the child runs into the street, is hit by a car, and was laid in a casket. It was a vivid and disturbing scene and one that lead her to believe her baby would die. You see, my mother was a prophetic dreamer.

Two to three times a week she would wake terrified. She kept silent about her dream, not wanting to tell my father, not wanting to acknowledge her fear. She prayed everyday asking God to spare her little girl, to keep her safe, promising everything she could think of to persuade God to change his mind. The dreams continued. By the eighth month, she was completely overwhelmed and my father found her in tears.

She poured her heart out to him, the dreams, the prayers, the fear, wanting him to take away the pain in her heart, wanting him to tell her it's only a dream. The silence got her attention. She looked up through her tears and was unprepared for what she saw. He was standing very still, his face ashen and his eyes filled with tears. He just stared at her unable to speak. He slowly sat down next to her and in a small weak voice told her she just described the very dream he was having. For six months, their dreams were the same, the baby was a girl, she grew to three years old, she ran into the street, was hit by a car, and then she was in her casket. They held each other and cried for they knew in that moment that it was all true. They would have a baby girl and she would die.

When I was born, it was no surprise to my parents that I was a girl. They already knew what I looked like before my big arrival. They were joyful and heartsick at the same time and devoted to teach me never to run into the street. Even after they brought me home the dreams continued like a beating drum. The message always the same; "She won't be here long".

I was a welcome addition to the family. My sister was thrilled and thought I was her baby doll and my brother, well, he was just happy he could get away with a little more. My mother was too busy to watch his every move. My Aunts and neighbors dropped by daily to help my mother and play with the new baby. All was well in our house in spite of the dreams.

The first few pictures my parents took of me did not turn out well. They were either blank or very blurry. At first they thought the camera was broken until they realized the pictures taken at the same time of my sister and brother were fine. They tried several times to get a picture of me all to no avail. They took that as a sign that God was sparing them further heart break in the future.

They became protective when they noticed how people were un-naturally drawn to me. In the grocery store, restaurants, even out for a stroll, strangers approached wanting to touch or hold me. By the time I was six months old, two neighbors approach my mother and ask to adopt me. Each stating their love and adoration, and the fact that my parents could always have more children. Needless to say those friendships ended and my parents became very cautious. Again they took all this as a sign. They thought I was shining a special light, one that said " I'm going home soon, I'm very close to God". The dreams continued.

We lived in a quiet neighborhood with little traffic. From the time I started to walk, my training started. Never, never, never was I to take a step into the street without someone with me. It got to the point that I feared stepping off the curb and I was terrified of the street. When I was three years old it happened. I wanted to go visit a little girl friend across the street. They lived in the corner house and my friends' mother was waiting for me in her front yard. I remember stepping off the curb and she yelled at me to stop. My training went into action and I immediately jumped back up on the curb. Just then a young man on a motorcycle came around the corner very fast behind me. I can still remember the wind washing over me as he passed, that is how close he came. He did not have his blinker on and she just intuitively knew he was going to turn.

That was the day the dreams stopped. My parents knew that was the incident they were being forewarned about. God had answered their prayers. They stopped worrying about me, however, I kept the fear of stepping off the curb into my adulthood.

Years later I was to learn the truth of the warning dreams my parents experienced...

It started with my very first hypnosis session when I was 40 years old. I had severe medical issues and one of the symptoms was memory loss. Although I wanted help with my memory, I got more than I ever thought possible.

My hypnotist was seven months on the job when I went to his office. We talked for a bit and we started the session. As soon as I went into trance, I experienced two past life regressions and then felt my self shift and make room for an entity who wanted to talk... That's when I met MROTZ, a soul guide. I later learned this is called "channeling" and at the time, I was unaware I had this ability.

As she moved in to talk, static electricity filled me and the room. She said we had been together for eons and in this life time was connected to my left arm. She said she was here to help me stay grounded due to the difficulties from the walk-in experience when I was seven years old.

At first I was confused. Walk-in? What is that? Then she helped me remember. At seven, I was laying on the living room couch sleeping. We had a newly adopted kitten curled up and soundly sleeping under the coffee table. She suddenly woke up, started making loud noises and ran over and attacked me. Biting and clawing my arm, she held tight, screaming her kitten voice and had to be pried off. The shock of the attack put my body into convulsions and I woke with my father holding me over the kitchen sink while he ran cool water over my head. My arm was a mess and my parents were distraught over the kittens attack. They had never seen an animal wake from a deep sleep and act like that. They came to the conclusion the kitten was mentally disturbed and had it put to sleep. As a child, I felt guilty. I loved the little kitten and blamed myself for her fate.

MROTZ went on to explain that I was a walk-in soul and the soul exchange took place on that couch. The kitten could sense and see the energy exchange and got frightened. Because of the attack and my body going into convulsions, the energy exchange did not go smoothly and it left me with a few problems in my body. This rang true to me as I had experienced several illnesses in my life that had no medical cure or explanation. I was amazed with this information, however, the best was next.

She showed me who warned my parents in dream form about my early demise...

It was me!!! I warned them.

She introduced me to the soul that left my body so many years ago. This soul explained that it only needed a baby experience and was planning to leave. However, I approached and asked if I could have the body if it could be kept alive. It was a perfect match. I did not need the baby experience, just the childhood and adult. The family dynamics were also perfect for all the lessons I needed to learn in this life. After much negotiation with all parties involved, the answer was yes. All I had to do was keep the child's body alive and hopefully without any damage. So I communicated with my parents through dreams so they would be able to teach me not to go into the street. It was a success. I also met the kitten who witnessed the soul exchange. She was happy and I was able to let go of my childhood guilt.

When I came out of trance, I opened my eyes and found my Hypnotist with his eyes wide and his hair standing on end. There was still static electricity in the room. This was his first experience with spontaneous past life regression and channeling, he was very excited. He did a wonderful job and I will forever be grateful to him for his wise guidance.

Since that time, I studied and became a Transpersonal Hypnotherapist. Helping people explore the spiritual aspects of their lives is now my passion. I continue to channel, and with help from MROTZ, other spiritual guides, and life mentors my body adjusted to my soul presence and is now healthy.

About Kathi Kenedi

Kathi Kenedi is the founder of Bottom Line Hypnosis.   She is Board Certified Transpersonal and Clinical Hypnotherapist, Board Certified Hypnosis and Spiritual Counselor Instructor, and Reiki Master Teacher. Kathi has a practice in Northern California and international through the internet and can be reached at 530-264-8885. Visit her web site at www.bottomlinehypnosis.com or email at Kathi@bottomlinehypnosis.com.

SECTION V

SCIENTIFIC RESEARCH

AND

METAPHYSICAL EXPERIENCES

FRANCIS & O'MALEY

INTRODUCTION

MARRIAGE OF SCIENCE AND SPIRITUALITY

BY DR. CAROL FRANCIS

Arrogance, dogmatic opinions, and egotistical political alliances have alienated spiritual explorations from scientific investigations off and on throughout time. Off and on, religion has oppressed scientific discoveries and scientific communities have berated spiritually-based practices. Political correctness has kept apart the Romeos from the Juliette's of science and spirituality for too long. Now, scientists have to hide their spiritual practices and perspectives and spiritually minded go underground, disinclined to be called fools by those scientific rigidity.

History fortunately also reveals that science and spirituality have been betrothed, even married. Chemistry, astronomy, architecture, medicine, meteorology, advanced mathematics, and now quantum physics each rose, incorporated and advanced due to spiritual curiosity, meditation and lucid dreaming.

Both science and spirituality benefitted the other's investigations and applications. Yes, both explored apparently unreasonable topics as well. This capacity to urge each other forward, like lovers in a competitively playful bliss, allows both to be challenged and expanded. Effort, strain, sweat and rest builds muscles; in like manner, the productive point-counter-point between science and spirituality has evolved our understanding and powers within this universe vastly faster than the ridiculous bickering and condescension.

Additionally, science and spiritual pursuits are in search of understanding and harnessing the invisible forces of the Cosmos in which we all live. Their goals are the same. Interestingly, some of their techniques are the same as well. For example, meditation of the Dalai Lama and deep theoretical contemplations of advanced mathematicians, physicists, biologists, et cetera, are the same mental and emotional exercises when examined with brainwave equipment. Both rely upon collection of narratives to sway belief toward a perspective. Scientists collect repetitive data after establishing their hypothesis (their predictive belief about the nature of the data they are about to collect). Then, scientists record narrating results arise from statistically normed groupings of events. Then, scientists create theoretical interpretations which seem to summarize and integrate statistically analyzed data with hypotheses.

Spiritually inclined researchers, collect data from experiences and experiencers too. These experiences are analyzed as more narratives come to the front. Analyzed experiences are coalesced into common and dissimilar categories which correspond or challenge theories about the unseen.

One primary modern example of interweaving science with spiritual perspectives has risen in the last two years with Resuscitation Medicine. The preponderance of subjective reports of near death experiences became interfaced with medical investigations which then gave birth to the new medicine of reviving the dead.

Ultimately both science and metaphysics create tools and teaches perspectives based on the interpretations of collected findings. Both rely on experiences being collected, shared, confirmed, adjusted, questioned, re-examined and tested for veracity. Both wish to understand the universe and answer what's, why's, how's. Both wish to offer solace, healing or remedy. Both schools of researchers write prolifically as if revealing ultimate truths which merely lead to the next unfolding of more data and experiences.

Not too different.

As a scientist focused on human development, and as a spiritual teacher focused on human development, I blend and spin between these realms daily. My spins into the scientific realms include studying and applying findings of neurology, psychopharmacology, neurobiology, physiology, biochemistry, physics, sociology, experimental psychology, sociology and evidence-based therapeutic techniques, and experimental laboratory based psychology, to name a few.

My spins into the mystical domains include investigations and experiments with channeling, spirit guide connections, mediumship, shamanism, psychic phenomenon, out-of-body processes, multiple religious teachings and doctrines, prayer, after-death, energy work, personal belief systems, or healings.

Of course, I spin into applying techniques of many psychotherapies to help patients and clients breech their sorrows and break out of self-imposed limits. These psychotherapies are based on medical models, statistically organized research, theoretical interpretations of scientifically collected data, spontaneous human responses in my office, and the objective analysis of patients and their families. Interestingly, many of these psychotherapies are historically sourced in Hinduism and Buddhism, Judeo/Christian/Muslim traditions, Shamanism, herbal medicine, and many other archaic traditions of Spiritualism. That is another discussion all together yet illustrates how science, spiritual teachings, and application of both for human development are unknowingly interwoven.

These worlds co-exist. Life coalesces. All researchers in all fields are entangled, coherent, and superpositioned. These worlds are married and interfaced beautifully with each other especially when the differences and similarities are embraced. They are integrated in reality. They both attempt to describe the complexities of many perspectives within reality. They are synchronized in human experiences and nature.

Separating fields of research from one another has allowed science and spirituality to explore the cosmos separately. Integration of science and spirituality allows interwoven dances of dialogue with agreements, disagreements and intriguing ponderings. My toast to this once again re-wedded couple: Let their awkward marriage of diversity and similarity begin, again.

Enjoy the following three chapters about science interfacing with spirituality:

Cynthia Sue Larson, graduate of UC Berkeley in Physics and possessing myriads of other academic degrees, explores in this section how findings of the last hundred years in the field of Physics pertains directly to spiritual manifestation. This chapter, **Welcome to the Quantum Age** is an excerpt from Cynthia Sue Larson's many works, and is a small taste of her amazing best-selling book, *Quantum Jumps: An Extraordinary Science of Happiness and Prosperity*. Integrating life and all its fields of exploration is what many hope Quantum Mechanics and its discoveries will allow.

Examining the spiritual paths which are revealed in nature and revealed in hard sciences is the focus of the chapter which follows. **Interdisciplinary Consciousness Nature, Science, Aesthetics and Spirituality** is adapted from the book *Spiritual Gurus, Spiritual Paths: Your Choice* by **Dr. Carol Francis**.

During the last 60 years, overwhelming scientific research confirms spiritual or metaphysical concepts such as multiverses, parallel universes, life after death, law of manifestation through thought and emotion, power of prayer, ESP, PSI, Reiki, effectiveness of meditation, remote viewing, holographic data likened to Akashic records, bi-location, synchronicity, healing via belief and much more.   The final chapter in this section, **Science of Metaphysical and Spiritual Phenomenon: A Brief Annotated Bibliography** by **Dr. Carol Francis** will act as a reader's guide for those of you who are keenly intrigued by the scientific investigations of metaphysical practices and phenomenon.

This chapter parallels this book, *Your Soaring Phoenix.*

In *Your Soaring Phoenix* each spiritual tool or metaphysical tool has a corollary to the scientific research findings revealed in this bibliography. In other words, each experience revealed in this book, has scientific research associated with that tool. Perhaps up to now you thought this book was merely experiential, narrative or fanciful.   To the contrary.   Now you will see how each chapter links to the discoveries of science within the fields of Cosmology, Mathematics, Quantum Physics, Molecular Biology, Cellular Biology, Neurology, Psychology, Anthropology, Sociology, and Medicine. Additionally, each tool has meta-data research with statistical and probability analysis, and experiments conforming to strict scientific methodology within laboratory testing situations which verify the phenomenons.   The bibliography in this section, is meant to trigger your awareness and curiosity. Go and read on your own.

FRANCIS & O'MALEY

CHAPTER 36

WELCOME TO THE QUANTUM AGE: QUBITS, COMPUTERS, SPIRITUALITY

BY CYNTHIA SUE LARSON, M.S.

Scientists are now observing quantum behavior once thought to be relegated exclusively to submicroscopic realms such as entanglement, superposition of states, coherence, tunneling, and teleportation in our everyday world at a very human level. New interdisciplinary branches of science are springing forth that invite us to recognize our quantum biological nature, harness the phenomenal power of the placebo, and discover how we can take positive actions to change our reality.

While it is true that we just left the Industrial Age behind a few short decades ago as we entered the Information Age, the times are again changing, as we are now arriving at the Dawn of the Quantum Age.

Such a bold statement demands an explanation, I realize. Like most changes in eras of time throughout human history–from the Stone Age to the Bronze Age to the Iron Age to the Industrial Age and the Information Age–this one too is based on new ideas and technology. There is right now a race to build quantum computers, which is driving forward a staggering number of new discoveries in the realm of quantum physics on a weekly basis.

These new Quantum Age computers are to our current classical Information Age computers as typewriters are to laptops: a technological leap forward in exponential orders of magnitude. This race to build the first working quantum computers is rocking our world to its very foundation, as quantum processes are being demonstrated at room temperatures on the macroscopic scale in repeatable laboratory conditions.

You can better appreciate the origins of our current Information Age by taking a look at the first classical computers. Our first computers became commonplace in the 1930s and 1940s, with the hefty accomplishments of the ENIAC computer's memorable debut. This gigantic milestone computer weighed in at thirty metric tons. Although it needed to be rewired in order to be reprogrammed initially and operated without any operating system, the ENIAC captured public attention and helped popularize the idea of computing as essential to everyday business and life. These first computers changed peoples' lives and way of thinking far beyond what was originally envisioned, making the world better connected and informed than at any previous point in history.

Quantum Age Computing: The Power of the Qubit

Whereas classical computers are based on a principle of recordable, reproducible facts in the form of flat, two dimensional worlds of zeroes and ones, Quantum Age computers are based on the physics of possibility. And what makes Quantum Age computers possible is a brand new idea we will become much more familiar with as we move more fully into the Quantum Age–the qubit.

The qubit, or quantum bit, is the simplest building block of quantum information. Qubits are designed to handle simultaneously superimposed possibilities, working together in entangled clusters of computational coherent complexity. A single quantum memory is capable of envisioning, for example, every single possible path home you can take during rush hour–all at once–so a quantum computer can instantaneously select the fastest possible route. Whereas classical computers have difficulty solving practical problems such as these, these real-life problems are tailor-made for quantum computers. The same is true in nature. Natural quantum computational capabilities are built into the photosynthesis process in plants.

Another mind-boggling difference between classical computers and Quantum Age computers is that qubits are much more than the sum of their parts. Whereas the bits and bytes of classical computers become just slightly more interesting and complex when more of them come together, truly mind-bending possibilities arise when two or more qubits are working together. Qubits work together in ways unlike anything ever seen in classical computing, beginning with entanglement, so that any single-qubit measurement performed will give a totally random result, whereas any time such a single-qubit measurement is performed on two entangled qubits, the two measurements will give opposite results. If you picture two entangled qubits as entangled coins being randomly flipped some great distance apart, so that whenever one came up Heads, the other would always be Tails, you see how very different the basics of Quantum Computing are from Classical computing.

Feeling the Pulse of Various Parallel Realities

One of the basic aspects of quantum computing is that energy is required to make a jump from one state to another. When quantum particles are observed to make a quantum jump, they can be seen to blink out of and into existence, like bright flashes of light, as they make the jump. There is an "oscillating phase" of vibration associated with each energy level state. So the faster the vibration, the higher the level of energy required to exist in that state. And whenever the energy of any one of the entangled particles in an entangled state increases energy, the entire entangled group of particles beat faster in that potential reality.

The Impact of Quantum Computing on Daily Life

The very existence of qubits and entanglement is already having a powerful impact on society, in similar fashion to the way the advent of ever-smaller classical computers and the internet has had on our lives in the past several decades. While most people might not be able to explain the difference between a bit and a byte, or explain the difference between RAM and ROM in a computer, there is now a great reliance upon global communication via a freely accessible internet for communication of news from person to person and group to group.

First proposed in the 1980's, quantum computing is expected to change everything from the way the stock market functions to every aspect of information security, weather forecasting, and trend analysis. Thanks to quantum superposition of states, quantum qubits contain information in all possible states, and entangled qubits thus have the capability to efficiently compute optimal solutions for some of the most complex, vexing and currently "unsolvable" problems known to man.

The first quantum computers for sale fetched fifteen million dollars, and were purchased by NASA and Google. The size of a large garden shed, the Canadian D-Wave-Two is the first commercially available quantum computer to hit the marketplace, and heralds the start of a brand new age of computing... and civilization.

The Quantum Age Mindset

The Zen of qubit processing logic can be more easily understood from an Eastern fourfold logic view. Rather than adopting a simple Yes/No, Zero/One, True/False dichotomy of classical computing bits, qubits exist in the realm of such possibilities as: True, False, True-and-False, and Not-True/Not-False. Such a lack of certainty in favor of optimization may seem strange at first, but this seemingly fuzzy logic is one of the core foundational aspects of the new Quantum Age.

The Quantum Age invites us to embrace uncertainty, recognize interconnectedness, and raise our level of energy in order to experience a better way of life. Through quantum entanglement, we find a mechanism by which to comprehend intuition. Through quantum teleportation we see how we can sometimes travel farther in less time. Through quantum coherence we better understand synchronicity and coincidence, and through quantum superposition we glean insights into spontaneous remissions from disease that can occur when people are in lucid dream or near death experience (NDE) states of mind.

Note added by Dr. Carol Francis: Cynthia Sue Larson continues to reveal the metaphysical and Quantum Age link in her newest book, *Quantum Jumping: An Extraordinary Science of Happiness and Prosperity* (2013). Her book explores the intriguing implications of Quantum Mechanics and associated mathematical analysis applied directly to psychic phenomenon such as PSI, ESP, Remote Viewing and Astral Projection. Examination of the subatomic physics combined with mathematical examination of Cosmological Science is starkly similar to Shamanic Journeying into multi-verses or parallel universes. Processes associated to bio-cellular shifts at this quantum level keenly address the work of alternative healing arts and energy work. That the evolving computer age as discussed here by Cynthia Sue Larson can also pertain to our metaphysical perspectives such as synchronicity, healing arts, near death experiences, astral projection, psychic powers, or lucid dreaming demonstrates one more way in which science and spirituality converge.

References

Larson, Cynthia Sue (2013). <u>Quantum Jumping: An Extraordinary Science of Happiness and Prosperity</u>. Reality Shifters: United States.

About Cynthia Sue Larson:

This article is reprinted from Cynthia Sue Larson's from Reality Shifters.com.

Cynthia Sue Larson is a comprehensive and sophisticated Spiritual Coach, Best-Selling Author, International Keynote Speaker, and Graduate from University of California, Berkeley, in Physics.

Publications from Cynthia Sue Larson include: Aura Healing Meditations CD, *Quantum Jumps: An Extraordinary Science of Happiness and Prosperity, Reality Shifts: When Consciousness Changes the Physical World, AURA ADVANTAGE: How the Colors in Your Aura Can Help You Attain Your Desires and Attract Success, Karen Kimball and the Dream Weaver's Web, Sacred Shift: Co-Creating Your Future in a New Renaissance,* and 2012: *Creating Your Own Shift.*

CHAPTER 37

INTERDISCIPLINARY CONSCIOUSNESS NATURE, SCIENCE, AESTHETICS AND SPIRITUALITY
BY DR. CAROL FRANCIS

Echoing rustles of eagles
in duskY hues.
Whisper flutters of
sapphire dragonflies.
Radiant glories of
sun-drenched petals and
bold cratered moons.

Resonate oscillation of
electrons shifting.
Breathless pauses
within molecular spaciousness.

Explore soulfully
magnificent unknowns.
Yield wisdom, Nature and Science,
Mystic Sages of Truths.

Nature ceaselessly instructs those humbly poised to absorb Her grandeur and minutiae. Nature, or Mother Earth or Pachamama (Incas), beacons humans to know magnificence greater than mankind can create or grasp. Whether vacationing or studiously analyzing molecular structures, or polluting and exploiting Her resources, Her domains are open for all to discover.

Our source of food, shelter, safety, pleasures and each breath is entirely contingent on Mother Nature. All science focuses on Her structures and processes. Industries completely deal with Her resources and Her temperament. We can simultaneously master and dominate Nature while resonating with Her powerful peacefulness or harmonizing with Her plentiful resources. We are never away from Nature, She is our Omnipresent Guru.

Whether you are pantheist, atheist, monotheist, spiritualist, polytheist, or agnostic, Nature is factually, materially, soulfully, aesthetically Omnipresent. To meditate on the experience of Omnipresence, is in a fashion to be in the presence of the consciousness or subjective experience of the Divine for each of us. Such meditations produce the AWE or the OHM of the Soul whether with tools of science, hiker's boots, spiritualist's rituals, or the lens of a camera. Perhaps, She, and the AWE She inspires, is our Great Unifier. Even the atheistic researcher embraces this pantheistic AWE so evident in Nature.

Interdisciplinary Consciousness
Autobiography First
Permit me a moment of meaningful nostalgia.
Nature
Pine forests kissed my childhood's grassy backyard fence. Snow draped willow trees. Santa-friendly reindeers nibbled blades peeking through the ground-cover. Bald eagles silently circled mountain rabbits. Native residents sculptured jewelry from turquoise and silver, hand-mined from local mesas.

This daily paradise, my home town, also housed an international contingency of scientists and their families. They tested bombs, atomic reactions and survivability co-efficients. Late at night, nuclear waste was trucked out of town past the trees, eagles, deer and me who dreamt about shamans in Los Alamos, New Mexico.

Nuclear Physics

Those scientists I met or heard tales about, were earnestly interested in the magnificence of their discoveries. They gerrymandered Mother Nature to their intentions. Power was unleashed. AWE impacted each observer of those bellowous explosions, including my father. Part of the AWE was sheer terror; part was reverence.

My nuclear physicist father supplied nightly dinner entertainment with table salt, forks and water glasses. He would display natural phenomenon which seemed like magic or violations of Newtonian Laws. Science during dinner evoked my wide-eyed AWE too.

Music

Baroque rhythms, fiery Rachmaninoff, or romantic Chopin would awaken me on weekend mornings as my mother's nine-foot Steinway Piano or Concert Cello lured me into the living room to soak in her rhapsodies. Yet another AWE! My mother communed with music written by others, yet their music was channeled through her all-knowing fingers.

Religion and Spirit

Sunday mornings, at age four and five, I would be shuffled to services where I would openly question their portraiture of God and wondered if those teachers were oppressed by their dogmas. Yet at night, the moon dominated the blackness, the Milky Way poured swirls in the pure mountain sky, and the sound of swooping-hooting owls reverberated through the pine canyon. I communed with my Spirit--Omnipotent and Endless-- with the

Spirits of Mesa Indians summoned by wooden flutes, or with the Christo of gentle Latin souls I would meet in the town.

Interdisciplinary Consciousness

My childhood nirvana simultaneously interlaced the AWE of Science, Nature, Human created aesthetics, and Spiritual teachings. I lived Interdisciplinary Consciousness, including the spirituality of the AWE each discipline inspired.

As a child, science for me was marvel, destruction, power, explanation, unknowns, and experimental intrigue. Science is one of my Spiritual Gurus, along with Nature, Human Master Teachers, Aesthetics, Mystical Esoterics, Ethereal Guides and Omnipresent Spirit.

Barriers to Interdisciplinary Consciousness

Science, as a spiritual path, has changed so much through the millenniums of human development. At times, it has been the expression of Spiritual pursuits. Chemistry was part alchemy which was part magic. Ethereal space was the region of spirits and the study of gaseous forms of matter, magnetics and electricity. The laws of nature were the laws of an orderly God on the Earthly plain. During those eras, being a scientist allowed seekers to touch God's omnipresence and omnipotence, too.

Science as a Path has also been the harsh critic of Spiritual pursuits. Indeed, religion overstepped its ability to define truth by implementing unreasonable dogmatic doctrines and single-minded rigid perspectives. Later, religion allowed no room for new discoveries and alternate points-of-view. Eventually, secretly, many scientists pursued both the Path of Science and the Spiritual Paths.

Yet some scientists have become the dogmatic doctrinaires they once despised. These scientists have disallowed a spiritual

290

interpretation of natural principles or explanations of the unknown, similar to how religion disallowed scientific understanding of phenomenon to be honored.

If those scientists among us who wish to also pursue a Spiritual Path mistakenly disavow the Path of Science, we all will lose and become blinder. We know too little. There is no room for dogma, decree or definitive closed-mindedness whether in the fields of science or the fields of spiritual teachings. There is plenty of room for discovery and descriptive interpretative hypotheses. We need everyone's effort to understand the forces, or Forces, that have made this existence possible.

Many scientists desire to reveal the charlatans who exploit and pander naïve foolish students who forget to be discerning. These scientists may opt to believe that all Spiritual pursuits pander to fools. However, even those scientists are driven to discover the intricacies of the visible and invisible, the tangible and intangible, the sources and causes as well as their effects and consequences.

The why's, what's, how's, when's, and where's of Nature all need to be answered by the curious scientist, so why not the Who's of Nature too? Scientists of all spiritual persuasions often hypothesize and theorize about the unifying principles, the ultimate prima facie perspectives, which will explain Nature in all of Her macro or micro subdomains. In their search, they are in pursuit of perhaps the unifier.

Yogananda described the need for Interdisciplinary Consciousness between sciences and spiritual practices elegantly:

"It is the Infinite, the Ocean of Power, that lies behind all phenomenal manifestations. Our eagerness for worldly activity kills in us the sense of spiritual awe. Because modern science tells us how to utilize the powers of Nature, we fail to comprehend the Great Life in back of all names and forms.

Familiarity with Nature has bred contempt for her ultimate secrets: our relation with her is one of practical business. We tease her, so to speak, to discover the ways in which she may be forced to serve our purposes; we make use of her energies, whose Source yet remain unknown. In science our relation with Nature is like that between an arrogant man and his servant; or, in a philosophical sense, Nature is like a captive in the witness box. We cross-examine her, challenge her, and minutely weigh her evidence in human scales that cannot measure her hidden values nor her Source.

On the other hand, when the self is in communion with a higher power, Nature automatically obeys, without stress or strain, the will of man. This effortless command over Nature is called 'miraculous' by the materialist.

Some students of science and nature assert that God has never been proven and therefore does not exist. However, perhaps they have not proven their specific "God-Construct," and perhaps that is why it seems science has not yet found the "WHO" of the all they explore. Is it their conceptualization of God they cannot prove? Or perhaps, it is just a matter of time before the tools of science touch the hem of God with clarity; or, perhaps the hem of God has already been touched by scientific tools multiple times without yet being recognized as such by the scientifically minded."

(Yogananda, 1946, p289-290.)

References

Francis, Carol (2011). *Spiritual Gurus, Spiritual Paths: Your Choice.* Rancho Palos Verdes, Make Life Happen Publishing.

Yogananda, Paramahansa (1946). *Autobiography of a Yogi.* Authorized by the International Publications Council of Self-Realization Fellowship.

About Dr. Carol Francis

In addition to her spiritual counseling and intuitive work with metaphysically inclined seekers, Dr. Carol Francis has practiced for 37 years as a Clinical Psychologist, Life Coach, Clinical Hypnotherapist, and Marriage, Family & Child Counselor. She assists individuals, couples and children who seek to optimize their current situation and overcome complications of daily living. These individuals seek deep relief and growth for depression, anxiety, stress, career moves, family discord, child and parenting issues, relationship dissatisfaction, habit control, and the psychology of financial success. Practicing and licensed in Southern California for over 37 years, Dr. Carol Francis can be reached at drcarolfrancis.com or 310-543-1824.

Publications by Dr. Carol Francis

Study Skills for Successful High School and College Students

Helping Children with Divorce

Schizoid Anxiety

Helping Children with Natural and Manmade Disasters

"Horrific Parental Imaginings"

"Therapist's Countertransference with Abuse Couples"

KISS Method for Stop Smoking and KISS Cigarettes Goodbye

If You Can't Stop Eating, Maybe You're Hungry: Reset Your Cravings

Re-Uniting Soldiers with Families

Evolving Women's Consciousness: Dialogue with 21st Century Women.

Spiritual Paths, Spiritual Gurus: Your Choice

Astral Projection and Spiritual Journeys

Your Akashic Records

Media Productions of Dr. Carol Francis

Dr. Carol Francis Talk Radio has been active since 2008 with hundreds of thousands of listeners across the internet planet. Archived programs are available at DrCarolFrancisTalkRadio.com and BlogTalkRadio.com/dr-carol-francis.

Dr. Carol Francis has interviewed internationally on KABC, KLOS, KROQ, and Associated Radio Programs as well.

Her *Spiritual Readings Radio Show* is live and archived at BlogTalkRadio.com/spiritual-readings.

For even more helpful information, Dr. Carol Francis Videos, Lectures, Dr. Carol Francis Television Shows and Presentations are archived at YouTube.com/Dr. Carol Francis or Vimeo.com/Dr. Carol Francis

CHAPTER 38

SCIENCE OF METAPHYSICAL
AND SPIRITUAL PHENOMENON:

A BRIEF ANNOTATED BIBLIOGRAPHY
BY DR. CAROL FRANCIS

Wealth of research articles and books now delineate the interface of modern science and spiritual, metaphysical or "consciousness" practices. In this chapter, each topic covered in *Your Soaring Phoenix* is correlated with scientific research findings. Fortunately there are so many scientific researchers sharing their findings, it is impossible to dedicate one book, much less a chapter, to discuss these correlations. We decided, therefore, to provide you with an annotation of significant books and researchers so you can further your investigations and be amazed how science and spirituality are once again communicating. I believe this is truly the era of Interdisciplinary Consciousness.

Science of Consciousness and Intelligence
Within The Cosmic Design

Schools of metaphysics and spirituality typically embrace the belief that Divine Consciousness, Source, God, and ethereal realms have intelligence, emotions and personalities. These following authors examine if we live in a universe of choices, decisions, reflections or consciousness based on the scientific disciplines of cellular biology, quantum physics, neurobiology, and supramolecular investigations in medicine.   Does the soul, spirituality or consciousness exist based on scientific research? These authors explain the scientific investigations currently evidencing the soul, consciousness, and spirituality in the human being.

Measuring the Immeasurable: The Scientific Case for Spirituality is a profound compilation of key researchers who integrate scientific methodology with spiritual processes. Topics well discussed include the alternative healing practices, the effects of emotions, prayer, meditation, and intentionality on local and nonlocal situations, and the consciousness as correlated with neurology, cellular sciences, medicine and quantum research.

Stephen C. Meyer's *Signature in the Cell: DNA and The Evidence for Intelligent Design* details cellular biological research which reconfigures the reductionistic interpretations of Darwinian evolutionary theory. Explaining the social and political pressures to conform to popular opinion within the scientific communities, Meyer illustrates that certain rigid beliefs have inhibited scientific research and misdirected interpretations of statistical results away from a Divine Consciousness perspective.   Reconsidering old research findings and connecting such with new scientific findings, Meyer uncovers the bio-cellular reflection of intelligent design and cellular personal consciousness.   His research is relevant to the meta-studies of consciousness, spirituality or the soul.

The God Effect: Quantum Entanglement, Science's Strangest Phenomenon by Brian Clegg examines the progressive field of Physics to reveal the interactions between subatomical particles which seem to communicate or have mindful exchange on subatomical, atomical, molecular and cellular levels. The Quantum Entanglement research does not necessarily indicate the presence of consciousness, willfulness or voluntary selections but may reasonably suggest that such is one very likely understanding of nature. His work is relevant to remote healing, prayer, astral projection, shamanic healing, remote viewing, psychic interchange and synchronicity.

His Holiness The Dalai Lama integrates the investigations of science and the Buddhist's perspectives on the meaning of life and suggests that the singularity of the Universe is essentially spiritual and physical simultaneously in *The Universe in a Single Atom*. During the last two decades. The Dala Lama has interfaced with many notable scientists within the research community studying consciousness and meditation alongside biochemistry, neurobiology and nonlocal events.

Stuart Hamaroff, an anesthesiologist and professor at the University of Arizona, is known for his studies about consciousnesses. His decades of research have led to examining pre-death and post-death quantum particles existing in our brains. These particles may house our consciousness or our soul or the aspects of humans which continue after death. His papers, lectures, and interviews are worth absorbing as he integrates Near Death Experiences, subatomical quantum physics, resuscitation medicine, and neuroscience. He explores consciousness on the supramolecular level.

Candance B. Pert, Ph.D., is well known for her studies of molecular biology and discoveries of cell receptors and "feel-good" chemicals and molecular sites. Consider *Everything You Need to Know to Feel Go(o)d* and her *Molecules of Emotion: The Science*

Behind Mind-Body Medicine. Her research and analysis is very relevant to energy workers, faith healers, and light workers.

Science and Psychic Phenomenon, PSI, ESP, Mediumship

Scientific studies regarding psychic phenomenon are conducted at many universities, governmental programs, and private sector facilities. Observational research, collaboration of experiences, and statistical analyses are primary methodologies considered by the following researchers.

Michael Talbot's *The Holographic Universe* is a well respected treatise detailing scientific studies about psychic phenomenon. While this book does not include the last two decades of amazing findings, it provides history and synopsis of rigid scientific research including neurology, cosmology, physics, PSI laboratory investigations, and probability analysis. Talbot weaves the unusual and bizarre events reported by multiple observers in with theories and discoveries reported by scientists. I consider this book a primer and backbone for all metaphysical and spiritually inclined investigators.

Erasing Death: The Science That is Re-Writing the Boundaries Between Life and Death is essential reading for anyone facing Death, all of us. Sam Parnia is a medical doctor on the forefront of Resuscitation Medicine. As a consequence, he has established rigorous research models which investigate the Near Death Experiences and the other-worldly experiences now so commonly reported. Sam Parnia actually renames NDE the After Life Experiences based on his findings. The implications for mediums, speaking with loved-ones passed-over or communications exchanged between those alive with those who have died is starkly evident.

Astronaut Edgar C. Mitchell founded IONS, International Organization of Noetic Sciences, discoverable at Noetic.org. IONS provides an international platform for researchers to organize, conduct, and share results associated with psychic processes, mind over matter, spontaneous healings, and nonlocal conscious connections. Their Chief Science Officer, Dr. Dean Radin, encouraged IONS to adhere to strict scientific methodology. Dean Radin's specific research findings are well delineated in his latest book, *Supernormal: Science, Yoga, and The Evidence for Extraordinary Psychic Abilities.*

Profound Implications of Quantum Physics, Cosmology, and Mathematics For Each Spiritual Practices Discussed in *Your Soaring Phoenix*

Validating spiritual tools and experiences has become easier since Quantum Physics has revealed that our subatomical universe actually functions the way spiritualists have been describing for thousands of years. These researchers examine complex and expanding discoveries of Quantum Physics. They then interface such findings with other fields of science. Then they ponder implications for spiritual manipulations or metaphysical discoveries which are explored in *Your Soaring Phoenix.*

Michio Kaku brings the wonders of physics alive in each of his books. Check out *Physic of The Impossible: A Scientific Exploration into the World of Phasers, Force Fields, Teleportation, and Time Travel.* Kaku's *Hyperspace* and *Visions* also integrate research and mathematical discoveries with phenomenon clearly connected to astral projection, time travel, remote viewing, bi-location, distance healing, energy and vibration work, and psychic activities. His latest, *The Future of the Mind* is dedicated to telepathy, psychic phenomenon, time travel, remote viewing and other fascinations which he grounds in various forward looking fields of science.

Our Mathematical Universe: My Quest for the Ultimate Nature of Reality by Cosmologist and Physicist Max Tegmark, boggles the reader with a collaborative examination of cosmology, astronomy, atomic and subatomic sciences, and mathematical deductions. Tegmark then investigates multi-verses, time travel, multi-dimensions, and the potential leap of consciousness. Through Tegmark's explanations, readers peek into research from MIT, Stanford, Berkeley and a host of other prime research universities.

Frank Wilcze examines the essential energetic nature of all form and formlessness in *The Lightness of Being: Mass, Ether and The Unification of Forces.* His purely scientific explorations have implications for energy and light workers and those traveling without regard to mass or physicality.

Cynthia Sue Larson, a contributor to *Your Soaring Phoenix* is both a spiritual teacher, guide, and an author who succinctly converges physics, computer science, and biology with psychic phenomenon, aura reading, spontaneous healings, laws of attraction or manifestation, and nonlocal processes such as astral projection, remote viewing, time travel, and multi-dimensional travel. Her personal experience seeing and communicating with nonphysical realities is wonderfully and easily paired with sound discussions of quantum mechanics discoveries. She discusses coherently spiritual practices associated with Quantum Entanglement,

Quantum Superposition, Quantum Tunneling, Quantum Coherence, Quantum Superposition, Quantum Teleportation and Quantum Jumping. Two of her many books to consider are *Quantum Jumps: An Extraordinary Science of Happiness and Prosperity* and *Reality Shifts: When Consciousness Changes the Physical World.*

Other books to add to this list would be *Physics of the Soul,* by Amit Goswami, *Science and the Akashic Field,* by Ervin Laszlo, and *Wholeness and The Implicate Order*, by David Bohm.

Science and The Powers of Healers, Energy Workers, Law of Attraction, Hypnosis, and Regression Therapies

How does science explore the spontaneous healing associated to energy and healing work or explain the power of suggestion or regression to change physical and emotional situations? These researchers have extended these questions into empirical analyses.

Bruce Lipton spearheaded the research indicating that beliefs altered cellular processes. *Biology of Belief* and his subsequent books and papers were initially considered fiction but now are embraced as fact. These findings are scientifically observable, repeatable, and usable information in all fields of scientific research and medicine. The implications of his work clearly address faith healers, spontaneous healings, energy workers, Reiki, Reconnective Healing, Huna Healing work, and other spiritual practices including meditation, yoga, hypnosis, regression therapy, and the power of intentionality.

Lynne McTaggart's *The Intention Experiment: Using Your Thoughts to Change Your Life and the World* is one of many of her works which clearly indicates that our minds, thoughts, emotions, intentions, observations and presence have direct impact on modifying what occurs around us. The brilliance of her work is that scientific repeatable studies, statistical analysis, and multi-observable situations are investigated to support her findings. Implications for healing, hypnosis, and Laws of Attraction, Manifesting or Intentionality, which are popularized in spiritual teachings, are quite excitingly evident now in science.

This list is resoundingly incomplete. Yet, these authors and titles will produce a cascade of other materials for the eager reader who is excited to know that spiritual pursuits no longer need to be hidden behind the Wicca bushes or secret lodges because of embarrassment, fear of being burned at the stack, or dismissed as merely fantastical.

About Dr. Carol Francis

In addition to her spiritual counseling and intuitive work with metaphysically inclined seekers, Dr. Carol Francis has practiced for 37 years as a Clinical Psychologist, Life Coach, Clinical Hypnotherapist, and Marriage, Family & Child Counselor. She assists individuals, couples and children who seek to optimize their current situation and overcome complications of daily living. These individuals seek deep relief and growth for depression, anxiety, stress, career moves, family discord, child and parenting issues, relationship dissatisfaction, habit control, and the psychology of financial success. Practicing and licensed in Southern California for over 37 years, Dr. Carol Francis can be reached at drcarolfrancis.com or 310-543-1824.

Publications by Dr. Carol Francis

Study Skills for Successful High School and College Students
Helping Children with Divorce
Schizoid Anxiety

Helping Children with Natural and Manmade Disasters

"Horrific Parental Imaginings"

"Therapist's Countertransference with Abuse Couples"

KISS Method for Stop Smoking and KISS Cigarettes Goodbye

If You Can't Stop Eating, Maybe You're Hungry: Reset Your Cravings

Re-Uniting Soldiers with Families

Evolving Women's Consciousness: Dialogue with 21st Century Women.

Spiritual Paths, Spiritual Gurus: Your Choice

Astral Projection and Spiritual Journeys

Your Akashic Records

Media Productions of Dr. Carol Francis

Dr. Carol Francis Talk Radio has been active since 2008 with hundreds of thousands of listeners across the internet planet. Archived programs are available at DrCarolFrancisTalkRadio.com and BlogTalkRadio.com/dr-carol-francis.

Dr. Carol Francis has interviewed internationally on KABC, KLOS, KROQ, and Associated Radio Programs as well.

Her *Spiritual Readings Radio Show* is live and archived at BlogTalkRadio.com/spiritual-readings.

For even more helpful information, Dr. Carol Francis Videos, Lectures, Dr. Carol Francis Television Shows and Presentations are archived at YouTube.com/Dr. Carol Francis or Vimeo.com/Dr. Carol Francis

SECTION VI

HUMANLY GROUNDED WHILE SPIRITUALLY SOARING

FRANCIS & O'MALEY

INTRODUCTION

LIFE CHORES AS TOOLS FOR

SPIRITUAL GROWTH

BY DR. CAROL FRANCIS

Birds
Flexibly run on sandy shores,
Float upon rocky waves,
Perch on slanted branches,
Soar on invisible, windy currents
While
Eating Worms
Nesting Hatchlings
Fighting off Prey
Pruning Parasites
Finding Refuge

Walk solidly on Earth during this life. Effectively interface with your physical demands. Why? One reason is because effective physical living supports your spiritual expansion, as explained by each author in this section.

Earning a living, dealing with family demands, paying bills, exercising daily, eating nutritiously, resting your body, driving safely, reducing stress or sadness, having functional relationships, and cleaning messes are on your list of daily physical human demands. Gregg Braden noted that our twenty-first century vision quests include our everyday life activities. (1)

Buddhist monks, shamans, or swamis select eager students into their mentorship programs yet often they require eager and diligent dedication to chores. (2) "Meaningless chores" is not the perspective of these teachers who use chores to build character qualities such as focus, gratitude, servitude, generosity, humbleness, tenacity, mental clarity, and physical strength. "Doing" daily life effectively while "being spiritual," however, is challenging for some of us. Yet, daily life can be the perfect realm in which to become more spiritually enlightened.

Some indigenous cultures required their spiritual leaders to be highly successful. They were to be healthy, wealthy, and accomplished in their villagers' eyes. Their material success verified the authenticity of their spiritual gifts. Perhaps such is still true for each of us?

Moving the energies of the universe for healing, conversing with elevated powers, or traveling with your astral self, have huge implications that also impact our materialistic realms. Clearly, followers of Illuminati, Golden Dawn, Wicca and such traditions sometimes ceremonially harness metaphysical tools to dominate the materialistic realms. Yes, spiritual tools can powerfully impact physical properties, for good or for malevolent intent. Yes, physical success can vibrate in harmony with your spiritual practices. Laws of attraction, intentionality and manifestation follow these principles as well.

Therefore, if you are grooming your spiritual tools and enlightenment authentically, your life as a grounded human being can be effectively and authentically enlightened, that is, successful. In essence, one verification of spiritual strength is your ability to harness physical health. This is not about creating guilt or inadequate feelings if your physical health appears unsuccessful. Rather, this is about learning to utilize all your physical and spiritual tools to live healthy, grounded, and elevated, simultaneously.

Law of Manifestation, Law of Attraction, Law of Intentionality, Prosperity Gospel and similar spiritual teachings attempt to integrate spiritual thinking with creating physical wealth. Yoga and pranic breathing attempt to combine physical exercise with spiritual enlightenment. Vegetarian or vegan eating, praying before meals, or even ceremonies enacted before and after a hunt, combine eating with spiritual consciousness as well. Dr. Moto's scientific research about water crystals being modified by written words on containers suggests that physical structures are affected by our spiritual gestures. (3) Spiritual tools do impact physical domains and using spiritual tools to do so is another important form of expanding your spiritual enlightenment.

So in this last section **Humanly Grounded While Spiritually Soaring**, your human need for money, exercise, food, breath, psychological health, and rest are set before you as yet other ways to expand your spiritual consciousness in your vision quest as an Earth-bound physical form.

First, best-selling author **Belinda Ferrell** integrates emotional and psychological health with spiritual awakening, Huna style, from her inspiring book, *Find Your Friggin' Joy* in her chapter **Shifting from Anger, Fear, and Guilt, The Huna Way**.

Nutrition Expert and Alternative Treatment Practitioner, **Mary O'Maley** holistically examines nutrition as the multi-leveled process of simultaneously feeding our body, mind and soul with more than merely good whole foods in **Holistic Health Primer.**

Health and fitness coach and author, **Edie Summers**, weaves physical exercise with nutrition, spiritual mindfulness and soulful connections in **Eating, Exercising, and Sensing within the Body-Mind-Spirit Triad**.

Dr. Carol Francis examines strategies for building businesses, wealth, and attaining goals with 14 steps including spiritual consciousness, Laws of Manifestation, Attraction and Intentionality. This last chapter, **Spiritual Mindful Tools for Financial and Business Growth,** is adapted from her book *Spiritual Gurus, Spiritual Paths: Your Choice*

References

(1) Braden, Gregg (2001). *The Isaiah Effect: Decoding the Lost Science of Prayer and Prophecy.* Harmony.

(2) Yogananda, Paramahansa (1946). *Authobiography of a Yogi.* Authorized by the International Publications Council of Self-Realization Fellowship.

(3) Emoto, Masaru (2004). *The Hidden Messages in Water.* Hillsboro: Beyond Words.

CHAPTER 39

SHIFTING FROM ANGER, FEAR AND GUILT

BY BELINDA FERRELL

The Great Secret Teachings: Missing Links Revealed*

Recently I found myself in a conversation with three gentlemen. Almost immediately I sensed a tension in the elder gentleman and told him I was writing a book about cleansing your soul in order to find your joy. He revealed he had too many regrets about his past to feel he could ever find any joy. Most of his life he had been a judge in a military tribunal, and some of the past events were coming back to haunt him. He believed it was too much to overcome. When I told him the book would give him ways to connect with his Higher Self, which would assist him in forgiving himself of his past, he was interested in reading the book.

You don't have to be stuck in the past. There is an easy way to be in the present and to be joyful. It's found in the ancient Huna teachings born in the beauty of Hawaii.

When I was first introduced to Huna almost 20 years ago, I was intrigued by its definition: "leading a hurt-less life." What did that mean? Well, I came to understand it as one refraining from doing or saying anything to harm yourself or another. The word "Huna" – devised by the teacher and author Max Freedom Long to mean "secret" – is the name of the teachings of the ancient Hawaiian people.

Over thousands of years old, the teachings are comprised of the original teachings of the people of this Earth. Before 750 C.E. (Common Era) all the people of the Earth lived by the Huna teachings of a connection with the Higher Self and a balanced male and female energy system. At that time, people recognized that the real "power" came from the One Source called the "I'O." This knowledge was taught all over the planet in a way best understood by the native peoples. In approximately 325 C.E., a wave of male-dominate cultures presided over the planet and overthrew the balanced systems. The sacred original teachings were wiped out, such as those from the Native Americans and the Australian Aboriginals. As time progressed, people deviated from the early teachings, separating themselves from Spirit and creating new beliefs and doctrines. Over the years, Huna remained pure because the Hawaiian Islands were distant from other cultures. Fortunately, the wise teachers sent many of the sacred teachings underground, knowing the cycle would eventually shift back towards balance. Because of this, the teachings remained a secret and were considered to be the most direct link to the ancient wisdom. In Hawaii, the original teachings were hidden in chants and Hula dances. By 1820, the Christian missionaries began to eliminate the old "superstitious ways. "They considered these teachings to be "sorcery" and "witchcraft."

Anyone who was caught practicing these rituals was fined and imprisoned. This was the case especially for the Kahunas, the master healers of the order. Though misguided, the missionaries were simply living by their own dogma and control without any awareness of a Higher Consciousness. Before the missionaries came, the Hawaiians lived their lives relatively free of mental illness. They were aligned with the Great Spirit through their breathing and forgiveness practices. When they noticed that the missionaries were not fully breathing, and yet "telling" them about

God, the Hawaiians knew the missionaries couldn't send strong enough prayers to reach the God force. Consequently, the Hawaiians did not reveal their secrets.

The sacred word "I'O" which referred to the Highest Creation (Akasha/Void) was given the designation of "hawk" (one who flies to the higher limits) because they did not want their sacred word desecrated by the missionaries' lack of consciousness. The word for the missionaries became "haole" which meant "without breath." The non-native people in Hawaii are still regarded as "haoles" today by Hawaiians because of their shallow breathing.

It was considered illegal to teach Huna practices in Hawaii from 1820 to the late 1970's. The United States Government passed the Native American Religious Freedoms Act in 1979, which has allowed these ancient healing techniques to be practiced once more. Over the past 30 years, our entire planet has experienced a return to the ancient ways of connecting with Spirit and a higher energy. The old male-dominated institutions are presently crumbling primarily because they fail to teach cooperation, they subtly deny the rights of women (the feminine), and they negate Spirit in all its forms. Denying this Divine Connection has only brought us disharmony, dissolution, depression, despair and war.

We have all participated in this collective dream, and now this dream is presently coming to an end. Outdated models, like the dinosaurs, become extinct. As our awareness continues to unfold, we are realizing we are energy beings and that our thoughts have created our reality. All the scriptures tell us that at one time we were one, united "whole." But separation from Spirit arose from the belief that we were separate. The purpose of dominant societies was to create power struggles and separation as well as to keep people's minds controlled and in fear. When the mind is in fear, it is in opposition to the heart, which is total and complete love.

Fear blocks the heart from opening and trusting. When you are in fear, you can also be manipulated. We have seen this countless times in our history, with dictators taking over countries, governments waging wars and politicians leveraging their control. As Sir Winston Churchill wisely stated, "Those who fail to learn from history are doomed to repeat it."

And so, knowing about the past wisdom of Huna, knowing the results of a controlled culture, knowing the consequences of fear and separation on our souls and on our society, what shall we do?

In a word "forgive." Yet this endeavor – done quite simply and swiftly by the practitioner of the great secret Huna teachings – has been an arduous if not impossible one for most of us.

So how does this Huna forgiveness technique work, whereas other endeavors to forgive may not? Have you ever tried to simply and swiftly forgive an enemy or foe who may have done you "wrong?" Have you ever tried to pretend everything was "fine" in the face of your resentment over a past experience? Have you ever had a parental figure just say, "Tell him you are sorry" and then do so with a gut full of frustration? Such attempts at forgiveness and release are futile, for they are missing some vital pieces of the puzzle. And what are these missing links? Simply put here, and then revealed in depth for the remainder of this section are such pieces:

1) Being prepared mentally – using your free will to choose a path that will take courage to truly face what you have been avoiding

2) The power of the breath – using the "HA breath" found in the Huna healing process

3) The connection to your Higher Self or a supreme Life Force

4) The vital process of cutting and dissolving cords or negative ties to people and experiences

5) Embracing the stringent reality that this forgiveness is actually about you forgiving yourself for your perceptions – not the life experiences – that have hurt you

6) The continual, committed and routine practice of clearing negative ties, dissolving cords, and cleansing the soul

If one takes these steps, the pathway to freedom and joy will easily be secured. But it will take your choice born of bravery and courage. And so I say, make the decree, make the call! Call back your Spirit! This involves the decision – your choice now – to melt away the anger, fear and resentments that have calcified our hearts. As a nation, we will then be stepping into the higher vibrations of Divine Love and Compassion ... one person at a time. Already we feel the strong vibrations of the planet moving us away from war, greed and the ways of being that no

longer serve us. Countries dominated by dictators are falling because the people will not support them. The old dreams are shattering like bubbles bursting in the air. We are gradually beginning to incorporate what does work. New and harmonious ways of living together within the community of Earth provide us with a unity for all, a connection to a Higher Self, and respect for all of life.

References

This chapter is reprinted with permission from the author and publisher from the book, *Find Your Friggin' Joy.*

Ferrell, Belinda (2013). *Find Your Friggin' Joy.* Chapter 10. Balboa Press.

About the Belinda Ferrell

As a Certified Master Hypnotherapist, NLP Master Practitioner, Huna Practitioner, and Reconnective Healing Practitioner,

Belinda is effective at getting results and enhancing performance in people's lives. She graduated from the University of California at Berkeley with a B.A. in English and Spanish. After obtaining a Lifetime Elementary Teaching Credential at Cal State at LA, she taught third grade for five years in Puerto Rico and Los Angeles. She played the character Snow White at Disneyland, was a TV News Reporter for KABC Channel 7 in Hollywood, and was on staff for Senator Charles H. Percy (Illinois) in Washington, D.C.

Belinda trained with Anthony Robbins (author of *Unlimited Power* and *Awaken the Giant Within*), and has effectively used these skills in her own life. In addition to fire-walking (18 times), Belinda was a professional Precision Stunt Car Driver for TV commercials and films. Her credits include ads for Buick, Cadillac, BMW, Volvo, Nintendo, Audi, Toyota, Lexus, AC Delco Spark Plugs and many more. She was a film and stage actress, having co-starred on the television series Midnight Caller, dozens of industrial films, commercials, and voice-overs. Belinda is the mother of two grown children, loves to "workout," bicycle, rollerblade, snow ski, and just be healthy and have fun.

Belinda received her training in Huna on the Big Island of Hawaii. Huna means "secret," and the secrets were hidden in the chants. The ancient Hawaiian chants became part of her life. They bring down the Higher Self (Aumakua/5th Dimension) that is in all of us. These ancient healing techniques flourished at a time when there was no mental illness on the islands, before the missionaries arrived. "As a Huna Practitioner, I've been ordained to bring back these ancient healing secrets. Inner empowerment is our birthright. We are all powerful spiritual beings, connected as one," declares Ferrell.

Fifteen years ago, Belinda collapsed with herniated discs, spinal nerve damage and paralysis. She was told by medical doctors that she would not walk again without surgery. Instead, she utilized the ancient Hawaiian healing techniques and completely recovered within days. Even the scoliosis she had since birth disappeared.　　She retired from stunt car driving and began teaching these healing modalities full time.

Overcoming a lifelong fear of water, Belinda guided groups for 10 years to the Big Island of Hawaii to teach Huna and swim with wild spinner dolphins.　　Swimming with the wild dolphins of Hawaii reconfirmed the connection to the 5th Dimension, the Higher Self in each of us.　The dolphins remind us how we must work together harmoniously if we are to co-exist together and build a New World of peace and harmony living in the 5th Dimension.

Between 2007-2009 several personal events altered her destiny.　After moving to Santa Cruz in March 2009, a friend took her to see the movie "The Living Matrix" featuring Dr. Eric Pearl of The Reconnection.　　There was an instant attraction to the Reconnective Healing work and within a few weeks, Belinda was attending the seminar in Chicago and completed Levels 1, 2, and 3 in Reconnective Healing and The Reconnection.　"This new Light and Information beckoned me to climb higher, leaving behind old modalities and stepping into a multidimensional frequency. This is the frequency of the 5th Dimension combining color, sound and information that can regenerate the functions of the human body on all levels.　I am humbled to be a part of this shift in time and honored to share this healing experience with you."　　You can contact Belinda Ferrell at her new office in Santa Cruz, Ca. Toll Free (866) 583-8370 or e-mail: belindafarrell44@yahoo.com

FRANCIS & O'MALEY

CHAPTER 40

HOLISTIC HEALTH PRIMER

BY MARY O'MALEY, MSHN, CHTI

Unlike practitioners of Western medicine, holistic practitioners are taught to look at the entire human being. This includes helping clients make good nutritional choices regarding lifestyle and life stressors. I will explain the concept of holistic health by expanding the definition of nutrition. We feed ourselves much more than food. Our body and mind and spirit all need to be fed. The term "holistic" encompasses our entire being, all of which needs feeding and nurturing in order to create not only good health but also feelings of true vitality. Holistic health is entirely about how we take care of our whole selves.

I will endeavor to answer the most basic and frequent questions which I have been asked by clients, friends, family, and students who are desperately trying to take better care of themselves and their families. These individuals are confused by the constant barrage of media reports about health and nutrition. More than 75% of money spent on health care is for treating chronic diseases. The blame for this has been placed on obesity and inactivity, both of which we can completely control in our own lives!

You may remember learning about psychologist Abraham Maslow and his theory about the hierarchy of needs in Psychology 101 class. This hierarchy consists of five levels of needs that must be met before we move on to fulfilling our other higher needs. It is generally represented as a pyramid. The base of the pyramid consists of our basic or physiological needs, and includes the need for water, air, food, and sleep. Once those needs are met, we are able to concentrate on our security and safety needs, like obtaining shelter, steady employment, and health insurance. The next level involves our social needs. They include the need for belonging, love, and affection. Esteem needs are next; self-esteem, personal worth, social recognition, and accomplishment are the focus of this level. Finally, we meet our self-actualizing needs, in which we become self-aware, concerned with personal growth, and able to fulfill our potential.

I mention this hierarchy of needs because how well we meet these needs can also affect our experience of moving up the pyramid steps. I believe it is the job of everyone in the health field, including both Holistic and Western medicine practitioners, to make sure clients and patients are educated properly. We can take back our health and vitality through self-responsibility. What exactly do we need to feed ourselves? Let's get started!

Nutrients of Air

Yes, air. We cannot live long without air!

In his book *Never Be Sick Again*, Raymond Francis, M.Sc., states that 96% of our nutritional intake comes from air! (1) Most of us would never think about air as a nutrient. Breathing not only keeps us alive, it also can help us relax, reduce our reaction to stress, ease pain, and give us energy and mental clarity. We can live for weeks without food. We can go days without water. We, however, can only live for a few minutes without oxygen. Air is our greatest source of energy. It is the number one nutrient required for the proper operation of all of our body. Of course, breathing clean air is preferable, but many of us are stuck inside buildings all day long, breathing recycled air. Whenever we can, we need to get outside around trees. Trees and plants help to detoxify and fortify the air.

The most commonly taught breathing exercise is to inhale slowly all the way down to the abdominal area, filling it with oxygen. Hold your breath for a moment, and then exhale slowly. However, recent advice suggests that it is more natural for us to breathe deeply into the abdominal area using the nose only, exhaling immediately and completely, and only resuming the inhale when the lungs demand it. Both techniques seem to work well, so give them both a try to see which feels best.

Nutrients of Water

About 60% of your body weight is water. Every system in your body depends on water. We can only live about five to seven days without it. Water flushes toxins from our body and lubricates our body. Water carries nutrients to our cells. We need between 8 and 12, 8-ounce glasses of water per day, depending on the size of our body. Food contains water; fruits and vegetables contain up to 90% water. While there are many other liquids that contribute to your water requirement, water remains the best source of hydration. How much you actually need depends on many factors, such as exercise, environment, weather, health conditions, and pregnancy or breast-feeding.

Some of the danger signs of dehydration include feeling dizzy and light-headed, producing less urine and darker urine, anger, impatience, fatigue, flushed face, irritability, anxiety, depression, snoring, insomnia, and short attention spans. More major health issues associated with dehydration are asthma, allergies, heartburn, migraines, constipation, obesity, fibromyalgia, high blood pressure, lower back pain, and even Type 2 Diabetes.

Nutrients from the Sun

Humans obtain 90% of our Vitamin D naturally from sunlight exposure to our skin. Ultraviolet B exposure to the skin naturally initiates the conversion of cholesterol in the skin to Vitamin D3. Since sunscreen has been introduced and touted as the only way to prevent skin cancer, our society has become increasingly Vitamin D deficient.

Extreme vitamin D deficiency shows up in children as bone deformities and rickets. In adults some of the symptoms include depression, weak immune system, skin problems, dental issues, osteoporosis, heart problems, and other chronic diseases. Fifteen minutes of sunshine on the legs and arms is enough exposure for most people. Dark-skinned people, the elderly, and people who are obese usually need more time. One rule of thumb is to be exposed to the sun for about half the time it would take to sunburn. Some Vitamin D can be absorbed from wild salmon, fortified milk, or multivitamins. Look for supplements containing D3.

Nutrients of Sleep

Sleep deprivation causes fatigue, clumsiness, weight gain or loss, and impairs brain and cognitive functions. Generally, we need from seven to nine hours of sleep per night. Less than seven hours is not enough, and more than nine hours can be too much. It is also quite natural for us to need a nap or rest in the middle of the day. Many societies and cultures include such siestas during the day!

Sleep apnea is another common problem, especially with obese people. It can lead to many dangerous health issues, including hypertension, heart attack, stroke, depression, muscle pain, cardiac arrhythmia, inefficient metabolism, loss of short term memory, weight gain, high blood pressure, diabetes, severe anxiety, concentration and intellectual deterioration, mood swings, insomnia, and impotence. Clearly, sleep is an important nutrient!

Nutrients of Exercise

It seems as though enough cannot be said about the benefits of exercise as a nutrient. Exercise increases our levels of energy, self-esteem, mental focus, strength, and stamina. It decreases depression, stress levels, a multitude of heart health issues, osteoporosis, and has even been proven to reduce breast cancer and the onset of dementia.

My mom once took her car in for servicing to get it ready for a vacation road trip. The car was about four years old and had less than 15,000 miles on it, but still needed belts and tires replaced. When my mom questioned the mechanic about all the repairs on a vehicle with so little mileage, the mechanic replied, "You've got to drive the car, lady, to keep the parts flexible and lubricated." This is a great metaphor for the need to move our body, many times a day.

Nutrients of Foods, Macronutrients and Micronutrients

By now I bet you have been wondering when I would get around to discussing food! Food as a nutrient is broken down into macronutrients and micronutrients. Macronutrients are carbohydrates (primarily found in fruits, vegetables, and grains), proteins (found in meats, fish, beans, and other plant foods), and fats (found in nuts, seeds, avocados, olive oil, nut oils, and coconut). From macronutrients we receive our micronutrients: vitamins, minerals, amino acids, enzymes, and the like.

In the United States we have a big problem with food addiction. Many of our foods have been processed with added sugar, salt, and fat. The chemical changes that are produced from this processing dull the neural pathways that tell us when we have taken in enough food. In the land of plenty, widespread malnutrition is caused by eating chemical waste products instead of natural foods full of worthy nutrients.

Portion sizes have increased threefold over the years to the point we feel cheated when served a normally portioned plate. Foreign proteins have been introduced into our crops and livestock to make them less susceptible to insects and disease. While that may generate more money for the chemical companies and farming corporations, it has created food allergies and possibly higher cancer and other disease rates at an alarming pace. The only way to be in control of the effects of our food consumption is to eat whole, fresh, and organic food that is prepared in our own kitchens.

Nutrients of Thoughts and Emotions

Our thoughts, especially our unconscious thoughts, rule our lives and how we experience the moments of our lives. They determine whether we view our day through fear or joy. Thoughts come before feelings, so changing your thoughts can change how you feel and how you react to daily stressors. Our unconscious thoughts are often revealed by our actions. Many people who are dealing with addictions will tell you that they ate that cookie or drank the wine before they became consciously aware of what they were doing.

We also know that the direction of our thoughts and our expectations determine what we notice and create in our lives. If we expect to have a bad time at a party, then that is exactly what happens. If we believe we will have trouble finding work because of our age, then that is what we will attract.

Nutrients of Healing Attitudes and Energies

Everything is made up of energy, and we can be highly impacted by the energies around us. Being around a positive person makes us feel good; being around a negative person can leave us tired and feeling low. We can use and manipulate energy in ways that make us feel differently at any given time. We can pull wonderful energy from nature. Imagine a gentle ocean wave washing away all of your troubles and stress. Imagine you are a beautiful mountain to help you feel yourself become strong and grounded. Imagine being caressed by a gentle cool breeze when you feel too hot.

You can give healing energy to a friend or loved one. Feel it coming from your heart and solar plexus, and fill up your body-awareness with love and strength and peace. Notice what happens within yourself when you do this. We can fill our office space with healing energy before a client arrives. It can help a new client relax and feel safe. How you experience the energies around you is your choice and completely in your control.

Nutritional Spiritual Experiences

We all deserve to experience that feeling of not being alone and knowing that there is a power greater than ourselves working on our behalf. We find our spirituality in a myriad of ways. We find it in the beauty of our religions, in being with other people, and in the total love and devotion from our pets. We find it by connecting with nature or praying to the divine or our guardian angel. We see it in the eyes of a child and in the beauty of a sunrise. Avowed atheists, even, can experience a spiritual bonding with nature or through meditative breathing or poetry. Spirituality is a highly intimate experience, but it is also a necessary ingredient in feeding ourselves.

Feed Your Whole Being DAILY

I have found that we can help our clients and ourselves focus on how we feed our body, mind, and spirit by answering three simple questions every day.

1. What foods will I feed myself today?

Planning ahead helps to keep us from eating the fast and processed foods that are so convenient.

2. How will I move and strengthen my body today?

Exercise, even a short walk, will help us reduce the effects of stress on our mind and body. Exercise keeps the body machine in good working order. Walking outside helps us maintain healthy Vitamin D levels and connect spiritually with nature.

3. What positive thought will I concentrate on today?

Concentrating on a thought of one word or a short phrase which is positive helps us to reprogram negative unconscious thoughts, connect spiritually, and change the focus and experience of our day, each day.

Answering these questions before you go to bed at night or first thing in the morning will help keep you focused on your holistic health and well-being.

References

Francis, Raymond (2002). *Never Be Sick Again.* Florida: Health Communications, Inc.

About Mary O'Maley, MSHN, CHtI

Mary O'Maley holds a MS in Holistic Nutritional Health Science and is a Certified Hypnotherapist and Hypnotherapy

Instructor with International Hypnosis Federation. She is recipient of the prestigious IHF Award of Excellence & Chapter Woman of the Year from American Business Woman's Association. Mary specializes in Past Life Regression, Intuitive Nutritional Counseling, Life Coaching, five energy healing modalities, psychic and medium readings, and hosts various programs and events.

Mary O'Maley, as Life Coach, created the Retreat-Reconnect-Recharge-ReEmerge Coaching. This R4 Coaching provides in-depth, personal-retreat experiences which help you access, trust, and follow your inner wisdom.

Certified in Reiki, Access Energy Clearing, Matrix Energetics and Reconnective Healing, Mary O'Maley also developed and provides Crystal Chakra Balancing. Crystal Chakra Balancing was discovered through Mary O'Maley's Akashic Records work.

Mary O'Maley teaches basic and intermediate hypnotherapy through IHF, nutritional approaches to health at various medical facilities, and metaphysical information at various international conferences and local venues.

Mary O'Maley's metaphysical studies allowed her to reignite her psychic and mediumship gifts which she uses for home, gallery and individual readings given since 1997. She is certified and tested as a member of Best American Psychics. Mary O'Maley hosts and produces The Merry Medium Show. On The Merry Medium Show, Mary interviews many wonderful spiritual explorers from the metaphysical and holistic communities. Podcasts of The Merry Medium Show are available at blogtalkradio.com/the-merry-medium. She also hosts live events in the Los Angeles area: **The Merry Medium and Friends – Where Science and Spirit Meet Live Events.**

To reach Mary O'Maley for her alternative health services, psychic and mediumship readings, radio programs, live events,

materials, workbooks and books, contact her at
http://www.maryomaley.com or call 424-234-9260.

CHAPTER 41

EATING, EXERCISING, AND SENSING WITHIN THE BODY-MIND-SPIRIT TRIAD

BY EDIE SUMMERS, M.A.

Hard to remember why you started eating well and exercising in the first place? More importantly, remember how eating well and exercising make you *feel on a core level of being?* You know the practical benefits of eating well, exercising, and practicing self-care on a regular basis. You see how the results impact your life on many levels. You may feel better, look better, and manage your stress levels better, among many other benefits.

Unfortunately, our practices can become routine, boring, uninspiring. We can easily flow into repetitive patterns, mindless practices. So, how do you reconnect with your chosen practices - whether yoga, meditation, preparing your own food, hiking, running, Tai Chi, or rock-climbing – in a renewed, soulful, more conscious way?

We have a chance to experience joy and connection on a daily basis through the practices we have already chosen. How? Through your everyday senses: activate how you experience what you eat, how you move - what you see, touch, hear, touch, taste, and feel.

Practice on a deeper level, instead of just eating well and exercising on a regular basis. *Practice awareness and joy* through the cultivation of your senses and develop an intimate understanding.   ***Experience*** your amazing mind-body connection.

What exactly is the mind-body? What is this "mind" we find everywhere in the body?   What is this soulful energy that animates us? I believe the mind is found everywhere in the body. We have proof of this through science which indicates that each cell thinks. Each cell selects, rejects, communicates, and choses its identity within its organ-community.   Additionally, neurotransmitters (neuro-chemicals), wiring, and receptor sites facilitate intra-body communication, decisions, and actions. Now, some consider our second brain to be within our digestive tracts.   Others notice the human heart functions like a separate brain as well.

Our "minds" and bodies are more and more understood as the same phenomenon. Or, at the very least, mind and body are intimately intertwined.   Is our mind more than our bodies? Perhaps, we can link mind and body to consciousness itself. We cannot define consciousness. It is still an inscrutable mystery, just like life itself.

We may be able to define "mind," however at least in part, as being intimately tied into and connected with our emotional landscape.   One of the main reasons I practice yoga so much is that it allows me to feel and then release my emotions.   Through yoga, I have found that I can best access my emotional territory through my physical body.   It is not just practicing yoga that helps access my emotions, however. It is through my senses as well. When I check in and become mindfully aware of what I feel and experience - especially in my chosen self-care practices – I become more alive, engaged, aware, and I am appreciative of my own existence.

"Mind" may also be that which connects us to, or is connected to, the divine. The concept and experience of "mind" may be a field of awareness that is ever-growing and expanding. By paying attention to our sensory experiences and immersing ourselves into our sensory experiences, we also can access divine energy which may access our "mind" as well.

On the same note, "mindfulness" is the process of being deeply engaged with the present moment and accepting what IS. What better way to deeply engage with the present moment than through your senses and your self-care? What better way to accept what IS than to fully enjoy your organic coffee, your morning smoothie, and your sunrise yoga practice?

How can you deepen your experience of the mind-body connection and mindfulness through your self-care practices? Why are our senses a path to a deeper sense of spirituality? What emotions come up when we engage any of our senses? Are you ready and willing to dive deeper into the sensory portals of your own physical experience?

Here is something to ponder:

~The deepest part of the mind is deeply connected to our senses.~

When we cultivate a deep awareness of ourselves and our existence through the practices we have now dedicated ourselves to everyday, a deep awareness of the ecstatic universe begins to unfold.

You have the opportunity in any moment to connect with the subtle, yet ecstatic experience of being alive. Through the intimate, immediate, yet everyday experience of what we eat and how we move through our day, we can expand our awareness through our everyday senses. We connect both with our own innate spirituality, as well as the divine nature of the universe.

Waking up is a process of becoming more mindful and aware of the present moment. Nutrition and exercise and other self-care practices can give us unique opportunities to become more aware of this unique phenomenon known as the "mind-body."

Eating well becomes an opportunity to awaken our sense of taste and smell. We begin to appreciate the dense, cultivated energy we are consuming which animates our bodies and gives us more life-force. Every vegetable is grounding, and each fruit becomes orgasmic. We become immediately grounded by the food we eat. Yet, our sensory experiences of eating well raise our vibration, which in turn lifts our spirits up toward the heavens.

We have opportunity upon opportunity in our daily practices to feel more alive, more connected to ourselves and to Source. In turn, Source is more connected to us. It is a two-way street. Said differently, this is the "mind" (Universe)/body (You) connection.

Source, as Mind, is in us, beckoning to us, and enticing us to come closer via the pathways of our sensory experiences and practices. The Universe really is inside of us. As we dive deeper into the experience of being alive, our senses wake-up even more. Now we are more connected to our mind, our body, our Source, simultaneously.

Awareness of being and feeling alive becomes exquisitely real and sensitized by engaging in movement, stretching our bodies and minds, and enlivening our senses. Real, live, healthy foods, invigorating movements, even spa visits, awaken our senses through restoration. Awareness is exquisite, and being *exquisitely aware* is everything. It is life, it is life force. Engaging with your senses in everyday practices is a major gateway to the divine.

Engaging with your senses requires a firm commitment to practicing mindfulness. "Mindfulness" is being in the now, accepting the now, and also waking up to the bright light of awareness. What a comfort and joy it is to know we can wake ourselves up more and more through a deep engagement with our minds, bodies, and senses.

John O'Donohue, author of the book *Anam Cara* speaks about the way mindfulness is a gateway to both yourself and the divine: *"Your senses are your guides to take you deep into the inner world of your heart." (5)*

Our hearts are now said to have more neurons than our brains. Our "heart" may be the deepest expression of ourselves, and may also be another metaphor for the "mind." When we "come from the heart" or do anything with passion, such as committing to doing our daily yoga asanas or eating organically, we put our hearts and minds into it, yes?

How wonderful would it be if those of us who already take care of ourselves and others in so many ways, had the courage to go even deeper into the territories of our mind, body, heart, and soul? Who knows what lies in the deep recesses of the mind-body? Who knows what secrets our hearts have yet to reveal? Who knows what mysteries our daily practices have yet to reveal to us about our own current lives as well as the heavens and cosmos? I will see you on the mat, on the hike, in the spa, at the batting cage, on the mountains, out on the waves, at the gym, on the trail, and in the kitchen. . .

We together will invigorate our senses, move fluidly with our body and emotions, and enliven our experience of the divine which blends within our current body-mind matrix.

References

O'Donohue, John (1998). *Anam Cara: A Book of Celtic Wisdom*. Harper Perennial.

About the Edie Summers

Edie Summers is an author of two books, certified wellness coach, top-rated radio host, and yoga instructor. She is certified through WellCoaches, which is connected to Institute of Coaching, affiliated with Harvard Medical School. She is about to finish her M.A. in Counseling Psychology as well.

For over 18 years she has trained and served within the alternative health field including being a health consultant, lecturer, and broker for natural foods industries. She represented over 30 lines and serviced 50 chain and independent stores. Summers' expertise includes corporate wellness coaching, stress management, energy healing and medicine, herbs and super foods, nutrition coaching, natural foods coach, HABA care, food psychology, personal training and fitness coach. Before this, she was a professional dancer for ten years. You can join her for yoga videos, meditations and support groups at ConnektWell.com, PortlandWellnessCoach.com and blogtalkradio.com/thewellnesscoach.

CHAPTER 42

SPIRITUAL, MINDFUL, TOOLS FOR FINANCIAL, AND BUSINESS GROWTH

BY DR. CAROL, FRANCIS

One of the most articulate authors who addressed the practicalities of human power, within a Divine consciousness, was Napoleon Hill. Following the Great Depression and WWII, desperate people sought to rise above poverty trends and deprivations. Napoleon Hill rose from this era as arguably the most influential and accessible guru teaching how to create material wealth. Notably, his methodology included spiritual processes. He noticed the following characteristics were present in financially successful people who also had spiritual practices.

Compassion and Kindness

Feelings and Emotionality

Cognitive Functions

Subjective Mental Exercises

Mindfulness and Awareness

Creation of Mental and Emotional Intense Moments

Physiological Well-Being

Ecstatic Sensations

Information, Knowledge, Education

Savvy Business Planning

Self-Discipline

Follow Through

To increase your ability to make money, build business, and meet your Earthly life's goals, sixteen exercises are offered below. Some are inspired from Napoleon Hill and others lifted from interviews with rich and famous spiritually minded individuals of this Twenty-First Century era.

Each step has a spiritual relevance to *Your Soaring Phoenix*. Each exercise will enhance your spiritual walk. Also, each will help you ground yourself so you can successfully accomplish the daily tasks of living successfully, creating projects, meeting goals, earning money, and managing the business of life.   Enjoy practicing each of these exercises and apply them to your chores, business, family needs and spiritual growth.

Desire and Passion Building

Exercise:

Calm your being, your extrinsic thoughts, and your physical activities. Then, generate extreme emotionally charged feelings of optimism and excitement about your ultimate Goal. (Practice daily for few moments.)

Purpose of Exercise:

Live within this passion moment by moment with your memory, imagination and physical attention. Enliven this passion as much as possible. "ENTHUSIASM" means feeling the ecstasy of the divine within. Generating enthusiasm about your ultimate goal is the key to your success. For Napoleon Hill, it is first on his list. Passion supports motivation to work hard.

Faith and Confidence Building

Exercise:

Harness any sense of confidence in yourself and the people or "powers" you include in your support system. Focus upon these strengths. Build the emotional experience of believing that you and your team have what it takes to succeed. List your strengths. Describe those strengths and why they are relevant to your goals. Then, emotionally feel inside how you value those strengths. (Practice daily for a few moments.)

Purpose of Exercise:

Defining and feeling what your faith is built upon, helps you focus your unrelenting confidence in your efforts, passion, wisdom, skill-sets, fortitude, and foresighted spirit and actions. You will build your belief in yourself and your team remembering that you can actually produce results. Acknowledge and grow your sense of faith that your GOAL will materialize.

Auto-Suggestions with Self-Hypnosis Skill Building

Exercise:

Move deeply into your unconscious and subconscious realms. Do so by any of these tools: meditation techniques, repetitive self-affirming statements, deep-breathing exercises accompanied by 3-30 minutes of self-hypnosis recordings of you or a hypnotherapist, or use YouTube.com hypnosis recordings. While using these tools to move you deeply into your subconscious and unconscious, repeat your mantra or motivating phrase. Repeat your stated goals adding emotion and mental clarity. State your axiomatic positive and empowering statements of affirmation. Use guided imagery, progressive relaxation, or some form of auto-suggestion on a daily basis. (Practice daily for a few moments or more.)

Purpose of Exercise:

Hypnosis utilizes the various forces of

a) Persuasion (suggestions to the unconscious)

b) Will-power building (emotional and mental pumping, or motivational work)

c) Constructive solution-building through visualization of how the final outcome will appear once it exists

d) Focus, attention, and concentration as key mental and practical skills necessary to attain goals

e) Emotional, soul-filled, and personal commitment to the efforts associated to attaining your goals

f) Gathering of mental resources

g) Gathering of the physiological biochemicals which are stirred during meditation, self-hypnosis, progressive relaxation, or guided imagery. Your physical body thusly can also support the time, energy and stress of moving toward your goal.

h) Motivation to persevere and face fears, worries, doubts or failures

Specialized Knowledge Building

Acquire Schooling and Mentoring, Train, Study, Practice

Exercise:

While the magical stirrings of luck, providence, meditations, self-hypnosis, or self-blessings will assist you as you accomplish your goals, you can never passively sit-back and lazily expect servants to achieve your goals for you. Daily, then, you must also educate yourself about information that is specific and general to your goals. View yourself as always attending a school, always listening to teachers, always researching information, always testing your knowledge, always improving your skills and never assuming you know enough. Acquire mentors. Surround yourself with those who know more. (Daily, Schedule Formal and Informal Training.)

Purpose of Exercise:

Establish an honest, solid, genuine, growing knowledge-base and skill-set associated to your goal. This education also helps you 1) assure yourself that you truly have the skills to succeed and 2) build truthful trusting support from others as they see your growing level of sophistication or expertise. Others can sense a fraud, bluffing, or pretense, including you. Self-sabotage is often associated to feeling authentically ill-equipped.

Build with Your Imagination Weekly While Educating, Planning and Executing

Exercise:

Weekly, imagine what attaining your goal or success will be like during the next week. Imagine how it will taste, smell, look, function, feel, impact others, change you. Conjure as many details as you can during this exercise. Note that your imagination will begin to form a more solid foundational structure as you begin to actually build the various aspects of your goal while educating yourself soundly.

Also, note that your imagination will need to change and adjust as you open different opportunities or learn different facts about your situation. Flexibility needs to also partner with constructive structure as you move forward with your plans. In like manner, your imagination about the path you are taking toward your goal will change weekly; but it also will adhere to a sound path as you move forward knowledgeably. (Practice weekly for a few moments or more.)

Purpose of Exercise:

Build, weekly, a sounder image of what all aspects of your successful ending-point will be. You need to envision the ultimate outcome so you can steer your way more clearly each week. Base your imagination about your weekly activities upon your increasing education and experiences as well as your solid plans.

339

Organized Planning
Goals Set, Objectives Defined, Action Plans Prepared, Action Plans Revised, and Process-Steps Delineated

Exercise:

After you have written your plans, subdivide your plans into smaller goals. Define the actions that will be taken toward each of these tasks. You need to reread them weekly, revise them regularly, and improve them globally at significant times of your year.

These maps provide the instructions for getting to your destination. Make them clear. Divide each subgoal into doable activities. Be able to measure your successes, failures, approximate or partial successes, and adjust accordingly. Make sure your team knows these steps as well. (Practice weekly, monthly and annually.)

Purpose of Exercise:

Defining the steps you need to implement to reach your ultimate goals is essential and provides you with the following:

1) Clear and regular feedback as to your successes, failures and needs.

2) Keeps your team answerable toward their responsibilities associated to your goals. Since you are the prime person on your team, it keeps you answerable too.

3) Abates laziness, procrastination, distractions and stall-outs.

4) Reminds you of where your focus, attention, concentration, imagination, passion and desires need to reside.

5) Keeps ACTIONS as key parts of your daily meditations. No invention has ever occurred prior to thought but plenty of thoughts have never produced an invention. The key ingredient is purposeful actions.

Informed and Inspired Decisions Making

Exercise:

With steps 1-6 firmly in your consciousness, you will still need to make decisions about changes, materials, moneys, time management, employees hired or fired, etc. Imagine that you are driving a semi-truck in thick fog. You can only see ahead what you can see, perhaps 30 feet ahead. You can only know what traffic, road or conditions are which you have studied before, mapped-out and seen in the moment. You do not want to stop driving the truck because you are in fact moving toward your ultimate goal, but you are driving in a type of fog. So now, make decisions moment by moment with savvy alertness. (Practice based on situational needs.)

Purpose of Exercise:

Decisions result in minor and radical changes. Remember that if a ship is off its course by only one degree in the middle of the vast ocean, it may never get to its ultimate destination. Each decision changes your course and either moves you closer or farther away from your goal. View your decisions as pivotal; yet, make decisions and carry on forward.

Persistence, Tenacity, Fortitude, Flexible Movement Forward, and Taking a Rest

Exercise:

Taking a rest or vacation from a task can renew you so that when you return, you are energized to mobilize. Pausing to assess a necessary change of course or enabling other forces to position themselves favorably with you, is savvy timing. However, *failing* to press forward, seize opportunities, take chances, or complete a strenuous or unpleasant task, is not allowable when you are pressing forward toward your ultimate goal. So, scrutinize yourself whenever you are inactive and note whether it is a valuable rest or a worthless escape from necessary yucky or boring chores you need to finish to move toward your goal successfully. (Practice daily.)

Purpose of Exercise:

Ever pressing forward toward your goal, (your dream), creates the energy, attitudes, momentum, excitement and constructive results which keep your goal attainable.

Master YOUR Mind with Focus, Meditation, Discipline, Imagery.

Keep your Mind from distractions, fears or being stuck.

Let these reactions be attended to minimally.

Exercise:

View distractions, fears and being stuck as drowsy states of dreamy sleep from which you need to awake as quickly as you can so that you will not sabotage your goal. Remember when Dorothy, Toto and the Lion, in pursuit of the Emerald City and the Wizard of Oz, fell deep asleep in the Poppy Seed Field? They would have remained asleep forever in their drugged state if they had not had a friend, the Scarecrow, who was unaffected by the opiates of pleasure, laziness, or delusions of passive living.   Make sure that you have people and systems in place which wake you up when you fall prey to those allures distracting you.   (Practice daily, except during vacations.)

Purpose of Exercise:

Anticipation of needless distractions and allures will help you realistically establish those assistants who will help you and your team wake-up and continue on the path of motivated, fortitude and disciplined diligence.

The Mystery of Sexual Energies

Practice Transmutation, the Power of Kundalini with Energetic and Orgasmic Intensity.

Exercise:

This particular step makes tremendous sense to those who understand the power of passionate, libidinal, hungry drives which propel endless hours of pursuing one's goals. Beyond the Western viewpoint of sexual or erotic drives, psychologists like myself, have uncovered that such libidinal forces can be harnessed to enliven anyone's intensity of focus and drive to succeed. These energies are considered the forces of power. So capturing those energies, libidinal drives, and using them to move forward is quite dynamic. Powerful people are often quite sexually dynamic as well. There are reasons that power and sexuality are linked; physiologically having energy to do many activities and feeling attractive come together emotionally and in terms of health. Eagerness to make something happen is associated with health, good eating, exercise, sound sleeping, hydration, as well as confidence, eagerness, "can-do" attitudes, self-esteem that faces failures with solutions, curiosity, and a willingness to connect with others who can help out.

Eastern (initiated in Hinduism) practices that examine Kundalini or Chakra forces also delineate methods of harnessing these energies of power and sexuality. The Chakra energy work (Dr. Carolyn White's Chapter) and good living (Edie Summers' Chapter) are two examples of how to breed health, mental clarity, effective activity and enlivened spirituality. Consider your sexual, erotic or libidinal energies and those of others you study and take serious notes of how that dimension of life can boost your ability to attain your goals. (Practice weekly.)

Purpose of Exercise:

Harness the many forces of energy available to you in order to powerfully accomplish your goals. This will include your mental

343

focus, sexual energies, healthiness, rest and sleep, Kundalini meditations and yoga and Chakra work.

The Subconscious Mind Harnessed by Prayer, Hypnosis, Meditation, and Affirmations Daily

Exercise:

This step returns us to the need yet again to solicit the many layers of our awareness or non-awareness to collaborate on the imagery of our goal as well as the passion and plans associated to such.   Spend time rehearsing your emotional, personal, and pragmatic reasons for your goal as well as re-enliven the power of your passions, motivations, determinations, plans and focus. This a daily practice which can be exercised in a minute of intense self-hypnogogic or meditative steps.   (Practice daily in moments.)

Purpose of Exercise:

Re-ignite the depths, breadth and power of our entire personality and soul around our goal.

Your Brain's Neurological Wiring

Your brain supports the following: implementation of skill sets, neurological and psychophysiological speed of problem solving or actions taken, skills of learning and memorizations, implementation of trainings, and the cognitive interfacing of mind, soul, spirit and material brain functions.

Exercise:

Imagine for a moment your physical brain and notice how intricately wired (nerves) and biochemically active (message transmitters) your brain is.   Now imagine all your brain cells coordinating your actions, words, thoughts, feelings and passions associated to attaining your goal.   Interesting, now we can trace through SPECT Scans and other measuring devices how we truly do activate the relevant portions of our brain while we imagine doing an activity. Some neurologists suggest that our physical brain functions, chemistry, and anatomy do not seem to know the difference between actually doing something, seeing something done in a movie, or experiencing such in a dream. Psycho-cybernetics was developed in the 1960's used with athletes to mentally excel at their skills; basketball players scored more who imagined shooting successfully than those who practiced physically for the same hour. (Practice daily in moments.)

Purpose of Exercise:

Partner with your anatomy, specifically your brain's cells, neurological wiring, and biochemical transmissions, as you move forward toward your Goal.

The Sixth Sense Building

Cultivation of PSI observation, mindfulness practices, Spirit connection, intuition blended with collected information, subjective awareness.

Exercise:

Without becoming arrogant or believing that you can "read minds," cultivate your ability to listen to your intuitive side. Some experience this in dreams. Others call it a "certain vibe" or "just feel something." This subjective response to people, circumstances, or decisions has been described as listening to the synchronicity of every moment and heeding the potential guidance such moments can provide.

Bit of caution here. Never suspend education, knowledge collecting, fact testing, and sound questioning. Individuals can falsely judge others or misinterpret others. Such toxic "intuition" is more based on fears, prejudices, ungrounded hopes, laziness, or blind faith. Do not be blind, be aware; use intuitive skills to help you collect information and increase awareness. Always double check your "intuitive sense." Bleeps on radar screens may be missiles or they may be pelicans. Note your bleeps but do not fail to research what those bleeps really mean. (Practice daily.)

Purpose of Exercises:

Always increase all of your senses and cognitive faculties so that you can absorb as much information that your attentive intuitive skills will permit. These expanding skills, groomed by your awareness, will become more reliable with time, training and experience as you advance your goal.

Law of Attraction and Acts of Kindness

Those who have much can give much. Those who perceive they have only a little, will receive and give little because they are afraid of being without. Those, however, who perceive that they have enough to give, they are more likely to build a revolving exchange of giving and receiving in their life.

These three sentences above summarize why the Law of Attraction is directly linked with Acts of Kindness. Often in books such as *How to Become a Millionaire*, "get rich authors" correlate their success with their wiliness to give and their diligent actions of giving.

Exercise:

Decide what you most need in this moment or each moment you do this exercise. Next, create three ways you can provide for those needs for someone else. The first of these three ways should be huge and overly magnanimous. The second of these giving plans needs to be moderate and relatively manageable. The third of these three giving plans needs to be quick, easy and doable regardless of your financial or time limitations. These three ways of giving need to be respectful of the receiver's true needs. Do not expect the receiver to return any favors unless they so decide. Do not intrude. Do not assume. Now, within the next week, do the third and easiest of these plans and record what you did, how you felt during and after, and any consequences. (Practice weekly.)

346

Purpose of Exercise: Maintaining a constant conscious awareness of your needs and how your needs also can help you empathize with other's needs enables you to be kind, humble, and nonjudgmental. You will become more emotionally fluid with yourself when you shift into a needy state and more aware of those around you. You will also remove yourself from the self-consuming narcissistic trap of "woe is me," which often interferes with success.

Also, performing the easiest of your solutions helps you maintain a constant awareness as to how easy it is to help others and how easy it is for you to begin to meet your needs on the most basic levels. This sense of ease about your needs reduces anxiety, emptiness, depression, or being stuck in your personal life and in your business dealings.

Finally, through connecting with others and helping others, you will increase your circle of connections, increase your problem-solving skills, and increase your ability to create the all-important cycle of giving-and-receiving.

Buddha Laughing

The big bellied Buddha with the wide-open mouthed, laughing-toothy smile sits on my bathroom counter reminding me that laughing, having fun, not taking myself too seriously, and enjoying the wealth of any enthusiastic emotion in each moment will help me during both good and bad times.

Exercise: Laugh every chance you get with your mouth open, your belly jumping and your heart engaged.

Purpose of Exercise: You will be less likely to take another's issues personally and avoid being caught in their games or complications. You will be less likely to become stuck in cruel self-judgment or impossible perfectionistic pits. You will breed joy and pleasure so that others can feel your magnetic and attractive qualities. You will rise yourself out of a self-centered, bluish moments and help others rise up as well.

Conclusion

Choose from these 14 exercises which tools match your personal weaknesses, needs and your personality. Be mindful that meeting your goals, financially or in business or health, can be a type of spiritual awakening. Enlightenment and soulful connections are part of each endeavor, each struggle, each boring necessary task, each brave step, each careful planning session, and each action taken. Every business decision and action can be connected to your spiritual ascension with the use of these tools.

About Dr. Carol Francis

In addition to her spiritual counseling and intuitive work with metaphysically inclined seekers, Dr. Carol Francis has practiced for 37 years as a Clinical Psychologist, Life Coach, Clinical Hypnotherapist, and Marriage, Family & Child Counselor. She assists individuals, couples and children who seek to optimize their current situation and overcome complications of daily living. These individuals seek deep relief and growth for depression, anxiety, stress, career moves, family discord, child and parenting issues, relationship dissatisfaction, habit control, and the psychology of financial success. Practicing and licensed in Southern California for over 37 years, Dr. Carol Francis can be reached at drcarolfrancis.com or 310-543-1824.

Publications by Dr. Carol Francis

Study Skills for Successful High School and College Students

Helping Children with Divorce

Schizoid Anxiety

Helping Children with Natural and Manmade Disasters

"Horrific Parental Imaginings"

"Therapist's Countertransference with Abuse Couples"

KISS Method for Stop Smoking and KISS Cigarettes Goodbye

If You Can't Stop Eating, Maybe You're Hungry: Reset Your Cravings

Re-Uniting Soldiers with Families

Evolving Women's Consciousness: Dialogue with 21st Century Women.

Spiritual Gurus, Spiritual Paths: Your Choice

Astral Projection and Spiritual Journeys

Your Akashic Records

Media Productions of Dr. Carol Francis

Dr. Carol Francis Talk Radio has been active since 2008 with hundreds of thousands of listeners across the internet planet. Archived programs are available at DrCarolFrancisTalkRadio.com and BlogTalkRadio.com/dr-carol-francis.

Dr. Carol Francis has interviewed internationally on KABC, KLOS, KROQ, and Associated Radio Programs as well.

Her *Spiritual Readings Radio Show* is live and archived at BlogTalkRadio.com/spiritual-readings.

For even more helpful information, Dr. Carol Francis Videos, Lectures, Dr. Carol Francis Television Shows and Presentations are archived at YouTube.com/Dr. Carol Francis or Vimeo.com/Dr. Carol Francis

OTHER BOOKS BY DR. CAROL FRANCIS

SPIRITUAL GURUS, SPIRITUAL PATHS: YOUR CHOICE

*SPIRITUAL JOURNEYS: ASTRAL PROJECTION,
SHAMANISM, AKASHIC RECORDS*

EVOLVING WOMEN'S CONSCIOUSNESS

LOVE – THE SUPREME SPIRITUAL TOOL

SPIRITUAL RADIO SHOW

BLOGTALKRADIO.COM/SPIRITUAL-READINGS

SPIRITUAL VIDEOS

YOUTUBE.COM/SPIRITUALJOURNEYTOOLS

SPIRITUAL BLOG

SOULJOURNEYTOOLS.COM

CONTACT THROUGH

DRCAROLFRANCIS.COM

DRCAROLFRANCISTALKRADIO.COM

FRANCIS & O'MALEY

ABOUT THE EDITORS

DR. CAROL FRANCIS AND MARY O'MALEY

Dr. Carol Francis

In addition to her spiritual counseling and intuitive work with metaphysically inclined seekers, Dr. Carol Francis has practiced for 37 years as a Clinical Psychologist, Life Coach, Clinical Hypnotherapist, and Marriage, Family & Child Counselor. She assists individuals, couples and children who seek to optimize their current situation and overcome complications of daily living. These individuals seek deep relief and growth for depression, anxiety, stress, career moves, family discord, child and parenting issues, relationship dissatisfaction, habit control, and the psychology of financial success. Practicing and licensed in Southern California for over 37 years, Dr. Carol Francis can be reached at drcarolfrancis.com or 310-543-1824.

Publications by Dr. Carol Francis

Study Skills for Successful High School and College Students

Helping Children with Divorce

Schizoid Anxiety

Helping Children with Natural and Manmade Disasters

"Horrific Parental Imaginings"

"Therapist's Countertransference with Abuse Couples"

KISS Method for Stop Smoking and KISS Cigarettes Goodbye

If You Can't Stop Eating, Maybe You're Hungry: Reset Your Cravings

Re-Uniting Soldiers with Families

Evolving Women's Consciousness: Dialogue with 21st Century Women.

Spiritual Paths, Spiritual Gurus: Your Choice

Spiritual Journeys: Astral Projection, Shamanism, Akashic

Your Akashic Records

Dr. Francis has contributed since 1977 to numerous newspapers and magazines, chapters in professional psychology anthologies, and blogs on family issues, personal development, and problem-solving concerns.

Media Productions of Dr. Carol Francis

Dr. Carol Francis Talk Radio has been active since 2008 with hundreds of thousands of listeners across the internet planet. Archived programs are available at DrCarolFrancisTalkRadio.com and BlogTalkRadio.com/dr-carol-francis.

Dr. Carol Francis has interviewed internationally on KABC, KLOS, KROQ, and Associated Radio Programs as well.

Her *Spiritual Readings Radio Show* is live and archived at BlogTalkRadio.com/spiritual-readings.

For even more helpful information, Dr. Carol Francis Videos, Lectures, Dr. Carol Francis Television Shows and Presentations are archived at YouTube.com/Dr. Carol Francis or Vimeo.com/Dr. Carol Francis

Mary O'Maley, MSNH, CHtI

Mary O'Maley holds a MS in Holistic Nutritional Health Science and is a Certified Hypnotherapist and Hypnotherapy Instructor with International Hypnosis Federation. She is recipient of the prestigious IHF Award of Excellence & Chapter Woman of the Year from American Business Woman's Association. Mary specializes in Past Life Regression, Intuitive Nutritional Counseling, Life Coaching, five energy healing modalities, psychic and medium readings, and hosts various programs and events.

Mary O'Maley, as Life Coach, created the Retreat-Reconnect-Recharge-ReEmerge Coaching. This R4 Coaching provides in-depth, personal-retreat experiences which help you access, trust, and follow your inner wisdom.

Certified in Reiki, Access Energy Clearing, Matrix Energetics and Reconnective Healing, Mary O'Maley also developed and provides Crystal Chakra Balancing. Crystal Chakra Balancing was discovered through Mary O'Maley's Akashic Records work.

Mary O'Maley teaches basic and intermediate hypnotherapy through IHF, nutritional approaches to health at various medical facilities, and metaphysical information at various international conferences and local venues.

Mary O'Maley's metaphysical studies allows her to reignite her psychic and mediumship gifts which she uses for home, gallery and individual readings given since 1997. She is certified and tested as a member of Best American Psychics. Mary O'Maley hosts and produces The Merry Medium Show. On The Merry Medium Show, Mary interviews many wonderful spiritual explorers from the metaphysical and holistic communities. Podcasts of The Merry Medium Show are available at blogtalkradio.com/the-merry-medium. She also hosts live events in the Los Angeles area: **The Merry Medium and Friends – Where Science and Spirit Meet Live Events.**

355

FRANCIS & O'MALEY

To reach Mary O'Maley for her alternative health services, psychic and mediumship readings, radio programs, live events, materials, workbooks and books, contact her at http://www.maryomaley.com or call 424-234-9260.

356